Daniel Dorchester

Romanism Versus the Public School System

Daniel Dorchester

Romanism Versus the Public School System

ISBN/EAN: 9783337044039

Printed in Europe, USA, Canada, Australia, Japan

Cover: Foto ©Suzi / pixelio.de

More available books at **www.hansebooks.com**

PREFACE.

IN writing my late book, *Christianity in the United States from the Earliest Settlement to the Present Time*,* much material came into my hands which could not be appropriately introduced into that volume, but which is of value to American citizens.

Valuable articles in the editorial and other columns of the *Christian Union*, in May, June, and July, 1888, have rendered much aid to the author.

The recent agitation of the Catholic school contest, in Boston and elsewhere, prompted me to enter into the discussion, for the benefit of my own congregation, and also for the public at large. The result is this little book, which I hope will help to an understanding of the questions involved; questions soon more fully to engross public attention.

The discussion, it is hoped, will commend itself to all as candid and fair, if not as sharp and severe as

---

* Phillips & Hunt, 805 Broadway, New York city. 800 pages, 8vo, 1888.

some would desire. Yet it is not wanting in positiveness.

There are points of radical divergence, indicating that two peoples are struggling in the womb of the nation. Vituperation and abuse cannot settle these points, but may postpone the settlement. In some localities the contest is hot. The author has decided views, and he does not intend to put either shavings or kerosene upon the fire, but rather the solid fuel of facts and principles.

Many American citizens do not yet seem to realize the need of awakening to these matters. The history, the expansion, and present proportions of this contest have, therefore, been sketched at considerable length, that all eyes may be fully opened. While the author does not share in the alarm of many good people, as to the country at large, he does, nevertheless, think that there are localities (and the number will soon be increased) where the case is urgent. Our greatest fear is from the political maneuvering of Rome.

DANIEL DORCHESTER.

Boston, Mass. (Roslindale P. O.), Nov. 10, 1888.

CONTENTS.

	PAGE
PREFACE	3

PART I.

History of the Contest.

SECTION 1.	Its Inception	9
" 2.	The Expansion	26
" 3.	The Bible in Schools	40
" 4.	Attempts at Compromise	55
" 5.	Attempts to get Public School Funds	63
" 6.	Constitutional Amendments	81
" 7.	Recent Papal Acts and Utterances enforcing the Parochial School System	94
" 8.	Statistical Exhibits of the Parochial Schools of Romanism in the United States	120

PART II.

Questions Involved in the Contest.

1. As to the Right and Duty of the State to Educate	135
2. As to Religious Instruction in the Public Schools	150
3. As to a Parochial School System for all Parties	171

	PAGE
4. As to whether the Public School Funds can be Divided	186
5. As to whether, as a Matter of Comity, we ought not to find some way to Divide the School Funds	204
6. Is a Compromise Possible?	211
7. Can both Parties patronize the Public Schools Harmoniously, and on what Basis?	224
8. What may we expect Romanists to do in the Future, and how shall we Preserve our School System?	238
9. As to the Pretensions of Rome as an Educator	243
(1.) The Historic Record of Rome in Respect to Education	244
(2.) Rome's Record in Respect to Education in the United States	255
(3.) The Quality of the Education afforded by the Roman Catholic Church	258
(4.) The Roman Catholic Church does not Believe in the Education of the Masses	291
10. Has Romanism Adopted a More Enlightened and Liberal Policy in our Times and in our Country?	295

PART I.

HISTORY OF THE CONTEST.

PART I.
HISTORY OF THE CONTEST.

SECTION I.
Its Inception.

A SKETCH of the history of the Roman Catholic school contest will help American citizens to more fully understand the character and proportions of this great struggle, and the unyielding spirit with which it is pushed. The struggle had its origin in the city of New York, and Bishop Hughes was its first conspicuous Roman Catholic champion.

Many may be surprised to learn that the first appeal for a division of the public school funds in this country was made by a Protestant denomination, and the first sectarian division actually made was to that body. The other Protestant Churches, instead of objecting, attempted to obtain their share of the public school funds. At that early period, and back into the last century, it was a common thing for legislative bodies to grant pecuniary aid to the higher educational institutions, such as academies and colleges, many of which had grants of public lands. These were not aided out of public school funds raised by taxation, but they were denominational institutions and were officially aided.

There is one instance in which specially-designated school funds were divided in the interest of a sectarian school of a Protestant denomination, the other Protestant bodies assenting, and even desiring to receive their share also. This occurred before the Roman Catholic school contest came on, and before the American people saw what it might lead to. That very act was the means of opening the eyes of Protestants to see the practical results of such a course—the destruction of the common school system. It was this act which Bishop Hughes, of New York, cited when he made his first demand for a part of the school money for Roman Catholic schools.

It should be premised that in the early part of this century, prior to the establishment of the common school system for the State of New York, which occurred in 1812, the raising and distribution of school funds was by methods very different from those of more recent years, and more irregular. The whole matter varied greatly in different counties and localities, many things being left optional. In the city of New York the school funds could then be distributed among certain schools and societies named by the Legislature, and such incorporated religious societies as then supported or might thereafter establish charity schools. This system was defective on account of the inequality of the distribution, the absence of inspection and accountability, and a liability to abuse.

It was while this system was in operation that an organization which for about a half a century performed a most beneficent work was formed in the city of New York.

The New York Public School Society

was an association of benevolent gentlemen, formed in 1805, for the education of poor and neglected children. In its schools probably a half million of children received the elements of a sound education connected with instruction in the holy Scriptures. It was largely aided by the School Fund of the State. Besides educating poor and forsaken children, it performed two other important services—it trained up many excellent teachers and watched over the general interests of the educational cause. This latter function brought it before the public on many very important occasions. Its annual expenditures amounted to about $130,000.

The first ripple of disturbance in the management of this society, it should be said, came from the

Protestant denominations, when the Baptist Bethel Church, in 1823, sought and obtained its share of the public money for its schools. An agitation was awakened all the steps of which need not now be distinctly traced; but the question went to the Legislature in some form, where it was argued, and a provision enacted that once in every three years the Common Council might name such schools and institutions as should be entitled to receive the school moneys, the city Corporation being still responsible to the State for the faithful application of its funds. The disbursement of the greater part of the funds was intrusted to the Public School Society, incorporated for the purpose, which, in addition to the public moneys, obtained other loans from life membership fees, etc. By the act of the Legislature, the question of a division of the funds was to be decided by the Board of the City Corporation. That body appointed a committee to hear the parties to the case. It is remarkable that the Episcopalians, Methodists, Baptists, and Roman Catholics, at that time, sought for a participation in the School Fund, just as the Roman Catholics have since done. After the hearing, the committee made a report which settled the principle for the time, that sectarian schools were not to be sustained or aided from the public money. This decision seems to have "convinced every body of the impolicy and injustice of such a division of the school money, except the Roman Catholics."

In 1831 the "Roman Catholic Benevolent Society" succeeded in obtaining, through the "Sisters of Charity," the grant of $1,500, which has been annually made by the Corporation of the city for a long series of years, for the orphan asylum schools under their care, notwithstanding the opposition of the Public School Society. This, however, did not satisfy the Roman Catholics.

Up to 1840 the Public School Society had established about one hundred schools; but the Catholics continually complained that Protestant ideas were more or less inculcated in the public schools. The Romanists had then had a considerable number of parochial schools in operation for, probably, twenty years, and the number was constantly increasing.

It is correctly claimed by intelligent Roman Catholics that this controversy did not begin with them, but with the Baptist Bethel Church already referred to. They also justly claim that certain influential Protestants, at the opening of this controversy, gave them encouragment. Among these the distinguished Rev. Dr. Eliphalet Nott, for a very long period president of Union College, at Schenectady, is cited as one who was open in the advocacy of a denominational school system, by which each denomination would share, in due proportion to its pupils in schools, in the common school fund. He is said to have even advocated the providing of schools for children of different nationalities.

Rev. Dr. Nott and Hon. William H. Seward.

Dr. Nott had been the tutor, and was the life-long friend and adviser, of Hon. William H. Seward, and frequently expressed his views on the school question to that eminent statesman, during his occupancy of the gubernatorial chair of the State of New York.

Governor Seward, it is said, on one occasion requested Dr. Nott to reduce his views to writing, promising to embody them in a message to the Legislature and to recommend their adoption. This he did in 1839, before Bishop Hughes had entered into the contest, and the Governor, in his message to the Legislature in January, 1840, presented the subject in the following remarkable passages:

> Although our system of public education is well endowed, and has been eminently successful, there is yet occasion for the benevolent and enlightened action of the Legislature. The advantages of education ought to be secured to many, especially in our large cities, whom orphanage, the depravity of parents, or some form of accident or misfortune seems to have doomed to hopeless poverty and ignorance. These intellects are as susceptible of expansion, of improvement, of refinement, of elevation, and of direction

INCEPTION OF THE CONTEST. 15

as those minds which, through the favor of Providence, are permitted to develop themselves under the influence of better fortunes; they inherit the lot to struggle against temptations, necessities, and vices; they are to assume the same domestic, social, and political relations; and they are born to the same ultimate destiny.

The children of foreigners, found in great numbers in our populous cities and towns, and in the vicinity of our public works, are too often deprived of the advantages of public education in consequence of prejudices arising from differences of language *or religion*. It ought never to be forgotten that the public welfare is as deeply concerned in their education as in that of our own children. I do not hesitate, therefore, to recommend the establishment of schools in which they may be instructed by teachers speaking the same language with themselves *and professing the same faith*. There would be no inequality in such a measure, since it happens from the force of circumstances, if not from choice, that the responsibilities of education are in most instances confided by us to native citizens, and occasions seldom offer a trial of our magnanimity, by committing that trust to persons differing from ourselves in language or religion. Since we have opened our country and all its fullness to the oppressed of every nation we should evince wisdom equal to such generosity by qualifying their children for the high responsibilities of citizenship.*

These passages do not present the grounds on which Roman Catholics base their claims, namely, the rights of conscience, as obedient children of

---

* *Assembly Documents.* 1840. Vol. I, p. 5.

Rome, and the equal rights of citizenship; nevertheless they open the door sufficiently wide to admit what the Romanists ask for.

Father Schneller, pastor of the Roman Catholic Church at Albany, after conversation with Governor Seward and other officials at the State-House, wrote to the Very Rev. Dr. Power, then administering the concerns of the New York diocese during the absence of Bishop Hughes in Europe, expressing the opinions entertained in Albany, that if petitions were presented asking for the participation of Catholic schools in the School Fund the measure could be carried. The trustees of the Catholic churches in New York city were called together and the subject laid before them. Dr. Power visited Albany and, from personal interviews, inferred the probability of success. Returning to New York, a Roman Catholic Association was formed in order to secure uniformity and concert of action. Weekly meetings were held, and a petition for a share of the School Fund was presented to the Board of Assistant Aldermen. Nor were the Catholics the only parties in this movement. Other religious bodies also participated. The Board denied these petitions, but the agitation continued, with much diversity of sentiment and recrimination. A Catholic paper, *The Truth-Teller*, charged the leaders with political designs, which was like a fire-brand thrown into the already excited meetings.

Bishop Hughes.

At this time a stronger hand took up the contest. In 1838 Rev. John Hughes was appointed coadjutor bishop of the New York diocese, on account of the failing health of Bishop Dubois. To obtain pecuniary aid for his diocese Bishop Hughes visited Europe in 1839, returning early in July, 1840, at the time when the school contest was well under way. An important meeting was held by the Catholics on the 20th of July, the Very Rev. Dr. Power presiding, and Bishop Hughes, for the first time, addressed his people on the subject, advising careful but firm action. August 10 the Roman Catholics issued an address to the public, to which the Public School Society made a reply. In a general meeting, on the 21st of September, the Catholics adopted a petition to the Common Council for relief, complaining of the sectarian character of the public schools, on account of which the Catholics had been compelled to erect schools of their own, which they offered to submit to the conditions of the law in regard to religious teaching. They specified seven Catholic schools which they prayed the Council "to designate as among the schools entitled to participate in the Common School Fund, upon complying with the requirements of the law," or "for such other relief as should seem meet." This petition was followed by two remonstrances, one by the trustees of the Public School Society, and the other by a committee of the pastors of the Methodist Episcopal churches of the city.

At this time the Protestants had fully thought out the question of the integrity of the public school system, and had reached the conclusion that there could be no successful maintenance of that system if the funds were divided among the different denominations. That would end the system.

The Debate.

The Corporation determined to have the question discussed before the full Board of Aldermen and Assistant Aldermen, which was done in the evenings of Oct. 28 and 29, 1840. In behalf of the Catholics Bishop Hughes appeared. In behalf of the Public School Society, Theodore Sedgwick, Esq., and Hiram Ketchum, Esq. On subsequent evenings Revs. Drs. Thomas E. Bond, Nathan Bangs, and David Reese, M.D., appeared for the Methodist Episcopal Church. Rev. Dr. Gardner Spring, for the Presbyterians; and Rev. Dr. —— Knox, for the Dutch Reformed Church. When the others had ended Bishop Hughes replied at length, from which, in justice to the Roman Catholics, an extract is given :—

It is the glory of this country that when it is found that a wrong exists there is a power, an irresistible power, to correct the wrong. They have represented us as contending to bring the Catholic Scriptures into the public schools. This is not true. They have represented us as enemies to the Protestant Scriptures, without "note or comment;" and on this subject I know not whether their intention was to make an impression on your honorable body or to enlist a sympathetic echo elsewhere; but, whatever their object was, they have represented that even here Catholics have not concealed their enmity to the Scriptures. Now, if I had asked this honorable Board to exclude the Protestant Scriptures from the schools, then there might have been some coloring for the current calumny. But I have not done so. I say, Gentlemen of every denomination, keep the Scriptures you reverence, but do not force on me that which my conscience tells me is wrong.

I may be wrong, as you may be; and, as you exercise your judgment, be pleased to allow the same privilege to a fellow-being who must appear before our common God and answer for the exercise of it. I wish to do nothing like what is charged upon me; that is not the purpose for which we petition this honorable Board. In the name of the community to which I belong I appear here for other objects; and, if our petition is granted, our schools may be placed under the supervision of the public authorities or even of commissioners to be appointed by the Public School Society; they may be put under the same supervision as the existing schools, to see that none of those phantoms, nor any grounds for those suspicions, which are as uncharitable as unfounded, can have existence in reality. There is, then, but one simple question—Will you compel us to pay a tax from which we can receive no benefit, and to frequent schools which injure and destroy our religious rights in the minds of our children, and of which in our consciences we cannot approve? This is the simple question. *

Roman Catholics have claimed that their position in this stage of the contest has been misunderstood. DeCourcy says: †

While they proposed to keep their own schools they proposed to conform them to the law, to subject them to State supervision, to arrange the instruction according to the State requirements, and did not ask for the exclusion of the Bible from the schools of the Public School Society, but asked for their share of the public money.

Pending the decision, negotiations for a compromise were interchanged, in which the Catholics offered to appoint no teachers except such as the Public School Society upon examination should find duly qualified; to afford every facility for visitation and inspection to the duly-appointed agents of the Board; to guard against abuses, and to render their schools in every respect free from objection. The Public School Society also offered terms—to let the schools be attended and managed as they were carried on, but to strike out of the school-books all pas-

---

* Report, p. 4. Also works of Archbishop Hughes.
† History of the Catholic Church in the United States. p. 417.

sages to which the Catholics objected, and to have only such passages of the Bible read as are translated the same way in the Protestant and Romish versions. But no agreement was reached; and so, after numerous hearings, negotiations, and visitations of the schools, the case was decided adversely to the Roman Catholics, Jan. 12, 1841. But the Catholics did not rest their case at this point.

Hon. John C. Spencer.

Petitions were thenceforth drawn up and presented to the Legislature, headed by Bishop Hughes. The memorial was referred by the Senate to Hon. John C. Spencer, Secretary of State and *ex-officio* Superintendent of Public Schools. The report of Mr. Spencer proposed an entire change in the system: that a Commissioner of Public Schools was to be elected in each ward of the city; to these Commissioners the Public School Society was to be transferred, and the general School Laws of the State were to be extended to the city. The Commissioners were to receive and apply the public moneys to the support of the public schools, which were to be placed under their control.

Seeing that it was impossible to carry their measure for a participation in the Public School Fund the Catholics advocated Mr. Spencer's proposition, on the ground that it was the least objectionable system they could get, and at least possessed the merit of excluding sectarianism from the schools. The Catholics favored the measure; Protestants opposed it. Controversy ran high. The newspapers were full of it. A disgraceful "*bull of excommunication*" from "Tristram Shandy" appeared in the *Journal of Commerce*. The result in the Legislature was the postponement of the question from May, 1841, to January, 1842, in order that the intervening State election might afford an expression of the popular sentiment.

In the election following (November, 1841,) Governor Seward narrowly escaped defeat, because of the stand he had taken on the school question. The Catholics ran independent candidates for the Legislature in New York city, because both the political parties held mixed positions on the school question, not making it an issue, and 2,200 votes were cast for the independent ticket—a significant lesson to the old parties. In his message Governor Seward reiterated the views uttered the previous year, recommended the abolition of the Public School Society and the creation of a Board of Commissioners, to be elected by the people, whose duty it should be " to apportion the school moneys among all the schools, including those now existing, which shall be organized and conducted in conformity to its general regulations and the laws of the State in the proportion of the number of pupils instructed."

His recommendations were in substance adopted. The school system of the State was extended to New York city. This led to the formation of "Ward Schools," under the direction of officers chosen in each ward, while those of the Public School Society remained under its control, the two systems operating side by side. As might have been expected, however, experience soon demonstrated that such a plan was attended with many difficulties. This led the Public School Society to propose to retire from the scene, which was allowed; and on the 22d of July, 1853, it transferred its schools and property to the Corporation of the city, to be managed by the Corporation's Board of Education, just as the ward schools were administered. The surrender was made after forty-eight years of valuable service to poor and neglected children, and after a long resistance against the demands of the Romish hierarchy, under the leadership of Bishop Hughes. At that time the Bible had been ejected from more than eighty of the public schools in New York city. The Romanists had not succeeded in obtaining a division of the School Fund for the benefit of their sectarian schools; but the disbanding of the Public School Society was a Roman Catholic triumph. In this contest Bishop Hughes managed with consummate tact, persistence, and ability, sustaining his cause in the Municipal Council and in the Legislature, and teaching the politicians the value of the Roman Catholic vote—a lesson which they soon learned to appreciate.

End of the Public School Society.

On the occasion of the delivery of the Public School Society property to the Corporation of the city Hiram Ketchum, Esq., delivered an appropriate address, in which he used the following language:

Now, my friends, I have to say here, and I hope that it will pass throughout the country, that there is no satisfying the Roman Catholics on this subject; and here I would proclaim loud enough, if I could, to be heard in California, that the Roman Catholic priesthood are opposed to Protestant children and Roman Catholic children sitting side by side in common schools and learning from the same forms. That is the objection. They did not want to expel the Bible; they did not want to blot out the offensive passages; but they wanted to separate their children from the Protestant children of the country, and to receive a portion of the School Fund to enable them to educate their children by themselves. For this object, we may rely upon it, the Roman Catholic priesthood will steadily and perseveringly exert themselves. I say the "priesthood;" for I do not believe the Roman Catholic laity desire any such separation. They, with us, desire that the children of this republic may study side by side in common schools, in order that they may have the advantage of all that union of sentiment and feeling that grows from boyish intimacy.

Mr. Ketchum terminated his speech with the following serious words, which deserve to be well pondered by every friend of our public schools; in fact, by every true friend of the country:

In this great struggle, which is to shake the country from Maine to California, we must stand up and oppose error with all our force, and cleave it down in its place, and preserve the purity and integrity of our institutions. For, if this republic is not preserved, where shall we go? What shall we do? What will there be left for our children? Let us, then, contend always for the right, being assured that such labor is never finally lost.

SECTION II.

The Expansion.

SOON after the closing up of the Public School Society the New York *Independent* said:

Now the question is, Are our public schools still to be tampered with at the instigation of Romish priests? And how far is this pusillanimous compliance with their demands on the part of our School Commissioners to be carried? Shall the whole system be first sacrificed and then Romanized? The object of this crusade against the public schools is, first, to bring them into contempt and suspicion, as irreligious and ungodly, and, next, to build up Romish schools on their ruins.

. . . .

The instinctive hatred and jealousy of Romanism against the Bible teach us very clearly the power of an education in which scriptural truth is an element and a fixture. . . .

"Expel the Bible from our schools!" exclaimed Mr. Choate. "Never, so long as a piece of Plymouth Rock remains big enough to make a gun-flint out of!"

The *American and Foreign Christian Union* the same year said:

Not content with the right which the Roman Catholic Church has, in common with every other religious denomination in the land, to establish as many schools as she can, at her own expense, and conduct them in any manner she pleases, she has the presumption to think that Protestants will consent to the destruction of our public schools—conducted, as at present, on a non-sectarian basis—and to allow her a share of the public school funds proportionate, not to the taxes which Roman Catholics pay (which are for the most part very far less than those of the Protestants), but to the number of children which they have, or which they may be able to gather into their schools. In other words, they wish to make Protestants contribute largely, directly or indirectly, to sustain their sectarian schools.

There is unmistakable evidence that a concerted movement has been set on foot which ramifies throughout every portion of our country where a public school system exists. The agitation has been commenced and prosecuted with vigor at Boston, New York, Newark, N. J., Detroit, Chicago, Cincinnati, Pittsburg, and Baltimore. It is the old war-cry of Rome against all education except what is carried on under her own control and direction. The first charge against the public schools was that they were "sectarian," because the Bible was read daily at the opening and closing of them. Well, after having succeeded in getting a faithful superintendent put out of office, and a tool of the priest chosen in his place, and the Bible banished from eighty schools, the charge is now made that the public schools are "godless."

After the act of 1842 Bishop Hughes devoted himself more fully to the establishment of Catholic schools for Catholic children, calling to his aid in the work of instruction the Brothers of the Christian schools and the Sisterhoods of the Church. The Romanists have paid their proportion of taxes for the support of the public schools, in which they say "they cannot conscientiously educate their children," and at the same time have provided parochial schools of their own.

It has been stated by a good authority that in the year 1853 the Roman Catholics demanded State aid for their schools in eight different States—Massachusetts, New York, New Jersey, Pennsylvania, Maryland, Michigan, Ohio, California. Since that time the demand has been repeatedly made elsewhere in some form.

In the same year that the Public School Society surrendered its property in New York city, in Michigan, and Ohio, the subject was carried to the polls, but the result was unfavorable to the Romanists. The existing school law was sustained by large majorities, the German Catholics in great numbers standing with the Protestants. The attempt was repeated in Maryland. Hon. Mr. Kearney, member of the Legislature from Baltimore, introduced into that body a bill, accompanied with a flourishing report, to make a similar division of the school moneys, as asked for in New York city. The movement met with great opposition in Baltimore, one-fourth part of whose population were Roman Catholics. An immense mass-meeting was held in the hall of the Maryland Institute. Addresses of great power were delivered by Rev. Drs. Plummer, Fuller, Johns, and others, and the proposed measure was unanimously condemned.

At the time the Public School Society surrendered itself and its position (1853) some kind of distinctly Roman Catholic schools had been in existence in New York city something over twenty-five years. The first school established by them was on Prince street (between Mulberry and Mott streets,) some time prior to 1830. In 1830 St. Paul's School, Brooklyn, St. Peter's, on Barclay Street, and St. Stephen's, East Broadway, were opened. Two more commenced in 1833. St. John's College (Jesuit) was opened in 1841 and raised to the rank of a university in 1845. The College of St. Francis Xavier soon followed. What was their number at this time?

A STATEMENT FOR 1854.

The editor of the *American and Foreign Christian Union*, a very careful, reliable magazine, for January, 1854, said:

We have in our possession a most remarkable document. It is a tabular view of the Roman Catholic schools and institutions, both those held during the week and those held on the Sabbath, in the city of New York, including Harlem. This document was prepared by a trustworthy person, who took pains to visit all these schools, and make the requisite inquiries on the spot. We have no doubt it is as accurate as it is possible to make such a statement. We will give a summary of this document in as few words as we can, and accompany it with a few remarks.

1. These schools and institutions are 28 in number, and are connected with Roman Catholic churches, and bear the names of these churches—such as St. Vincent, St. Bridget, St. Nicholas, St. Anne, St. Patrick (the Cathedral), St. John the Baptist, St. Stephen, etc., etc.

2. The number of these schools which have *boarders* as well as *day-scholars* is six, and the number of boarders is 920.

3. The number of pupils is 10,061, including the 920 boarding-scholars.

4. The number of youth in the Sunday-schools attached to these churches, and held, we believe, in the same school-rooms, is 9,649.

5. The number of priests who have the charge of these schools, either as instructors or directors, or both, is sixty.

6. The number of teachers in these schools, male and female, is 143.

7. In 22 schools the instruction is in English; in four it is in English and German; in one it is in French and English, and in one it is in German.

8. The teachers belong to *five* orders—*Christian Brothers, Sisters of Charity,* etc.

9. Four of these schools are called "District Schools," and receive aid, if we are rightly informed, from the public treasury. These are (unless we have

been misinformed) the schools of St. Mary's, St. Francis Xavier's, St. Patrick's, and St. Vincent de Paul. We believe that Mr. Ketchum explained this in his speech last summer (see *American and Foreign Christian Union* for the month of October).

10. In several of these schools are children belonging to various Protestant denominations! How many it is not possible to ascertain; but the number is believed to be considerable. And this in a city where no Protestant family can possibly live very remote from a good public school, in which, whatever may be taught, or not taught, as it regards religion, their children would not be exposed to being made acquainted with the dreadful errors of Rome.

11. In not one of these twenty-eight schools, it is believed, is either the Bible or the New Testament read by the scholars or read to them by the teachers! When the Protestant version is used in any public school, the Romish hierarchy cry out that this is sectarianism! When the Bible is put away to please them, then they cry out that the school has become godless! But when they establish their own schools, expressly on the ground that the public schools are godless, then they will not use in them even the Douay version or any other! So true is it that Rome dreads the Bible in any translation whatever! To this conclusion we have to come at last.

12. The books used in these schools are elementary primers, spelling-books, catechisms, grammars, geographies, etc., about which there is little to say. Occasionally one finds in the geography used (that of Pinnock) some statements which show, as might be expected, a Romish bias; but in the main the book is sufficiently correct. The reading-books found in these schools are three: *The Third Book of Reading Lessons; A New Treatise on the Duty of a Christian*

towards God, and *The Doctrinal and Scriptural Catechism; or, Instructions on the Principal Truths of the Christian Religion.*

The first of these books was compiled by the Brothers of the Christian Schools. The second is "an enlarged and improved version of the original work of the venerable J. B. de la Salle, founder of the Christian Schools." The translation is from the pen of Mrs. J. Sadlier. The third is a translation (also by Mrs. Sadlier) from the original French work of the Rev. P. Collot. The first is a collection of pieces for reading in schools, and has but little that is objectionable in its character. The last two are, of course, full of the peculiar doctrines and practices of the Roman Catholic Church. They are duodecimo volumes of some 350 or 400 pages. The third and last, we will only add, is a very complete, and even minute, exhibition of the dogmas and sentiments of the Roman Catholic Church on every topic supposed to be connected with the Christian system of faith and morals. All the exclusiveness of Rome is here fully developed and inculcated, as well as in the smaller catechisms. The child is taught that there is no salvation out of the Church (of Rome), and that there is no hope for what she calls "heretics" and "schismatics." No less than twenty-two pages of this *Doctrinal and Scriptural Catechism* are devoted to the subject of baptism, seven to confirmation, forty-seven to the eucharist, thirty to penance, and thirty to other subjects. The reader will conclude from this that the work descends to the usual explanations and subtle distinctions of the Romish doctors.

Our chief object is to give our readers some idea of the character of the instruction in the schools for which the Roman hierarchy demanded the aid of the

State in New York, Massachusetts, Michigan, Ohio, Pennsylvania, Maryland, New Jersey, and California, last winter, and will demand it again! It is our opinion that the State should aid no sectarian schools, whether Protestant or Roman Catholic.

A Statement for 1858.

	Pupils.	Teachers.
In higher schools for females	708	84
" Colleges and higher schools for males	530	48
" Free schools for females	6,100	84
" " " " Males	4,800	54
" Orphan asylums, etc	800	46
Total	12,938	316

Capital Invested.

Female high schools	$780,000
High schools for males	250,000
Female free schools	228,000
Male " "	228,000
Orphan asylums	462,000
Total	$1,948,000

About half under mortgage. *

The editor of the *American and Foreign Christian Union* (April, 1858), made a statement that shows the rapid progress the Roman Catholics were making in the control of the public schools in that city:

We will state, upon what we regard as good authority, that the papal members of the Board of Education amount to about *one quarter* of the whole number; that the papal members of the ward

---

* The above statement has been abridged from the *New York Herald*, January 22, 1858.

boards amount to *nearly one half* of their number respectively, and that at least *one third* of all the teachers now employed in the public schools are members of the Romish organization." "It is manifest that Rome is making gigantic efforts to establish herself firmly in this land." "At least 150,000 children are more or less affected by this state of things in New York, every day."

A Statement for 1871.

The New York *Daily Tribune*, September 11, 1871, under the head "*Public School Abuses*," gave an exhibit for that time. Some idea of the article may be judged from its sub-headings: "Decrease in Attendance;" "Corruption in the Board;" "The Old Board of Education Destroyed that the Ring might Rule;" "The Extravagance of the New Board Fully Revealed;" "A New Field for Ring Corruption," etc. It shows very clearly that the Board of Education was under the control of the same spirits who had so manipulated the city finances as to pocket scores of millions of the people's money. It reveals also how entirely subservient to Roman Catholic influences was the management of the Public School System. We insert the part of the article under the sub-head, "*The Bible in the Schools.*" It says:

Section 44 of laws governing the public schools reads thus:

"All the public schools of this city under the jurisdiction of the Board of Education shall be opened by the reading of a portion of the Holy Scriptures, without note or comment."

It is well known that this rule is gradually becoming obsolete, principally through Catholic influences. There is much difference of opinion, among the most religious people even, as to the propriety of enforcing this rule, and it is no part of the plan of this article to war against the disposition to exclude the Scriptures from the schools. The facts in the case will be brought forward to help in the presentation of a complete illustration of the illegal and fraudulent methods used by the opponents of the present school system to break it up. The state of affairs in this connection in several of the wards is as follows:

In the Sixth Ward the Catholics make up three fourths of the population, and these are controlled by the priests. Here Mr. Mullany, who has been principal of Ward School No. 23 for twenty-five years, says that the Bible has not been read for twenty years at least; and yet he reports his delinquency every month. There was a disturbance about the matter in 1861, and the salaries of all the teachers in the schools of the ward where the reading was not maintained were suspended for six months; but the dereliction was finally acquiesced in. Mr. Mullany said that his school and that in Elm Street would be closed in a month if the Bible was read in them. "Father Curran, of the church across the way, has no parochial school, but if he hadn't perfect confidence in us he would open one and reduce our attendance by three fourths in a single week." Sometimes a rumor would be started that Curran was to begin a school, and all the teachers of the public schools were at once in terror for fear they would lose their places. James Campbell, who has a grog-shop at No. 82 Centre Street, is one of the school trustees in the Sixth Ward. He said to a reporter, "Whin I went into my place here, an' that's a-goin' on eight year, the Bible wasn't a bein' read; an' shure I didn't ax any questions about it. I guiss it's all right, it is, and they've fixed it up wid the Board of Eddycashun so as there won't be nothing said about. Anyhow I couldn't, 'pon me honor, tell ye any thing about it, sur." The power of Catholicism is so great in this ward that a vote of censure was nearly passed in 1868 by the male principals against Thomas Hunter, principal of Grammar School No. 35, for ridiculing the style of teaching in vogue in Catholic schools.

In the Twenty-first Ward, Sara J. J. McCaffrey, Principal of Primary School No. 16, uses a Catholic Bible, and is in high glee because, after long badgering the Board of Education, she and her backers in the ward obtained the book from the Department of Instruction, it being duly labeled by them, and they paying $25 20 for it.

In the Fourth Ward schools there has been no Bible-reading for eleven years. Here again the pay of teachers was stopped on account of the omission. There was much excitement, and the teachers brought suit for their salaries. The suit finally went by default. In one case a trustee carried off a Bible from School No. 1 under his arm, to decide the matter. An evidence of the real animus and intention of the Romanists is found in the fact that a reporter, visiting this school, *found the pupils engaged in celebrating the Catholic festival of Ascension Thursday, by singing and other exercises.* The teachers in this ward are nearly all Catholics.

In the Fourteenth Ward there is no Bible-reading.

EXPANSION OF THE CONTEST. 37

In School No. 21, this has been the case for fifteen years. The teachers are nearly all Catholics, but they are very jealous of the parochial schools. All the trustees are also Catholics.

The five schools of the Nineteenth Ward are ruled by Catholic and Democratic trustees, with one exception. The priests are trying hard to build up parochial schools here, and keep their children away from the public schools on religious holidays, and also keep them at home for months together to prepare for yearly confirmation or "first communion." Nothing but the great superiority of the public schools enables them to withstand the competition of the parochial schools. Some parents even pay the price of tuition in the latter while they send their children to the former.

In the Twenty-first Ward two schools still use the Protestant Bible. The recitation of the Lord's Prayer ceased in 1870. John Stephenson, the car-builder, fought for this custom, and, though a warm friend of the schools and a trustee for many years, has not since been returned to office. Nearly all the trustees are Catholics. The priests of St. Gabriel's Church fight the public schools very hard. They induce the children who attend their schools to call all who go to the others "Little Protestants," and one of their preachers proclaimed in the pulpit that parents who wished their children to "learn to steal or swear, or do all kinds of evil, should send them to the public schools." One priest came near being expelled for speaking favorably of the free schools.

In the Sixteenth Ward an illiterate Irish Catholic named McNiernay proclaims himself the champion of Romanism, and strives in every possible way to drive out Protestant teachers and observances. He has kept up a sort of guerilla fight against one principal—has used his influence to so break down the standing of the school that the principal would be forced to resign. The means he has used have been the forcing of incompetent teachers and a worthless janitor upon the school.

The Fifth Ward was formerly strongly Protestant, but the Catholics are getting the upper hand. A specimen of what American Democrats may expect from their Irish political associates is shown by the following reply of the "Hon." Mike Murphy to the friends of a stanch American Tammany Democrat, who had been a trustee and wished the nomination again: "Yis, gintlemin, this is all very good, beshure, but the time is past whin American Dimicrats are agoin' to be elicted to offices in the Fifth Ward; an' bedad, ye may make yer minds that it won't come again very seon. We don't want any American Dimicrats; bedad an' we don't. We kin git along widout 'em."

Father Quinn, of the First Ward, who is a candidate for the Bishopric of New York, delivers furious tirades against free schools, and frightens hundreds of children into his own by this means. The trustees of this ward are prophecies of the good time coming. They are Peter Disch, emigrant boarding-house keeper; Patrick Baldwin, liquor dealer; William Kenny, ostensible undertaker, is a gentleman at large, with political influence; John O'Connor, junk-store and politics, and Dennis Keenan, liquor-dealer.

The wards mentioned are some of those that are most thoroughly under Irish Catholic influence; but many others are rapidly running in the same direction.

This was five years after Hon. V. M. Rice, Superintendent of Public Instruction of the State of New

The Expansion.

York, had rendered an official decision against the use of the Bible in the public schools. The year following the date of the document just quoted, in 1872, Hon. Mr. —— Weaver, Superintendent of Instruction of the State of New York, officially pronounced a similar decision.

SECTION III.

The Bible in Schools.

THE rejection of the Bible from the schools of New York was clearly contrary to the intentions of the founders of the Public School System, and contrary even to many explicit legal provisions.

Governor George Clinton, of New York, in 1802 and 1803 recommended the subject of education to the Legislature because of the advantage which would come to morals, religion, liberty, and good government. Governor Lewis, in 1804, said:

> In a government resting on public opinion, and deriving its chief support from the affections of the people, religion and morality cannot be too sedulously inculcated. Common schools, under the guidance of respectable teachers, should be established in every village.

So prominent was the idea of inculcating morals as a part of common school education in the minds of the founders of this system.

The first law establishing the Common School Fund of New York State was passed in 1805, the same year in which was passed the act of incorporation of the Public School Society of New York City. In the first address to the public by the founders of the city free schools, dated May 18, 1805, it was stated that—

It will be a primary object, without observing the peculiar forms of any religious society, to inculcate the sublime truths of morality and religion contained in the holy Scriptures.

This object was kept in view, and the Bible was read and its lessons inculcated in an unsectarian way. In 1810 Governor Tompkins said :

I cannot omit this occasion of inviting your attention to the means of instruction for the rising generation. To enable them to perceive and duly estimate their rights, to inculcate correct principles and habits of morality and religion and to render them useful citizens, a competent provision for their education is all essential.

The next year Governor Tompkins renewed his appeal so effectually that five commissioners were appointed to report a system for the organization and establishment of the common schools in the State of New York. They reported the following year.

The remarkable success of the Public School Society of New York city, in the first seven years of its existence, was the strongest incentive to the Legislature, in 1812, to make provisions for free schools throughout the State. The idea of inculcating morality with secular education was prominent in the minds of the Commissioners, as is evident from the language of their report:

The expedient devised by the Legislature is the establishment of common schools, which, being spread throughout the State and aided by its bounty, will bring improvement within the reach and power of the humblest citizen. This appears to be the best plan that can be devised to disseminate religion, morality, and learning throughout the country.

Connected with the introduction of suitable books, the Commissioners take the liberty of suggesting that some observations and advice touching the reading of the Bible might be salutary. In order to render the sacred volume productive of the greatest advantage, it should be held in a very different light from that of a common school-book. It should be regarded as a book intended not merely for literary improvement, but as inculcating great and indispensable moral truths also. With these impressions the Commissioners are induced to recommend the practice introduced into the New York free schools of having select chapters read at the opening of the schools in the morning, and the like at close in the afternoon. This is deemed the best mode of preserving the religious regard which is due to the sacred writings.

In accordance with the recommendation of this report the common school system of the State of New York was founded in 1812. In confirmation of this view that eminent statesman, Hon. John C. Spencer, Secretary of State of New York and also Superintendent of Public Instruction, said, in 1839:

The people of this country have a right to bring up their children in the practice of publicly thanking their Creator for his protection and invoking his blessing.

Again, in a communication to the Legislature, April 26, 1841, called forth by the religious difficulty at the time in the schools in New York city, he said:

It is believed to be an error to suppose that the absence of all religious instruction, if it were practicable, is a mode of avoiding sectarianism; on the contrary, it would be in itself sectarianism, because it would be consonant to the views of a peculiar class and opposed to the views of other classes. . . . It is believed that, in a country where the great body of our fellow-citizens recognize the fundamental truths of Christianity, public sentiment would be shocked by the attempt to exclude all instruction of a religious nature from the public schools; and that any part or scheme of public education, in which no reference whatever was had to moral principles founded on these truths would be abandoned by all.

An act of the Legislature was passed April 11, 1842, which might at first thought appear to favor the exclusion of the Bible from the schools. By this act it is provided that

No school shall be entitled to or receive any portion of the school money, in which the religious doctrines or tenets of any particular Christian or any other religious sect shall be taught, inculcated or practiced, or in which any book or books containing compositions favorable or prejudicial to the particular doctrines or tenets of any particular Christian or other religious sect, or which shall teach the doctrines or tenets of any other religious sect, shall be used.

This provision was doubtless secured by the opponents of the Bible in New York city, with the intention of using it for the expulsion of the Bible and all other religious instruction from the schools. At all events, determined efforts were made in the city, under cover of this provision and other similar enactments, for the ejection of the Scriptures, which had been employed daily for nearly forty years. To meet the efforts an amendment to the law of 1842 was obtained in 1844, mainly by the efforts of Colonel Stone, City Superintendent, which declared:

Nothing herein contained shall authorize the Board of Education to exclude the holy Scriptures without note or comment, or any selections therefrom, from any of the schools.

Thus the efforts against the Bible resulted in the more explicit legal sanction of its use. Subsequently, however, this important feature of the law was in danger of being obliterated, and still later was utterly ignored. The opposition to the Bible gathered strength with every renewed attack upon it. After the Bible had maintained its place for sixty years, a decision from Hon. V. M. Rice, Superintendent of Public Instruction for the State of New York, was rendered against the use of the Bible in the public schools. This was in 1866. In 1872 a similar decision was obtained from Hon. Mr. Weaver, then State Superintendent of Instruction, who strangely misquoted Hon. J. C. Spencer as authority in support of his decision. Armed with such official documents, it is no wonder that school officers and teachers, especially in Roman Catholic wards, but not wholly confined to them, defied the law.

In the meantime the controversy which has been sketched in New York city had broadened out into the whole country, particularly into the large centers of population, in which the Roman Catholic Church was massing its people. In every instance, however, the first point of irritation was the use of the Protestant Bible in the public schools.

In Connecticut

the reading of the Bible, prayer, and other religious exercises, were neither required nor forbidden by law, these things being left to be regulated by school boards or the people of the various municipalities.

In Massachusetts.

As late as 1855 Rev. Dr. Sears, Secretary of the Massachusetts Board of Education, said:

The Roman Catholics seldom raise any objection to the use of the Bible in our schools. In one manufacturing town the school committee allow the children of Roman Catholic parents to use the Douay version if they prefer. In Lowell there is at least one Roman Catholic teacher, the children being from such families. But a single instance of the Romanists maintaining separate schools has been recently known, and that was in Fall River. The children have left those schools in many cases because they are inferior to the public schools.

The General Statutes of Massachusetts formerly read :

The School Committee shall require the daily reading of some portion of the Bible in the common English version; but shall never direct any school-books calculated to favor the tenets of any particular sect of Christians to be purchased or used in any of the town schools.

The first part of this section was distasteful to the Roman Catholics, but the State law did not specify whether the reading shall be by the teacher, or by one or more of the scholars, or by both teacher and scholars. In 1859 there was an organized resistance to "the enforced use of the Protestant version of the Bible," to the "enforced learning and reciting of the Ten Commandments in their Protestant form," and to the "enforced union in chanting the Lord's Prayer and other religious chants" as they were then practiced in the Boston public schools; and about four hundred pupils were, for a time, withdrawn or expelled from the schools; but the greater part soon returned.

In 1862 and 1880 the law was amended, and now reads as follows (Chap. 44, sec. 32):

The School Committee shall require the daily reading in the public schools of some portion of the Bible, without written note or oral comment; but they shall not require a scholar, whose parent or guardian informs the teacher in writing that he has conscientious scruples against it, to read from any particular version or to take any personal part in the reading; nor shall they direct to be purchased or used in the public schools school-books calculated to favor the tenets of any particular sect of Christians.

The Famous Cincinnati Contest.

We have referred to the question of the Bible in the public schools as it was agitated, in a mixed form, in connection with the question of the division of the school moneys in New York city. In some cities the Bible question assumed a more distinct form, as in the Cincinnati controversy in 1869. The reading of the Bible without note or comment had been a daily exercise in the schools of that city from their first establishment forty years before, and instruction in the elementary truths and principles of religion was always given without any sectarian interference with the rights of conscience. As early as 1842 Bishop Purcell complained that the school text-books contained passages obnoxious to Roman Catholics, that their children were required to read the Protestant

Testament and Bible, and that the district libraries contained objectionable works to which their children had access without the knowledge of their parents.

The School Board invited the Bishop to point out any thing that was offensive in the text-books in the English and German schools. They also ordered that no pupil be required to read the Testament or Bible, if his parents or guardians desired them excused from that exercise, and that no child should take books from the libraries, except at the request of the parent or guardian at the beginning of the session.

When the controversy was opened, in 1869, it was stated that the rule adopted in 1842 had long been inoperative, and had been for twenty-five years omitted from the standing rules of the Board. In 1852 the School Board ordered that the opening exercises of the schools should comprise the reading of the Bible and appropriate singing, the pupils to read such version as their parents or guardians might prefer; but that no notes or marginal readings be allowed, nor comments by the teachers. In 1862 the Board's report says there are intimations that the division of the School Fund will be again agitated, but that they are relieved from any apprehensions by "the fact that the Constitution of the State imperatively forbids the right or control of any part of the school funds by any religious or other sect." "The threat is accompanied by reproaches utterly groundless," because for twenty years the Board has had "a standing request that any offensive exercises or books, or passages in books, used in our schools be made known to us, which has never been answered; that for nearly ten years we have offered to supply teachers and schools in every orphan asylum whatever having a sufficient number of children to warrant the employment of a teacher; that we have always carefully excused pupils, whose parents desired it, from attending the religious exercises with which our schools are daily opened, and that in order to encourage pupils to attend the religious teachings which their parents prefer, we have expressly required that they shall be excused from school one half day or two quarter days each week."

The rule adopted in 1852 remained in force until November 1, 1869, when the Bible was formally excluded from the public schools of the city by the adoption of the following resolutions by "The Board of Education:"

Resolved, 1. That religious instruction and the reading of religious books, including the Holy Bible, are prohibited in the common schools of Cincinnati, it being the true object and intent of this rule to allow the children of parents of all sects and opinions in matters of faith and worship to enjoy alike the benefits of the Common School Fund.

2. That so much of the regulations, in the course

4

of study and text-books, in the Intermediate and District Schools (p. 213 Annual Report), as reads as follows: "The opening exercises in every department shall commence by reading a portion of the Bible, by or under the direction of the teacher, and appropriate singing by the pupils," be repealed.

These resolutions were adopted,* after a long and exciting contest, by a vote of twenty-two to fifteen. One member absent desired his name to be recorded with the minority. John D. Minor and others instituted a civil suit, and an order was issued the next day restraining the promulgation and enforcement of the resolutions. The case came for trial before the Superior Court of Cincinnati, November 30, 1869, Judges Storer, Taft, and Hagans being on the bench. It was ably argued by six lawyers, three on each side, and on the 18th of February following judgment was rendered for the plain-

---

* POLITICAL ANALYSIS OF THE VOTE.

For Rescinding.		Against Rescinding.	
Democrats	12	Democrats	3
Republicans	10	Republicans	12
Total	22	Total	15

RELIGIOUS ANALYSIS.

For Rescinding.		Against Rescinding.	
Catholics	10	Protestants	13
Free-Thinkers	3	Free-Thinker	1
Jews	1	Jew	1
Protestants	3		
Unknown	5	Total	15
Total	22		

tiffs. This judgment set forth that the resolutions were passed without warrant or authority of law and in violation of the seventh section in the first article of the Bill of Rights in the State Constitution, and are therefore null and void. Judge Taft disssented. A motion for a new trial was overruled by the court, and the reading of the Bible was practically restored.

It has been stated, on what seems to be good authority, that not more than two hundred petitioners asked for the exclusion of the Bible, and that a remonstrance against it was sent in with more than ten thousand names upon it. The leading person prompting and sustaining the onset against the Bible was Rev. Thomas H. Vickers, a free-thinking Unitarian minister. Rev. A. D. Mayo, D.D., a prominent Unitarian minister of the "right wing," was an able and efficient defender of the Bible in the schools.

Three weeks after the action by the Cincinnati School Board, and before the suit had been argued in the Court, the *Tablet** said (November 20, 1869):

If this has been done with a view to reconciling Catholics to the common school system its purpose will not be realized. It does not meet, nor in any degree lessen, our objection to the public school system, etc.

---

* New York City Roman Catholic paper.

December 25, the same paper said:

We hold education to be the function of the Church, not of the State; and, in our cause, we do not and will not accept the State as educator.

December 11 the *Freeman's Journal* said:

The Catholic solution of this muddle about Bible or no Bible in schools is "Hands off!" No State taxation or donation to any schools. You look to your children and we will look to ours. We don't want you to be taxed for Catholic schools. We do not want to be taxed for Protestant or godless schools. Let the public school system go to where it came from—the devil.

The *Catholic World* for August, 1871, shows how little was gained by the liberality which allowed the exclusion of the Bible from the schools:

This proposed remedy (says the *World*) will prove worse than the disease. . . . Exclude your Protestant Bible and all direct and indirect religious instruction from your public schools, and you will not render them a whit less objectionable than they are now, for we object not less to purely secular schools than we do to sectarian schools. . . . There is only one of two things that can satisfy us—either cease to tax us for the support of the public schools, and leave the education of the children to us, or give us our proportion of the public schools in which to educate them in our own religion. We protest against the gross injustice of being taxed to educate the children of non-Catholics, and being obliged, in addition, to support schools for our own children, at our own expense, or peril their souls.

THE BIBLE IN SCHOOLS. 53

Many will inquire, Does not this argument prove too much? Do not the things here claimed involve a recognition of a particular religion by the State and a discrimination in its favor which necessarily carries with it the converse right to discriminate against it?

THE NEW HAVEN CONTEST
will be related by another : *

You know what New Haven lately resolved on, after a keen debate between her Romish and her Protestant schools. There was a party, represented in that college city by honored men, in favor of excluding the Bible from the common schools, in order that Romanists might make no objection to the management of the education of the children. That party is not a weak one among Protestants in this country. It once mastered the city of Cincinnati. I suppose that I shall offend many if I say that political parties may easily connect their vote with strong ecclesiastical prejudices concerning the American school system, and that a great majority of our Romish population is in one of the political parties. I know over what blazing plowshares I am walking; but, as I am no politician, and have no political bias in what I am saying, you will pardon me for asserting that in such a city as Cincinnati a democratic municipal government is almost certain to be under the manipulation of Romish ecclesiastics. That is true in New York city. I will not say it is true in Boston or Chicago; but our great towns already occupy one fifth of the land, and the largest of them are notoriously under the control of the political party which has in

---

* Rev. Joseph Cook, December, 1879.

it friends of this foreign priesthood. In New York city about five sevenths of the most important offices are in the hands of Romanists. A practical division of the school funds has occurred in New York city in several cases.

New Haven had before her the same question which Cincinnati discussed, but she decided it precisely in the opposite way: to have the Scriptures read, and to have the Lord's Prayer offered by the children. The Scriptures are read in the Protestant version; but no teacher in New Haven has any objection to a Romish child reading out of the Romish version. There is nothing really sectarian in the present religious exercises, which New Haven, after long debate, has adopted, unless it be the exclusion of a prayer recognizing Mary, the virgin, as in some sense divine. That prayer was really recommended by one or two astute theologians in New Haven, and it is to the amazement of all America. Shut out, I say, from public use the prayers that represent sectarianism, not only in Romanism, but in Protestantism. I would take what is common to all sects—the Decalogue, the Sermon on the Mount, the Bible, as a text-book of morals—and I would sink them by public reverential exercises into the youthful heart of this nation. To that platform New Haven has come back after long discussion; but if you can't come up to that platform I will ask you to come up to one next to it—that is, local option. If I could only re-arrange our population, put the infidels in wards by themselves, the extreme Romanists in wards by themselves, and American Protestants in wards by themselves, I would allow the law of the survival of the fittest to determine whose schools are the best, and whose literature, whose newspapers, whose politics, whose science.

SECTION IV.

Attempts at Compromise.

ABOUT 1870 the impression was upon the minds of many intelligent Protestants, gathered from some things darkly shadowed forth by Roman Catholics, that papists were about to work out a plan which would modify the public school system, and furnish a common ground on which Protestants and Romanists could meet and better utilize the existing system, without impinging upon the rights of either. In view of the immense expense prospectively involved in undertaking to establish every-where a system of parochial schools, there was a strong inducement to Catholics to try to find some common ground.

Rev. Henry Ward Beecher, in the *Christian Union*, in 1870, said:

Their plan, which now for some time they have been discussing in secret conclave, is so admirable, that it will take time to thoroughly understand its character and appreciate its merits. We are not sworn to secrecy, and we speak what we do know.

The plan, then, which is now under consideration, and which awaits only some perfecting of details before it is officially promulgated, is this: It will be proposed that any private association may open a public school. Its doors shall be thrown open to the public. There shall be no conditions of admission other than those which the Board of Education may prescribe. Its teachers shall all be subject to the examination of the Board, and shall receive their certificates from it. The schools shall be at all times open to its visitation, and subject, within reasonable bounds, to such regulations as it may enact. In the school-house proper there shall be no religious teaching. But when the session is ended, the teachers may employ additional hours in giving such religious instruction as they see fit. Attendance on these extra hours shall not, however, be compulsory. Scholars may attend or not, at the option of their parents. Such schools, thus established, may draw from the school fund an amount in proportion to the number of scholars in actual attendance. Such, in its substantial features, is the plan at no distant day to be proposed as a compromise between the contending parties.

"The advantages of this scheme," said Mr. Beecher, "are manifest. It will involve the State in no additional expenditure. It will, indeed, save something, for the association will provide the rooms and the text-books. Secular instruction will be furnished at the expense of the State. It will be furnished under the direction of the State. At the same time an opportunity is afforded to the Church to instruct its own children in religious truth. Thus religious and secular instruction will go hand in hand. Protestantism and Romanism will live in peace. The lion and the lamb will lie down together, and a little child shall lead them."

This plan to which Mr. Beecher referred as inchoate in 1870, and in prospective development, had already taken a partial form in some cities in Connecticut. In New Britain, Conn., the Roman Catholic school was adopted by the town November 12, 1862, and was known as "the town school." It was supported by the town for the school year ending August 31, 1870, at an expense of over $3,000. It was then, as since, known and reported in the *Sadlier's Catholic Almanac* as St. Mary's Parochial School. In 1871 it reported, boys, 170; girls, 132, with lay teachers. Its male principal was a graduate of the State Normal School, with six female teachers, all Roman Catholics, selected by the priest or other authority, and approved by the school visitors of the town. It works under the general regulations of the other town schools, and was supported at public expense, but was a thoroughly denominational school. In 1888 *Sadlier's Almanac* gives the following item, under the head of "Parochial Schools": St. Mary's, New Britain, Sisters of Mercy, boys, 570; girls, 551.

In the city of New Haven the Roman Catholics gained their object at a school election, September 16, 1867, when their ticket was elected by a majority of seventy votes. The *New Englander*[*] said:

---
[*] October, 1867.

The day before the balloting two of the Roman Catholic pastors of the city exhorted their parishioners to show their strength against "the Yankees;" and in the third of the churches, the pastor being absent, the Catholic ticket was distributed through the children of the Sunday-school. One of the priests is reported to have said that he had been trying to secure public money for his parish school, and now was the time to demand it.

The Hamilton or St. Patrick's school was soon adopted and supported at public expense. The steps leading to its adoption are related in the Report of the Board of Education of New Haven, for the year ending September 1, 1868. They say:

Early in the year Rev. Matthew Hart, in behalf of parents residing in the eastern part of the district, made application to the Board to receive the pupils of St. Patrick's school (about six hundred children) and instruct them as pupils of the public schools. The Board, after due consideration, believing it to be their duty to provide for the instruction of all children, residents of the school district, who make application, so far as it is in their power, decided to comply with the request, if suitable accommodations could be secured. The reply of the Board was communicated in the following resolutions:

Whereas, Application has been made to this Board by Rev. Matthew Hart, requesting it to provide for the education of scholars now in St. Patrick's School, and for other children in that neighborhood now unprovided with seats in any school; and *whereas*, this Board recognizes the duty of furnishing to all suitable applicants the opportunities for education in the

ATTEMPTS AT COMPROMISE.

public schools under its charge; and, *whereas*, it has at this time no suitable building immediately available for the purpose of a school in that part of the district; therefore,

Resolved, 1. That the Board is ready to rent for temporary use the building now occupied by St. Patrick's School, or any building eligible for the purpose, and to commence and maintain therein a public school for the children of that neighborhood, on exactly the same basis as all other schools under their charge.

2. That the Committee on School Buildings be requested to inquire and report to the Board as to a controlling lease of one or both the buildings now occupied by the St. Patrick's School, what alterations, if any, will be necessary to fit them for the use of a public school and the expenses attending the same; said lease to commence in time, so that the rooms can be prepared for occupancy by the district for the May term of 1868.

An agreement having been made for the rental of the building previously occupied by the school, after a thorough reconstruction at the expense of the owners, the school was opened under the charge and instruction of ten teachers,* who had been previously examined by the Superintendent of Schools and found duly qualified for their duties. The studies and exercises were regulated like all other schools of the district by "time-tables," containing a programme of recitations covering the whole time of each school-day. Frequent visits have been made by the Superintendent, members of the Board, citizens, and strangers from abroad, and the results thus far are quite satisfactory, exhibiting regularity of attendance, good

---

* All Sisters of Mercy.

order, and earnest attention to duties, highly commendable to teachers and pupils. In all respects the school has been conducted in the same manner and governed by the same rules as all other schools of the district.

Moreover, this school is understood to be an exclusively Roman Catholic school, the teachers being all Sisters of Mercy, and, with all the scholars, under the spiritual direction of the Roman Catholic Bishops, acting through the pastor of St. Patrick's Church, and securing to the pupils, by the opportunity of imparting religious instruction freely to the school out of school hours, a thoroughly Roman Catholic training. Under the head of Parochial Schools *Sadlier's Catholic Year-Book* for 1871 has "St. Patrick's, New Haven, pupils, 730, under the charge of the Sisters of Mercy." In 1888 the same appears: "Boys, 400; girls, 460." Here is a Roman Catholic parochial school, supported at public expense, complying with the letter of the school law, but holding religious exercises out of school hours.

In Waterbury, Conn., a parochial school was organized by Rev. Father Thomas F. Hendricken, pastor of the Church of the Immaculate Conception, but it was taken under the care of the Board of Education, of which Father Hendricken was usually a member, with the understanding that it was to consist, as before, of Roman Catholic children and teachers, and the opening and closing exercises were to be distinctively Roman Catholic, as they had been, though the school was to conform in all respects to the laws of the district. In 1871 *Sadlier's Catholic Year-Book* reported it under the head of Parochial Schools, with 200 boys and 175 girls. In 1880 it reported 1,100 pupils under lay teachers, Sisters of Charity.

In Manchester, N. H., according to *Sadlier's Catholic Year-Book*, for 1870 there were fourteen public schools kept by fourteen Sisters of Mercy. The Year Book for 1888 shows 2,665 pupils in parochial schools in that city taught by Brothers of the Christian schools, Sisters of Mercy, Sisters of the Holy Name, and Gray Nuns.

While the plan which Mr. Beecher, in 1870, more than hinted at was tentatively, but partially and informally introduced in some places, it has never been officially adopted or even recognized by the leaders of the Roman Catholic Church; and all hope of such a compromise measure has now utterly vanished. Probably there never was any good ground for Mr. Beecher's suggestion. He doubtless consulted chiefly with his hopes and his imagination. The truth is, the Church of Rome is *in toto* opposed to the American Public School System. She is fully intent upon educating her children in her own way, and means to gather them into her own schools. She hates our school system, and would be glad to overthrow it. Take out the Bible, and she is not then satisfied, as we have seen. The Roman Catholics do not introduce their own Bible, the Douay version, into their own schools. They have never been anxious to have their people read their own Bible. The reading-books in their schools have generally been such avowedly Catholic works as *La Salle's Treatise on the Duty of Christians towards God*, and *Collot's Doctrinal and Scriptural Catechism*, which were used as class-books for reading and study. Their schools are always strictly denominational schools.

The concessions to Romanists in New Haven and the other cities just cited was ill-advised, and never afforded any basis for any thing really hopeful, and it is, moreover, of doubtful legality. To consent to the use of public property and funds, directly or indirectly, in aid of sectarian schools is contrary to the spirit and letter of our unsectarian institutions.

SECTION V.

Attempts to Get Public School Funds.

WE have seen that as early as 1840, in New York city, many Roman Catholic children were taken out of the public schools and gathered into parochial schools. From 1840 to 1850 there was a similar movement in other large cities, though the number for the whole country was scarcely appreciable.

As the work of organizing parochial schools went on, demands were made for their portion of the public school money raised by taxation; not the portion raised from their own people, which would have been quite small, but in proportion to the number of children they could muster.

In 1853 this demand was made in eight different States—New York, Massachusetts, New Jersey, Pennsylvania, Maryland, Ohio, Michigan, and California. If they had succeeded in these demands they would have gained two important objects: they would have drawn large sums from Protestant purses to support Roman Catholic schools; and they would have thus effected a partial union between Church and State—objects dear to every Romanist. The money of the State would have been devoted to the payment of sectarian teachers, all of whom impart rigidly sectarian instruction. It was also expected that if they succeeded in this object, all other religious denominations would ask for their share of the public school money.

Thus, the funds provided in common for all being dissipated among the different sects, the Common School System would perish. This demand was not formally acceded to, but by degrees, in New York city and a few other places, the Catholics have succeeded in getting some appropriations of money which have aided their institutions.

As late as about 1860, it is believed, there was no sectarian instruction in the public reformatory and charitable institutions of New York. All denominations shared, without jealousy, in the work, in an unsectarian way. But in the year 1863, at the instance of Rev. Dr. Ives, a pervert to Romanism from the Protestant Episcopal Church, a charter was obtained for a "Roman Catholic Protectorate" for destitute or unfortunate children, to be supported by a public tax. All its officers and instructors were to be *of one faith*—the Roman Catholic, and they were to receive annually $110, instead of $70, *per capita*, as before. This was a papal triumph, invading the province of the Common School System.

On the 12th of May, 1869, the tax levy law for New York city was passed by the Legislature, allowing "an annual amount equal to twenty per cent. of the excise moneys received from said cities for 1868, to be distributed for the support of schools educating children gratuitously in that city." Another Roman Catholic victory.

Nearly all Protestants declined to receive these funds, protesting not only against the unequal distribution proposed, but also against the principle recognized in the "Bill," of appropriating money to sectarian schools, as fatal to the Common School System. The people thus found themselves taxed for the support of sectarian education, the Roman Catholic faith being taught in the schools thus supported. The State and the Church were virtually united. A powerful agitation followed, and, through the vigorous efforts of Francis Lieber, LL.D., and the Union League Club, this law was repealed in 1870.

There arose a demand that many Roman Catholic asylums, protectories, etc., should be aided from the public treasury. Many of these were in part charitable institutions, but a considerable number of them were of a mixed educational and industrial character, and some were purely parochial schools. Hon. Dexter A. Hawkins, A.M., a late member of the New York Bar, devoted much time to careful research into this subject, compiling data collected from the public records in the offices of the Comptroller of the city of New York, of the Board of Education, of the Board of Apportionment, of the Commissioners of Emigration, of the Comptroller of the State, and the State Commissioners of Charity, showing under what guises or names the Roman Catholic Church has drawn public money from the city and State treasuries. The following is a condensed exhibit: *

MONEYS DONATED IN SEVENTEEN YEARS (1869–1885, INCLUSIVE) TO THE ROMAN CATHOLIC CHURCH FROM THE PUBLIC TREASURY IN THE CITY OF NEW YORK.

Total for 17 Years, $10,915,371 81.	Total Amount paid to each Institution.
New York Catholic Protectory	$3,491,582 57
Foundling Asylum of Sisters of Charity	2,872,474 89
Institution of the Sisters of Mercy	
Sisters of Mercy	816,230 95
Institution of Mercy	
St. Elizabeth Hospital Dispensary	5,836 00
Society of St. Vincent de Paul of the city of New York	80,530 50
St. Vincent Industrial Home for Girls	8,547 00
St. Vincent Home for Boys	5,975 00
St. Vincent de Paul Orphan Asylum	21,445 43
Free School of St. Vincent de Paul	7,642 00
St. Vincent's Hospital	60,692 00
St. Vincent's Roman Catholic Orphan Asylum	15,000 00
Free School of St. Vincent	2,500 00
Home for the Aged of Little Sisters of the Poor	39,600 00
St. Stephen's Home for Children	205,061 24
St. Stephen's Orphan House	17,244 43
St. Stephen's Home	2,150 00

* See pamphlet by Mr. Hawkins. Phillips & Hunt, 805 Broadway, New York city, N. Y. Last edition, 1887, pp. 18-21. The last edition contains a reply to criticisms upon a previous edition made in the *Catholic World*.

ATTEMPTS TO GET PUBLIC SCHOOL FUNDS.

	Total amount paid to each Institution.
St. Francis's Hospital	$78,911 75
Sr. Francis's Male Parochial School	3,750 00
St. Francis's Female Parochial School	4,250 00
Roman Catholic Orphan Asylum	306,504 80
Asylum of the Sisters of St. Dominic	265,961 17
Sisters of St. Dominic	25,722 20
House of the Good Shepherd	297,983 36
Mission of Immaculate Virgin for Protecting Homeless and Destitute Children	308,532 15
Missionary Sisters of the Order of St. Francis	161,023 06
Sisters of the Holy Cross	750 00
House of Our Lady of the Rosary	6,125 25
Asylum of Dominican Convent of Our Lady of the Rosary	65,698 63
St. Joseph's Home for the Aged	46,154 57
St. Joseph's Industrial Home for Destitute Children	173,638 97
St. Joseph's Orphan Asylum	35,463 87
St. Joseph's Improved Institute for Deaf Mutes	151,792 69
St. Joseph's Hospital of the Poor of St. Francis	1,800 00
St. James's Home	49,457 38
St. Ann's Home	19,301 24
St. Agatha's Home	7,975 71
St. Michael's Home	2,504 15
Association for Befriending Children and Young Girls	57,352 43
Baby's Shelter and Day Nursery	1,310 00
Day Nursery and Lod'g House for Respectable Women	266 00

That the steady increase, year by year, during the last eleven years, may be seen, we give the yearly totals:

1869	$771,612 04	1878	$710,350 98
1870	676,495 55	1879	693,616 29
1871	502,592 65	1880	719,957 06
1872	421,674 03	1881	748,989 48
1873	338,336 24	1882	817,520 93
1874	326,797 90	1883	814,182 84
1875	459,187 48	1884	862,190 85
1876	554,285 98	1885	908,904 20
1877	588,677 31		

The next table will show no less than 56 Roman Catholic *schools*, besides other institutions, aided by donations from the public treasury in four years, 1869 to 1872, inclusive, all of which is additional to the preceding table.

Money Donated from the Public Treasury of New York City to the Catholic Church—*Continued.*

	Total Amount paid to each Institution.
St. Joseph's Church	$5,266 58
St. Joseph's Parish School, Manhattanville	12,954 00
St. Joseph's Parochial Male School	6,222 00
St. Joseph's Parochial Female School	6,852 00
Sisters of St. Joseph	10,000 00
St. Joseph's Industrial School	900 00
St. Joseph's German-American Industrial School	828 00
German Free Schools of St. Joseph's Church, 125th Street and 9th Avenue	420 00
St. Joseph's Home	12,000 00
Convent of the Sacred Heart	10,000 00
Charity Week-day School Academy of Sacred Heart	6,170 00
House of Mercy, Bloomingdale	12,500 00
Church of Dominican Fathers	5,549 46
Dominican Church, Lexington Avenue	7,000 00
School of St. Nicholas, Order of St. Dominic	6,800 00
St. Nicholas School	16,700 00
St. Nicholas Church	364 60
St. Patrick's Orphan Asylum	8,153 41
St. Patrick's Cathedral	17,857 68
St. Patrick's Cathedral School	19,830 00
St. Patrick's Orphan Asylum, Mott and Prince Streets	15,000 00
St. Bridget's School	58,168 00
St. Bridget's Church	5,000 00
Sister Helena	4,317 85
St. Teresa's School	22,135 00
St. Teresa's Church	1,280 00
School of St. Teresa's Chapel	5,000 00
In aid of school attached to St. Teresa's Church	5,000 00
St. Ann's Parochial School	9,890 00
St. Ann's Church, Eighth Street	2,173 33
St. Peter's Free School	17,015 00
German-American School, St. Peter's Church	1,500 00
German-American Free School	18,456 00
St. Paul's Church Parochial Schools	5,316 00
Free School of St. Mary's Assumption Church	840 00

Attempts to Get Public School Funds.

	Total amount paid to each Institution.
St. Lawrence Church	$1,500 00
St. Lawrence Parish School	15,118 00
St. Mary's School	55,122 00
St. Mary's Church, Grand Street	400 00
Sisters of Charity, St. Mary's Church	140 00
School of the Most Holy Redeemer	38,688 00
St. Michael's Parochial School	10,462 00
In aid of school attached to St. Michael's Church	5,000 00
St. Michael's School	5,000 00
St. Gabriel's School	34,840 00
Church of Transfiguration	387 75
Transfiguration Free School	39,596 00
St. James's Parochial Male School	12,900 00
St. James's Parochial Female School	31,548 00
St. James's Church	800 00
School of our Lady of Sorrow	22,400 00
St. Columba Charity and Week-day School	23,966 00
Church of the Holy Innocents	1,124 50
St. Andrew's Church	2,014 02
Church of the Immaculate Conception	5,182 43
School of the Immaculate Conception	38,878 00
Church of St. Paul the Apostle	10,004 64
German-American School, 19th Ward	5,850 00
Church of St. Boniface	965 70
St. John the Evangelist Free School for Girls	8,048 00
Parish School Church of the Nativity	639 60
Roman Catholic Church, Second Ave., Second and Third Sts.	645 45
Church of the Holy Cross	8,565 35
Parochial School Church of the Holy Cross	1,272 00
Church of the Holy Name, or St. Matthew	463 12
Church of the Assumption	918 26
Church of St. John the Baptist	1,035 31
Parochial School of St. John the Baptist	1,560 00
Free School of Sisters of Notre Dame	1,296 00
Free German School	13,080 00
German Mission Association	15,000 00
College of St. Francis Xavier	7,272 00
St. Peter's	1,042 90
St. Columba Church	1,987 28
Church of the Covenant	652 60
Church of the Nativity	645 45
Church of the Epiphany	765 71
School of Bethlehem	770 00
St. Boniface Church School	4,270 00

	Total amount paid to each Institution.
St. Patrick's Free School	$7,384 00
St. Francis Xavier Male School	3,861 00
St. Francis Xavier Female School	21,370 00
Sacred Heart Female Academy	3,000 00
Church of the Annunciation	3,174 00
Church of the Annunciation School	7,372 00
St. Gabriel's Male School	7,449 00
St. Gabriel's Female School	27,591 00
St. Alphonsus's School	8,524 00
Church of the Holy Redeemer	1,000 00
School of St. Francis of Assisi	8,140 00
School of the Holy Cross	9,741 00
School of the Nativity	700 00
School of St. Chrysostom	2,165 00
Orphan Asylum, Prince and Mott Streets	10,000 00
Sisters of St. Mary's	3,000 00
School of the Order of Sisters of St. Dominic	5,600 00
Other Roman Catholic Institutions, New York City	202,095 00
Total	$1,101,344 01
Total in the two tables	$12,016,715 82

Of the above $712,469 were given to schools, an amount much larger than the endowment of many Protestant colleges. When has Rome ever hesitated to put her hand into public treasuries?

Mr. Hawkins says:

Some of the Protestant religious denominations receive a small donation from the public treasury in this city for their charities, but they are opposed to the whole business, as recognizing the principle of a union of Church and State, and would be glad to have each tub stand on its own bottom—that is, each Church support its charities with its own money, and not with the money of others, but the Roman Catholics oppose it."

ATTEMPTS TO GET PUBLIC SCHOOL FUNDS. 71

Mr. Hawkins then shows:

HOW THE ROMAN CATHOLICS EVADED THE CONSTITUTIONAL AMENDMENTS.

In this city this Church was subsidized by the "Tweed Ring," and nearly $800,000 paid to it in a single year, 1869. In 1870 petitions from more than one hundred thousand citizens caused the Legislature to repeal the law, the repeal to take effect near the end of that year, imposing a perpetual tax of nearly $250,000 on this city for their parochial schools. Hence a falling off the next year, 1871, in the subsidy. On Washington's Birthday, 1872, a detailed exposure of this "Tweed Ring" subsidy for the three preceding years, to the extent of $1,396,389 51, was made by the writer, and the subsidy in consequence fell that year to $421,674 03. In the autumn of 1872 the "Tweed Ring" were driven from power in both the city and State. The writer remained at Albany nearly the entire sessions of 1873 and 1874, to expose and denounce this class of legislation, and the annual sectarian appropriation bills, that had grown to over $1,000,000, were wholly defeated. This subsidy in this city was in consequence reduced for 1873 to $338,336 24, and for 1874 to $326,797 90. Constitutional amendments were prepared in 1873, and finally adopted in 1874, which, had they not been interfered with, and two pestilent clauses Jesuitically introduced into the amendments to Article VIII, by the skill and influence of a Catholic member of the Constitutional Commission, would have cut those subsidies up by the roots.

These two legal wolves in sheep's clothing were the apparently harmless phrase, "and juvenile delinquents" in Section 10, and the sentence, "This section shall not prevent such country, city, town, or village from making such provision for the aid or support of its poor as may be authorized by law," in Section 11.

Under the "juvenile delinquents," this Church saved chapter 647, Laws of 1866, giving the Roman Catholic Protectory annually out of the city treasury $50 per head; and chapter 428, Laws of 1867, giving it annually $60 more per head (total $110 per head, or double the actual cost) of its inmates, thus securing a subsidy of from two to three hundred thousand dollars per year from the taxpayers, and, if well managed, a clear profit to the Church of at least $100,000. So profitable to this sect is this protectory that they keep sentinels on the watch at each police court to induce commitments to the protectory, and have had laws enacted compelling justices to commit to it. They made war on a public school connected with the city alms-house, and, by act of Legislature, broke it up, for the purpose of getting possession of a portion of the inmates to swell their own numbers and profits.

Charity is the using of one's own means for the good of others. It is the highest Christian virtue, and the duty especially of all Churches; but to get hold of and use the public money to make a profit and to build up a sect under the pretense of charity, is hypocrisy.

Mr. Hawkins further shows how the Catholics again got into the public treasury:

Immediately after the above amendment to Section 11 of the Constitution was adopted this Church made haste to set its skilled talent to devise schemes to connect whole broods of their institutions by a sort of sectarian suction-hose with the public treasury. It accomplished this under the word "poor" in the above sentence in

Section 11. It had the word "poor" defined by chapter 221, Laws of 1875, so as to include, among others, "the sick, destitute, friendless, and infirm," and the occupants of their enormous boarding-house, built on land given by the city, and improperly called the "Foundling Asylum of the Sisters of Charity;" and by the same statute they grabbed the excise moneys, thus adding several hundred thousand dollars more to their annual subsidy.

These so-called "foundlings" may be two years old when received by the "Sisters," and may board with them, or under their control, till eighteen years old, if girls, and twenty-one years old, if boys. They may be indentured to this institution, if half orphans, by either the father or mother, and the mother may board there also to look after the children. For every child boarding there these "charitable Sisters" draw from the city treasury $138 70 per year, and for every mother boarding there $216 per year; total for a mother and child, $354 70 per year, besides having the work of the children and mothers.

Most of the hard-working laborers throughout the country would be glad to turn "*poor*" and support themselves if they could draw from the city treasury at this rate. These advantages to this sect are secured by chapter 635, Laws of 1872; chapter 644, Laws of 1874, and chapter 43, Laws of 1877. The cost to the city treasury of this Church boarding-house of the Sisters of Charity is now between two and three hundred thousand dollars per year, and if well managed brings annually not less than $100,000 net profit to the Church.

By concentrating their forces, and by a change of name or of statement as to what they are doing, so as on paper to appear to be "aiding or supporting the poor," nearly all their organizations have got back into the public treasury again, and the annual subsidy to this Church is now as great as in the palmy days of the "Tweed Ring." In the last two years in this city it drew from the public money $1,403,967 27.

They may call any persons in their schools and institutions "the poor," and so pension them upon the public treasury. There is no investigation of their statements or accounts or supervision of their institutions by any public officer, as common safety requires where the public money is paid out to them; but whatever statement under oath they choose to make is accepted as the basis of payment to them.

An amount of public money equal to two and one half per cent. of the entire tax levy, or six per cent. of the administrative expenses of the entire city government, is thus paid annually to this Church in this city.

Any taxpayer can from his tax bills readily calculate how much of this is exacted from him; and this, too, in a country where a State Church is prohibited by the Constitution, and in a State where the organic law forbids "discrimination or favor" to any Church.

An examination of the roll of taxpayers in this city shows that those belonging to the Roman Catholic Church pay about one-tenth part of the public taxes; while they draw from the public treasury for the societies belonging to their churches nearly ten times as much as those of all the other religious sects together.

The fact that Roman Catholics excel all other sects in the number of their paupers and criminals, in this city, is no reason for thus pensioning this denomination upon the public treasury, but, on the contrary, is a reason against doing it; for the interests of the taxpayers, and of society, and of civilization all require that public support should not be given to a sect that has made such a signal failure in reducing pauperism and crime among its adherents.

There is but one effectual remedy for these subsidies, and but one effectual way of putting a stop to this indirect building up a State Church with the public treasure, and enabling its satellites and dependents to live on the public without work.

It is for the taxpayers and the opponents of a State Church and a State religion, and all friends of toleration in religion, to insist upon the striking out of these two Jesuitical clauses in the State Constitution, and the repeal of the statutes they protect.

The Roman Catholics have attempted to answer * Mr. Hawkins's allegations; but, having examined both statements, we are unable to see that Mr. Hawkins has been impeached.

In 1885 there was appropriated on State grants, out of the New York city treasury and from the Excise Fund, about $1,600,000. Of this amount about $224,000 went to non-sectarian institutions, about $92,000 to Hebrew institutions, about $356,000 to Protestant institutions, about $933,000 to Roman Catholic institutions.†

In the New York Legislature, January, 1887, a bill was introduced by Hon. Michael C. Murphy, which provided that "The schools established and maintained

---

*The Roman Catholic vindication, entitled *Grants of Land and Gifts of Money*, etc., was published in a pamphlet of 54 pages by the Catholic Publication Society Co., 8 Barclay Street, New York city, 1880.

† Rev. J. M. King, D.D., in an address before the Committee on the Affairs of Cities, Albany, 1885.

by the New York Catholic Protectory shall participate in the distribution of common school funds in the same manner and degree as the common schools of the city and county of New York "—a plain demand for sectarian appropriations and the destruction of the common school system. The bill failed, but it is a key to the purposes of the Roman Catholic Church.

In August, 1887, the Roman Catholics in Lowell, Mass., applied to the School Board of the city for a supply of school-books for their parochial schools, on the plea that they are bought by money raised by general tax for the free use of pupils. The reply was made that the Constitution of Massachusetts forbids the use of money raised for school purposes in aid of any denominational or sectarian schools.

A little later came the request of the Roman Catholics in the city of Malden, Mass., that certain unoccupied public school rooms might be leased for a compensation to the authorities of the Roman Catholic Church, for the use of their parochial schools. As these rooms had been emptied by the withdrawal of the children of Catholic parents from the public schools in order to place them in parochial schools, it was supposed that the same answer might have been returned as in the Lowell case; but a subservient city council granted, almost unanimously, the request, fixing the rent at a merely nominal sum. These incidents have served to arouse public attention to the encroachments of Romanism, and awaken apprehensions that in many places, through unscrupulous politicians, American institutions may be periled.

An important decision has just been rendered by the courts in Illinois adverse to the Roman Catholic Church, defeating a shrewd scheme for obtaining the public money for the support of their Industrial School for Girls. The result of the trial appeared in the *Chicago Tribune*, October 2, 1888. Under provisions of a law shrewdly pushed through the Legislature, presumably in the interest of the Romanists, dependent children can be committed to industrial institutions by the courts, their "tuition, maintenance, and care" to be paid for, by the county, at the rate of ten dollars per month. A large number of dependent girls were committed to the Roman Catholic Industrial School for Girls in Chicago. In process of time the managers of the institution presented a bill for settlement to the county treasurer, who declined to pay the bill. In the lower court the Roman Catholics gained their case. The Board of Commissioners of the county appealed to the Supreme Court, by which the decision of the lower court was reversed, on the ground that it would be an appropriation of public money in aid of a sectarian institution, which would be contrary to the Constitution of the State of Illinois. The third clause of the eighth article provides that "neither the General Assembly nor any county, etc., shall ever make any appropriation or pay from any public fund whatever, any thing in aid of any church or sectarian purpose, or to help support or sustain any school, academy, etc., controlled by any church or sectarian denomination whatever." It was fully shown in the trial that said institution was controlled by the Roman Catholic Church, and that the instruction it furnished was of a sectarian character. To pay said bills would be an appropriation of the taxpayers' money for sectarian purposes.

This question is likely to assume another phase, if we may accept what the *Freeman's Journal* says. They are aware that the public school moneys in a considerable number of States are guarded by constitutional * prohibitions against division for sectarian schools, and that if relieved from the burden of expense they must seek it in some other way. There are intimations that they will seek it by relief from what they call double taxation for schools. A very recent number of the *Freeman's Journal* says of the school question:

It is not really a question for the politicians, but a question for the courts. Can a large body of the people of New York and Brooklyn be forced to bear a double tax, because the authorities insist that they must accept a non-Christian education or go without any? This burden is forced on them now. How long, as the pro-

---

* See Section 6 of this volume.

testing population increases, and as public opinion becomes more enlightened, can it remain? If the Baptists, Methodists, and Presbyterians prefer Christless schools to the loss of money made necessary by the founding of schools of Christian morality, their demands for a share of the school fund, on conscientious grounds, might well be looked on with suspicion. In our political system numbers count. The majority is supposed to settle all political questions. But the opinion of a large minority has weight in proportion to its numbers. As Catholics we are bound to have what we want, for two reasons—we are right and we are numerous. Moreover, we have always been consistent on this public school question. Catholics ask for what they save the State. It is an enormous sum. With the multiplication of Catholic schools it becomes greater every year. If the Protestant Episcopalians build schools, let them have what they save the State. When the Congregationalists or the Hebrews can show schools like ours, they may consistently make the demand that we are making.

The *Catholic Citizen*, of Milwaukee, in a recent issue emphasized the statement that the Catholic parochial schools of that city save the city $15,000 a year. This is a bold hint that, therefore, they should be exempted from taxation for the support of the public schools.

The subject of relief from taxation will be discussed under Question IV, Part II.

As to the purposes of Romanists, Rev. Dr. McGlynn said : *

---
* *North American Review*, August, 1887, p. 199.

The hope is not concealed that when the so-called "Catholic vote" shall become larger, the politicians may be induced to appropriate, through State legislature or local government, all the funds necessary for the support of these schools. This has already been accomplished in Poughkeepsie, New Haven, and elsewhere, and for a brief period during the offensive and defensive alliance between a certain set of priests and the Tammany Ring of the days of Tweed, Connolly, and Sweeny, an appropriation procured by a legislative trick and fraud, under the management of Peter B. Sweeny, awarded several hundred thousand dollars to the parochial schools of New York city. . . . The extraordinary zeal manifested for the getting up of these sectarian schools and institutions is, first of all, prompted by jealousy and rivalry of our public schools and institutions and by the desire to keep children and other beneficiaries from the latter; and, secondly, by the desire to make employment for and give comfortable homes to the rapidly-increasing hosts of monks and nuns, who make so-called education and so-called charity their regular business, for which a very common experience shows that they have but little qualification beyond their professional stamp and garb. It is not risking much to say that if there were no public schools there would be very few parochial schools; and the Catholic children, for all the churchmen would do for them, would grow up in brutish ignorance of letters; and a commonplace of churchmen here would be the doctrine taught by the Jesuits in Italy, in their periodical magazine, the *Civilta Cattolica*, that the people do not need to learn to read; that all they do need is bread and the catechism, the latter of which they could manage to know something of even without knowing how to read.

SECTION VI.

Constitutional Amendments.

DURING the famous Know-Nothing excitements the need of constitutional prohibitions against the appropriation of school funds for sectarian schools was deeply felt and agitated. As the result, in some States, they were obtained. In 1855 the Constitution of Massachusetts was amended by adding the following provision:

ARTICLE XVIII.

All moneys raised by taxation in the towns and cities for the support of public schools, and all moneys which may be appropriated by the State for the support of common schools, shall be applied to and expended in no other schools than those which are conducted according to law, under the order and superintendence of the authorities of the town or city in which the money is to be expended; and such moneys shall never be appropriated to any religious sect for the maintenance, exclusively, of its own schools.

The new Constitution of Pennsylvania, adopted in 1874 by an overwhelming majority in the popular vote, contained the following:

ARTICLE X.

SECTION 1, The General Assembly shall provide for the maintenance and support of a thorough and efficient system of public schools, wherein all the children of this Commonwealth above the age of six years may be educated.

SEC. 2. No money raised for the support of the public schools of the Commonwealth shall be appropriated to or used for the support of any sectarian school.

In the winter of 1867-68, under the influence of the Roman Catholics, the following bill was introduced into the Legislature of New York, "referred to the Committee on Colleges and Schools, was reported back and printed." This bill, if it had been passed, would have ruined the public school system:

An act entitled, An Act to amend the School Laws of the State of New York. The people of the State of New York, represented in Senate and Assembly, do enact as follows:

SECTION 1. The schools of the various religious societies within the State of New York shall participate in the distribution of the school moneys in the same manner and to the same extent, so far as relates to the teachers of said schools, where the number of scholars regularly attending number 100 or more.

SEC. 2. The schools of the said societies shall be subject to the rules and regulations of the common schools in the said State, but shall remain under the immediate management and direction of the said societies as heretofore.

SEC. 3. That said societies furnish the necessary building for said purpose.

SEC. 4. This act shall take effect immediately.

The bill was defeated.

An amendment to the Constitution of New York was proposed in the Assembly, at Albany, by Mr. J. D. Brown, of Cayuga, January 3, 1872, forbidding an appropriation of public money for the benefit of sectarian schools, in these words:

That no gift, loan, or appropriation of public money or property shall be authorized or made by the Legislature or by the corporate authorities of any county, city, town, or other municipal organization, to, or in favor or aid of any institution, association, or object, which is under ecclesiastical or sectarian management or control.

On the 12th of April this amendment passed the Assembly, ayes 78, noes 14.

May 10, in the Senate, the amendment passed, ayes, 23; noes 5.

It was necessary for this measure to pass the Legislature the second year, but its history we have been unable to clearly trace. It appears, however, to have been swamped with some other measures near the close of the legislative session.

In the Congress of the United States several amendments to the national Constitution have been proposed, for the purpose of prohibiting the appropriation of public moneys to sectarian schools or institutions. April 19, 1870, Hon S. S. Burdett, of Missouri, proposed a new article to the United States Constitution, in the following words:

Section 1. No State or municipal corporation within any State of the United States shall levy or collect any tax for the support or aid of any sectarian, denominational, or religious school or educational establishment; nor shall the Legislature of any State or the corporate authorities of any municipality within any State appropriate any money or make any donation from the public funds or property of such State or municipality, for the support or aid of any sectarian, religious, or denominational school or educational establishment.

Sec. 2. Congress shall have power to enforce this article by appropriate legislation.

December 19, 1871, Hon. William M. Stewart, Senator from Nevada, proposed the following amendment to the Constitution of the United States:

Section 1. There shall be maintained in each State or Territory a system of free common schools, but neither the United States nor any State, Territory, county or municipal corporation shall aid in the support of any school wherein the peculiar tenets of any denomination are taught.

Sec. 2. Congress shall have power, etc.

Strong disapproval of the proposition was expressed by many, on the ground that such a measure was both unnecessary and mischievous—unnecessary because no danger could arise in any State from such action; and mischievous because it would only tend to provoke a controversy over a question which, by the silent consent of all, was acquiesced in, if not agreed to. But the trend in the direction of constitutional action was too

CONSTITUTIONAL AMENDMENTS.

strong to be at once suppressed. During the Centennial year the national perils and needs were closely studied, leading to a revival of this question.

The memorable utterance of General Grant during our Centennial year helped forward the movement. He said:

If we are to have another contest in the near future of our national existence I predict that the dividing line will not be Mason and Dixon's, but it will be between patriotism and intelligence on one side and superstition, ambition, and ignorance on the other. In this Centennial year the work of strengthening the superstructure laid by our forefathers one hundred years ago, at Lexington, should be begun. Let us all labor for the security of free thought, free speech, free press, and pure morals, unfettered religious sentiment, and equal rights and privileges for all men, irrespective of nationality, color, or religion. Encourage free schools, and resolve that not one dollar appropriated to them shall be applied to the support of any sectarian school. Resolve that every child in the land may get a common school education unmixed with atheistic, pagan, or sectarian teachings. Keep the Church and State forever separate.

On the 14th of December, 1875, Hon. James G. Blaine, in the House of Representatives in Congress, proposed the following amendment to the Constitution of the United States:

ARTICLE XVI.

No State shall make any law respecting an establishment of religion or prohibiting the free exercise thereof; and no money raised by taxation in any State for the support of public schools, or derived from any public fund therefor, nor any public lands devoted thereto, shall ever be under the control of any religious sect (or denomination); nor shall any money so raised, or lands so devoted, be divided between religious sects or denominations. (This article shall not vest, enlarge, or diminish legislative power in Congress.)

August 4, 1876, the above was reported from the Judiciary Committee, with the additions included in the brackets.

The record says, "After a brief debate," the resolution as reported, was agreed to, yeas, 180; nays, 7; not voting, 98.

In the Senate, August 7, the above article was referred to the Committee on the Judiciary, with several substitutes offered for it. August 9, Hon. Mr. Edmunds, from the Committee on the Judiciary, reported the joint resolution with an amendment, in the nature of a substitute, as follows:

ARTICLE XVI.

No State shall make any law respecting an establishment of religion or prohibiting the free exercise thereof; and no religious test shall ever be required as a qualification to any office or public trust under any State. No public property, and no public revenue of, nor any loan of credit by or under the authority of the United States, or any State, Territory, district, or municipal corporation, shall be appropriated to or made or used, for the support of any school, educational, or other institution under the control of any religious or anti-religious sect, organization, or denomination, or wherein the particular creed or tenets of any religious or anti-religious sect, organization, or denomination shall be taught. And no such particular creed or tenets shall be read or taught in any school or institution supported in whole or in part by such revenue or loan of credit; and no such appropriation or loan of credit shall be made to any religious or anti-religious sect, organization, or denomination, or to promote its interests or tenets. This article shall not be construed to prohibit the reading of the Bible in any school or institution; and it shall not have the effect to impair rights of property already vested.

Sec. 2.—Congress shall have power, by appropriate legislation, to provide for the prevention or punishment of violations of this article.

August 11 the subject was briefly debated, and the substitute of the committee was agreed to, yeas, 27; nays, 15. August 14 the Senate voted on the passage of the joint resolution as amended, when it was disagreed to, yeas, 28; nays, 16, two thirds being necessary. So the joint resolution failed for the want of two votes. In the House the political parties voted *pro* and *con* without drawing party lines; in the Senate every affirmative vote was Republican and every negative vote was Democratic.*

---

* These facts may be verified by reference to McPherson's *Hand-Book of Politics* for 1876.

In the platform of the national Republican party, in 1876, the following plank (No. 7) occurs:

The Public School system of the several States is the bulwark of the American Republic, and, with a view to its security and permanence, we recommend an amendment to the Constitution of the United States, forbidding the application of any public funds or property for the benefit of any schools or institutions under sectarian control.

The Democratic National Convention, held soon after, adopted the following plank, in which the above is specified and condemned as "a false issue:"

The false issue with which they (the Republicans) would enkindle sectarian strife in respect to the public schools, of which the establishment and support belong exclusively to the several States, and which the Democratic party has cherished from their foundation, and is resolved to maintain without prejudice or preference for any class, sect, or creed, and without largesses from the treasury to any.

In the platform of the national Republican party in 1880, after a plank on the general subject of education, comes the following:

4. The Constitution wholly forbids Congress to make any law respecting the establishment of religion; but it is idle to hope that the nation can be protected against the influence of (secret) sectarianism, while each State is exposed to its domination. We, therefore, recommend that the Constitution be so amended as to lay the same prohibition upon the Legislature of each State, and to forbid the appro-

priation of public funds to the support of sectarian schools.

In the same year (1880) the Democratic National Convention in its platform declared itself in favor of—

Separation of Church and State for the good of each; common schools fostered and protected.

In the platforms of the State Conventions of the Republican party in Massachusetts in 1887 and 1888 a strong utterance appeared against sectarian schools.

Thus it appears that the Republican party in Congress, in 1876, attempted to pass an amendment to the Constitution of the United States, prohibiting the appropriation of public moneys to any sectarian schools or institutions, and the measure, after passing with the necessary majority, in the House of Representatives, failed in the Senate for the want of two votes, the Democrats voting solidly against it, and the Republicans solidly for it; and, in the National Republican Conventions in 1876 and 1880 planks were put in the platform, calling in strong terms for such an amendment. In the year 1876 the Democratic National Convention put into its platform a plank protesting against such an amendment, and in 1880 it only very feebly declared itself in favor of fostering and protecting the common schools.

The question has remained an open one. The

danger to the common school system, from the division of its funds, should not be lost sight of. The enemies of the public school system are wide awake. They are too prudent to attempt to carry out their purpose at present, but they lose no opportunity to instill their ideas into the minds of those with whom they have influence. The Roman Catholic Church is persistently pushing forward to that end. There are, however, watchful statesmen who are ready for necessary action.

In the Senate of the United States, May 25, 1888, Mr. Henry W. Blair introduced the following joint resolution, proposing an amendment to the Constitution of the United States respecting the establishment of religion and free public schools. The resolution was read twice and ordered to lie on the table.

Resolved, by the Senate and House of Representatives of the United States of America in Congress assembled (two thirds of each House concurring therein), That the following amendment to the Constitution of the United States be, and hereby is, proposed to the States, to become valid when ratified by the legislatures of three fourths of the States as provided in the Constitution.

ARTICLE.

SECTION 1. No State shall ever make or maintain any law respecting an establishment of religion, or prohibiting the free exercise thereof.

SEC. 2. Each State in this Union shall establish and

maintain a system of free public schools adequate for the education of all the children living therein between the ages of six and sixteen years, inclusive, in the common branches of knowledge, and in virtue, morality, and the principles of the Christian religion. But no money raised by taxation imposed by law, or any money or other property or credit belonging to any municipal organization, or to any State, or to the United States, shall ever be appropriated, applied, or given to the use or purposes of any school, institution, corporation, or person, whereby instruction or training shall be given in the doctrines, tenets, belief, ceremonials, or observances peculiar to any sect, denomination, organization, or society, being, or claiming to be, religious in its character, nor shall such peculiar doctrines, tenets, beliefs, ceremonials, or observances, be taught or inculcated in the free public schools.

SEC. 3. To the end that each State, the United States, and all the people thereof, may have and preserve governments republican in form and in substance, the United States shall guarantee to every State, and to the people of every State and of the United States, the support and maintenance of such a system of free public schools as is herein provided.

SEC. 4. Congress shall enforce this article by legislation when necessary.

The author has been anxious to ascertain how many of the States have constitutional restrictions or prohibitions against the appropriation of public school moneys for sectarian schools. He is at last able to make a statement on a high authority. The case is well covered by the following classified summaries: *

---

* *American Statute Law*, by Frederick J. Stimson, 1886.

1. By the constitutions of *thirteen* States no public money can be appropriated for the support of any sectarian or denominational school.

    New Hampshire,   Texas,
    Massachusetts,   Missouri,
    Pennsylvania,   California,
    Illinois,   Colorado,
    Michigan,   Alabama,
    Wisconsin,   Louisiana,
        Minnesota.

2. By the constitutions of *fourteen* States no money can ever be taken from the public treasury in aid of any Church, sect, or sectarian institution.

    Pennsylvania,   Texas,
    Indiana,   California,
    Illinois,   *Oregon*,
    Michigan,   Colorado,
    Wisconsin,   *Georgia*,
    Minnesota,   *Mississippi*,
    Missouri,   Louisiana.

The *four* States printed in italics are not included in the previous list.

3. In six States money cannot be appropriated for sectarian purposes or education by any municipal corporation.

    Illinois,   Missouri,
    Virginia,   California,
    West Virginia,   Colorado.

The *two* States printed in italics are not included in either of the previous lists.

4. Nor in *six* States can *property of the State* ever be appropriated for such purpose.

Illinois,   Missouri,   California,
Michigan,   Texas,   Colorado.

5. Nor in *four* States can the *property of any municipality* be so appropriated.
Illinois,   California,
Missouri,   Colorado.

6. In *one* instance the State cannot accept or grant a bequest to be used for sectarian purposes.
Nebraska.

7. In *four* States no public money can be appropriated for any school not under the exclusive control of the State or its school department.
Massachusetts,   Pennsylvania,
Maine,   California.

Maine is not included in any of the previous lists.

8. In *four* States no sect shall ever have any exclusive right to, or control of, the State School Fund.
Ohio,   *South Carolina*,
Kansas,   Mississippi.

Here are three States not before mentioned.

9. In six States no sectarian instruction is permitted, directly or indirectly, in any of the State schools.
Wisconsin,   California,   Colorado,
Nebraska,   Nevada,   South Carolina.

10. In *two* States no money can be appropriated for religious services in the legislatures.
Oregon,   Michigan.

By looking through the foregoing lists it will be seen that the appropriation of moneys for the aid of sectarian schools or institutions is substantially prohibited in twenty States, by constitutional provisions.

SECTION VII.

Recent Papal Utterances and Acts Enforcing the Parochial School System.

THE official utterances of Rome have ever been unqualifiedly against the public school system. We have noticed that the First Provincial Council, in 1829, expressed the wish that "schools might be established where youth might imbibe principles of faith and morality along with human knowledge." The Second Council, in 1833, appointed a committee "to revise and enlarge the books intended for Catholic youth." The First Plenary Council, in 1852, condemned the system of public schools where children of all denominations are admitted and religious teaching is excluded, and the bishops were instructed, if possible, to establish a school by the side of every church.

In 1858 Bishop Hughes, in a public lecture in New York city, said:

The Public School System is a disgrace to the civilization of the nineteenth century; I hope to see the day when New York will look back upon it with shame and horror, that such a gross and miserable delusion could ever have been suffered to take possession of the public mind.

The pope, in his famous Encyclical Letter, issued December 8, 1864, specified certain "errors" which he officially condemned, among which are the following:

The entire direction of public schools in which the youth of Christian States are educated may and must appertain to the civil power, and belong to it so far that no other authority shall be recognized as having any right to interfere in the discipline of the schools, the arrangement of the studies, etc.

The most advantageous conditions of civil society require that popular schools, open without distinction to all children of the people, and public establishments designed to teach young people letters and good discipline, and to impart to them education, should be freed from all ecclesiastical authority and interference, and should be fully subjected to the civil and political powers, for the teaching of matters and opinions common to the times.

These principles, so fundamental to the educational system of the United States, are condemned as "errors" by the pope, and the Roman Catholics of our country are enjoined to oppose them.

Soon after the issuance of that famous Encyclical Letter the Second Plenary Council of the Roman Catholic Church in the United States assembled in Baltimore, in the autumn of 1866. In this Council "parochial and industrial schools were recommended and commanded, where possible, in two distinct decrees."

This subject is treated under Title IX : *De Juventute Instituenda Pleoque Emdienda.* The Council deplored that many Catholic children were exposed to evil influences in reformatory schools, in addition to the accumulated stock of such influences derived from their former habits of life. It was admitted in the Pastoral Letter of 1866 that it was a melancholy fact that a very large proportion of the idle and vicious youth of our principal cities were the children of Catholic parents, and it was there stated that the only remedy for the evil would be to provide Catholic protectories or industrial schools. Accordingly decrees as aforesaid were passed.

Other high Roman Catholic authorities follow. In March, 1870, the *Tablet* said :

There is no help but in dividing the public schools or in abandoning the system altogether.

In their periodicals and lectures the common schools have been ridiculed and denounced as "pits of destruction," and "public soup-houses where children eat with wooden spoons."

The editor of the *Freeman's Journal* said :

Every such school is an insult to the religion and virtue of our people.

A Roman Catholic orator said:

The prototype of the American school system is seen in the institutions of paganism.

During the winter of 1872–73 the Roman Catholic children were taken out of the public schools in Holyoke, Mass. The Bishop of Cleveland, O., just before the Lent season, in 1873, published a "pastoral" which attracted considerable attention. It required Roman Catholic parents to send their children exclusively to their own church schools, under severe threats. In case of refusal to comply, the bishop "authorized confessors to refuse the sacraments to such parents as thus despise the laws of the Church, and disobey the commands of both priest and bishop." The public press commented severely upon this action, and the bishop replied, giving his *ultimatum*, which we here insert as taken from the Brooklyn *Catholic Review*, March 22, 1873:

Finally the bishop submits the following propositions to the School Board of Cleveland, promising that if they are accepted he will put the Catholic schools under the control of the Board; if they are rejected, Catholics will know that they have nothing but injustice to look for:

1. We shall build our school-houses and collect into them our children. When there we shall place them and their teachers, during school hours, under the entire control of the School Board, receiving from the School Board such directions as it may give.

2. During school hours no religion or religious instruction of any kind shall be given.

For these concessions, which certainly are all that could be demanded, we will only ask that either before or after school hours we shall be permitted, in our own way, to instruct our children in their religion. And secondly, *that the teachers shall be Catholics and paid by the School Board.* The italics are ours.

At the opening of a new Roman Catholic school in Worcester, Mass., in January, 1875, Bishop McQuaid said:

We are going to have a desperate struggle on this question all over this country for the next generation. Not one with the musket, but with the ballot and all the levers of public opinion. I know the American people are sometimes slow to give up their strong prejudices, but they are always ready to listen to fair argument.

The Sacred Congregation *de Propaganda Fide*, in a letter to the bishops of the United States, in 1875, assigned two fundamental reasons for its condemnation of our public school system:

1. The system . . . excludes all teaching of religion.

2. Certain corruption likewise ensues from the fact that in the same schools, or in many of them, youths of both sexes are congregated in the same room for the recitation of lessons, and males and females are ordered to sit on the same bench (*in eodem scamno*); all which have the effect of lamentably exposing the young to loss in faith and endangering of morals.

The Last Plenary Council.

Much has been said of late about the action of the Roman Catholic Plenary Council in Baltimore, November, 1884. Its utterances were not new, but were more explicit and decided than those of previous councils, and it concerted measures for carrying out more fully the policy of Rome in regard to parochial schools.

In the Prize Essay before the Council, entitled, " The Catholic Church in the United States," by John A. Russell, A.B., we find the following declarations:

For thirty years and more the Catholic population of this country have been forced to pay tribute to a system of godless education of which no one can conscientiously take advantage. The Catholic protests against paying for the education of other than their own children were made in the earliest days of the Know Nothing era, and were hurled back as arguments in favor of the enmity of Catholics to free institutions. But Know-Nothingism has passed away, and the school question still remains in all its glaring injustice. Millions of money are annually taken from Catholics for the support of schools in which they have no interest. The Catholic considers it unfair to tax him for the support of schools from which all ideas of religion are excluded, nor can he accept those in which a false religion is taught; for between godlessness and error the choice is only slightly in favor of the latter.

The formal declaration of the Plenary Council of 1884 was:

The friends of Christian (that is, Catholic) education do not condemn the State for not imparting religious instruction in the public schools, as they are now organized, because they well know it does not lie within the province of the State to teach religion. They simply follow their conscience by sending their children to denominational (that is, Catholic) schools, where religion can have its rightful place. Two objects, therefore, dear brethren, we have in view—to multiply our schools and to perfect them. We must multiply them until every Catholic child in the land shall have within its reach the means of education. There is still much to do ere this be attained. There are still thousands of Catholic children in the United States deprived of the benefit of a Catholic school. Pastors and parents should not rest till this defect is remedied. No parish is complete till it has schools adequate to the needs of its children, and the pastor and people of such a parish should feel that they have not accomplished their entire duty until this want is supplied.*

In a sermon by Rt. Rev. Bernard J. McQuaid, D.D., Bishop of Rochester, N. Y., before the same Plenary Council, a freer utterance was given to the feelings of the Roman Catholics on this subject. He said:

Scarcely had the work of building churches for our rapidly-increasing population been taken in hand by priests and people than a yet heavier task was imposed upon them. Churches might suffice for the elders of the flock, who, trained to religion in a Cath-

---

* *Memorial Volume of the Third Plenary Council.* Baltimore Publishing Co. 1885. 8vo. Pastoral Letter, p. 17.

olic atmosphere at home, could neither be cajoled nor deterred from its practices; but what was to become of children growing up in an atmosphere not simply innocuous, but positively dangerous and hurtful? Bishops and priests were most unwilling to add to the burden already weighing down their congregations. They sought, as well in justice they might, that a portion of their own money paid to the State might come back to them. Unkindly, rudely, contemptuously, their reasonable request was spurned. Politicians and parsons were our fiercest antagonists. When passions are aroused, it is useless to argue. The passions of a nation cool slowly. There were some Catholics who hoped that an education purely secular might be made to answer. No doubt it will give to the children of secularists the husks of education—all they ask. They wonder that Catholics seek for more. They cannot comprehend our doctrine, that the school for the child is as necessary as the church for the parent. Without further argument or dispute, but, nevertheless, grieving and groaning under the wrong put upon us, by process of law and the vote of the majority, Catholics gathered their children into their own schools, that therein they might breathe a Catholic atmosphere while acquiring secular knowledge.

Without these schools in a few generations our magnificent cathedrals and churches would remain as samples of monumental folly—of the unwisdom of a capitalist who consumes his future, year by year, without putting it out at interest or allowing it to increase. The Church has lost more in the past from the want of Catholic schools than from any other cause named by me this evening. The 2,500 schools, with a half million scholars, which now bless our country, tell Catholics and non-Catholics that the question of religious education is settled so far as we are concerned. The good work so well advanced will not halt until all over the land the children of the Church are sheltered under her protecting care.*

OTHER CATHOLIC AUTHORITIES.

Not long ago the *Catholic Review* said:

There is no longer a school question for Catholics. It is closed. The door of discussion, which was slightly ajar prior to 1884, was closed, locked, bolted, and barred by the Plenary Council held in that year, which directed that Christian schools should be maintained by all the parishes in the United States not prevented by extreme poverty from carrying them on. The decree is law for priests and people.

In an address delivered in Boston on the 22d of December, 1887, Rev. Father F. T. McCarthy, S. J., read from a work by Father Connolly, S. J., the following:

The Sacred Congregation of the Inquisition in a detailed instruction to the bishops of the United States concerning the public schools, June 30, 1876, after quoting the last sentence of the above citation, adds the following words: These words, inasmuch as they are based on the natural and divine law, enunciate a general principle which holds universally, and refers to all places where this most destructive system has been unfortunately introduced. It is, therefore, necessary that the illustrious prelates should by all possible means keep the flock intrusted to their

---

* *Memorial Volume of the Third Plenary Council.* 1884. Baltimore Publishing Co., p. 174.

charge aloof from the corrupting influences of the public schools. In the opinion of all, nothing is so necessary for this end as that Catholics should everywhere have their own schools, and these not inferior to the public schools. Every effort must, therefore, be made to erect Catholic schools where such do not exist, or to enlarge them and make them more useful and efficient, that in the course and method of training they may be in no sense inferior to the public schools. The Sacred Congregation grants that there may be circumstances in which Catholic parents may in conscience send their children to American public schools; namely, when no Catholic school is at hand, or when that which is at hand is not fit to give the children an education suited to their station and conformable to their age.

Father McCarthy then proceeds:

It is to be remembered, however, that the frequenting of the public schools can be permitted even in these cases, according to the declaration of the Sacred Congregation, only when the danger of perversion can be rendered remote. On that the decision is left to the bishop, and not to the parents of the children. So that even in the circumstance that I have described, even where there is no Catholic school at hand, it is not lawful for Catholic parents to send their children to these public schools, unless they can and unless they will make the danger of perversion, from being approximate, become remote. And when there is a doubt at all with regard to the matter the judge in this case is not to be the parent; he is not to be the judge, but the bishop of the diocese.

Now, in order to show you that this legislation extends to the whole country and that it extends to this part of the country, I may mention a fact that ought to have a great deal of weight with you Catholics of the Diocese of Boston. In the synod which was held within the past year and a half in this diocese the archbishop expressly declared that in all parishes Catholic schools were to be built; that they were to be built as soon as possible; that they were to be under way, at all events, *within two years, and that a pastor having the ability to build such schools, and failing to do it, would give sufficient canonical cause for his removal from that parish.* This is the utterance of the highest ecclesiastical authority in this State of Massachusetts.

Now, dearly beloved, here is the sense of the Catholic Church. Here is her teaching from the pope and the council general, down to the bishops and to the priests, that Catholic schools are to be built, Catholic schools are to be supported, that the children of Catholics are to be sent to these schools and to no other, that religion must be taught in the schools, that religion and education must go hand in hand, that there is no education worthy of the name without the teaching of religion, and this must be done without any let or hinderance on the part of any one whatsoever. This is certainly to impose a great burden upon you. We appreciate it. But, dearly beloved, at the same time we impose a great burden upon ourselves. It would be a great deal more for our comfort if we were simply to allow our children to go to the public schools, to pay our school taxes, and to give ourselves no concern about the matter any further.

The *Record** (Boston) quoted the following late utterances from the *Freeman's Journal:*

---

* August, 1888.

Look at Catholic school-houses throughout the country, supported by the exertions of our priests and the hard work of our people, and say whether public opinion can consistently hold that Catholics have not proven their sincerity in the matter. They have gone down deep into their pockets. We want justice. We want a fair per capita share of the school funds. We want to be on an equal footing with our fellow-citizens, who, if they have children, receive a return for the taxes they pay. Let our Protestant friends awaken to the danger which godless schools threaten the American people, and join with us, insisting that the school is the church of the little ones, and that it should be sacred to Christ.

The *Transcript* * (Boston) quotes from the *Freeman's Journal:*

The Catholic attitude on the school question is uncompromising. We will not permit our money to be used for the propagation of lies like those noticed in Boston, and in Brooklyn by Father Donahoe. Ignorant Calvinistic ministers—and when they are ignorant how ignorant they are!—must broaden their views. They protest in vain. Swinton's lies about indulgences must be put out of schools for whose support we pay. Sectarianism shall not be taught in a professedly "colorless" school while there is justice in the courts. The State has no right to educate, but every right to protect itself against parental carelessness. As the State taxes us for schools we must be represented in them! As American citizens we cannot submit to taxation without representation. As Catholics we cannot allow the State either to teach sectarianism to our children, or to increase a school

---

* August 1, 1888.

system of which we cannot approve with our money. There is no divergence between our duty as citizens and our duty as Catholics.

ENFORCEMENT.

In the autumn of 1879 serious trouble occurred in St. Mary's parish, Cambridge, Mass., Father Scully pastor. Four or five years previously a parochial school had been established, and all Catholic parents had been ordered to send their children to the Church schools and to contribute to their support. The quality of the instruction imparted was soon found to be inferior to that of the public schools, on account of which some children were withdrawn, and sent again to the public schools. Against these parents Father Scully directed all the ecclesiastical weapons at his command. He taught his people to shun and ignore such parents and their children * as if they were Protestants, and refused them the sacraments. Some parents went to other priests in other parishes for the spiritual consolations which Father Scully denied them. These priests were openly blamed by Father Scully. He made war upon them, claiming that by the canons of the Church he had the sole charge of the people of his parish, and no one but he and his assistant could " forgive their sins and

---

* One boy is said to have been so severely flogged that he was unable to sit up for two weeks.

send them to heaven." For this claim to an exclusive celestial monopoly he cited the authority of the archbishop, and sent to him the names of all the offending parents, children, and priests.

It is a remarkable fact that Archbishop Williams seemed to give his support to the belligerent priest. He refused to receive a committee sent from the parish to present complaints against Father Scully, but a committee sent in his behalf he received, and said that Father Scully's course met his entire approval. In a speech in a parish meeting, Father Scully said that other priests in the diocese were about to follow his example, in the erection of parochial schools, and that for him to give the sacraments of the altar to those who were sending their children to the public schools would be "to incur for himself eternal damnation, and leave them without salvation, too." His short and distinct answer to those hesitating or expressing dissent, in his congregation, was, "Do as I bid you, and I will forgive your sins and send you to heaven; disobey me, and you will be lost."

A Boston daily, commenting on the case, said: "The archbishop, in our judgment, has made a serious mistake in sustaining Father Scully's mischievous procedure, by the sanction of his high authority." But the bishop's action, and Father Scully's action, too, are perfectly logical from the premises on which their religion is predicated."

The *Boston Journal* * said in an editorial:

There is some ground to hope that the more liberal and intelligent Catholics will not yield abject obedience to the new policy, and that there may be developed within the Catholic Church such a degree of resistance as may make the full execution of such measures impracticable. In Belgium the priests, being excluded from the control of the public schools which they have long enjoyed, have established schools of their own—many of them grotesquely weak and inadequate —and have ordered the exclusion from the sacrament of teachers, parents and children who continue to support or attend the government schools. The course of Archbishop Williams is calculated to make a Belgium out of Massachusetts. But the Belgian government schools are maintained, notwithstanding, and Catholic children are sent to them. There is at least as much liberty and individuality in Massachusetts as in Belgium, and it would hardly be supposed that a policy which proves too arrogant to accomplish its purpose among Belgian Catholics would be tried here. The attempt to do it is interesting, and in a certain sense startling, and the outcome of it will be closely watched.

This agitation led to a formal proclamation of the archbishop's views by his Vicar-General soon after, sustaining and enforcing the parochial school policy of the Church.

In 1879 the Very Rev. William Byrne, Vicar-Gen-

---

* November 12, 1879.

eral of the Archdiocese of Boston, prepared a paper upon the parochial school question, of which we give a part of the abstract as printed in *The Pilot* (Roman Catholic), November 15 :

From the decrees of the Second Plenary Council of Baltimore the following propositions are, we think, fairly deduced, and will be accepted by all Catholics:

1st. That the Church is solicitous for the proper education of the young.

2d. That she does not approve of a system of popular education that seeks to impart a knowledge of earthly things only, and that, too, apart from her oversight and influence.

3d. That pastors of souls may properly concern themselves with the education of the children of the flock.

4th. That the American Public School System is defective in theory, inasmuch as it does not provide for the culture of the moral faculties, and in practice tends to evil results.

5th. That this system, by its very nature, tends to indifferentism in matters of religion, and in the hands of designing men can easily be used as an engine of perversion.

6th. That the manner in which the public schools are, in most places, conducted, renders them a source of danger to the faith and morals of the Catholic children attending them.

7th. That Catholics should endeavor to correct the evils and counteract the dangers of the public schools.

8th. That the best safeguard against these dangers is the Catholic parochial school.

9th. That pastors and parents, where the public schools are, as a matter of fact, dangerous, and especially where these evils are great, should labor to the best of their ability and means to establish Catholic schools for Catholic children.

Where suitable Catholic schools are accessible the parents' duty is plain.

The practical question here arises as to whether we Catholics, holding these views, can with a safe conscience use the public schools at all, even in the absence of any better.

The question involves a matter of principle and a matter of fact.

The principle is settled, and is easily stated.

Where the public schools are in fact so dangerous that the result is, or, according to common experience, most likely to be damage to faith or morals, they cannot, of course, be prudently used, and must be avoided at all hazards and at whatever cost. No person can without sin voluntarily expose himself to the proximate occasion thereof.

Where the public schools are not positively harmful, and the danger is remote, they can be used in the absence of suitable Catholic schools, prudent precaution being taken to avert such danger as there is, and reasonable care being taken to supply the defects of the system in some efficient way.

The doubt hangs on the matter of fact.

Are our public schools here in Boston so dangerous that a prudent Catholic is in duty bound to keep his children away from them, where no Catholic schools exist and cannot conveniently be built?

This doubt has never been settled by any formal decision of a competent authority. The tolerated usage of the public schools that obtains here is the nearest approach to a solution that we have.

Rome has given no decision as to the gravity of the danger in this country, and, whenever appealed to, has referred this matter of fact to the judgment of the bishops in council, or to each bishop in and for his own diocese.

Several bishops have decided the case for their own dioceses, with a thorough knowledge of the facts as they were in their districts, and have declared that the obligation of withdrawing Catholic children from the public schools where Catholic schools exist was of the gravest character, and that the duty of providing Catholic schools was of such prime importance that the establishment of a school should accompany the erection of a church in a parish.

The Council of Baltimore has decided that danger inheres in the very system itself, but has not undertaken to say what the amount of danger is in any given place. Manifestly the system, as reduced to practice, varies enormously as to its danger, in different places, and even in the same place, for different persons.

The schools we are warned against, as specially and seriously dangerous, are those in which Catholic children are induced to read the Protestant version of the Bible, to join in heretical forms of prayer, and to sing the hymns of the sects, or where the Catholic religion is attacked, her doctrines controverted, and the facts of history distorted, to vilify and render odious the Catholic Church and her institutions.

Apart from the dangers inhering in the system itself, which arise chiefly from defect, most of these incidental evils are absent from the public schools of Boston. The children are not required to read the Protestant version of the Scriptures or to recite un-Catholic prayers. The books in use are now pretty thoroughly purged of all sectarian or anti-Catholic leaven; the mouth of the reviler is closed, and at least no open or direct attempts at proselytism allowed.

That the spirit of proselytism is abroad we know full well, and it has full play in some quarters, notably in the State Reform Schools. The proposed action of the Legislature would go far to remedy that abuse.

Our use of the public schools, or our co-operation in carrying them on, when given with a view of correcting the evils in them, cannot fairly be construed into an approval of them. I can use a poor road in the absence of a better without being said to approve the bad construction of the road or the ruts that infest it.

We are not quite content with the public schools as they are, and yet, in most of our parishes the burden of church debts carried, the pressing calls for the support of our hospitals, orphanages, asylums, and homes for the poor, are so urgent and imperative that little can be done toward establishing Catholic schools even by those who hold that they are the safest for our Catholic children.

We admit that the education of the children of the whole people, in schools common to all and frequented by all, has many temporal advantages, but we can never reasonably or conscientiously consent to sacrifice or seriously endanger our eternal interests for worldly advantage.

The rapidly-growing fairness of public opinion may ere long discover a way of making a system of common school education acceptable to Catholic minds and safe for Catholic consciences.

That the problem is not absolutely insolvable is shown by the success of some other countries in dealing with it in somewhat similar circumstances. Belgium, Holland, England, and Lower Canada, are cited as instances.

Prussia, before she became blinded by pride, was an illustrious example.

The foregoing document has been given at such length in the interest of fairness, and to facilitate the close study of the problem which many are deeply pondering.

About the same time *The Pilot* contained a statement, authorized by his Grace the Archbishop,* setting forth substantially what his vicar-general had given in his paper. He added that Catholics are agreed on the principle and purpose of establishing parochial schools, and " differ, if at all, only as regards the feasibility, opportuneness, or best methods of giving these principles practical effect;" and he urged that these schools " be established wherever practicable in every parish, and as far as possible made equal to the public schools." " Parochial schools are regarded as practicable," continues the archbishop, " where their establishment and support would not create any

---

* Rev. Joseph Cook, commenting upon the case of Father Scully, said : " When a boy is stretched on a table, yonder at Cambridgeport, and his back lashed till for two weeks the boy cannot lie down on account of his wounds [sensation], the eyes of the mother and father of that boy are very likely to be opened. His only crime was attending a public school, when the priest had given warning that he should attend the parochial. . . . Archbishop Williams, of Boston, whispers to Father Scully, of Cambridgeport, : 'Hist ! No noisy barking against the American public schools. A still-hunt is what the Church wants. The parochial schools are to be defended and the public schools assailed unflinchingly, but with prudence, with suavity, with opportuneness.' The manly outspokenness of the priest is preferred to the politic indirection of the archbishop. [Applause]. Bunker Hill, Faneuil Hall, the Old South, listen to this colloquy and whisper to each other: 'Whom the gods would destroy they first make mad.' O, Lord ! now let the prayers of our fathers be fulfilled abundantly, that the love of good learning may not be buried in their graves.''

8

serious financial embarrassment or impose too grievous a burden on the resources of the faithful." Further on we have these astonishing declarations, in which much is contained between the lines: "Any priest hearing confessions in the private tribunal of penance is free, in the exercise of his faculties, in this, as in all other cases, to give or withhold absolution, guided by the disposition of the penitent and his own judgment and discretion, and his knowledge of the facts and principles involved."

At West Chester, in Pennsylvania,* the priest of St. Agnes Church excommunicated two pew-holders, Philip Maguire and William S. Bowen, because they withdrew their children from a parochial school and sent them to a public school. The priest gave his reasons for this action at mass, and this is what the priest said:

These gentlemen were excommunicated on my own authority and the authority of the archbishop, with whom I had consulted in the matter. I took their pews from them, because I do not propose that any one shall hold a pew in this church who is in open rebellion against its laws, when there are faithful and obedient members who are willing to occupy them. Mr. Bowen had the audacity to apply for communion last Easter morning, and was publicly refused. I had consulted with the archbishop months before in reference to this matter, and it was on the strength of this, and of a letter from his grace, that the refusal was made.

---

* *The Boston Transcript*, June, 1888.

And this is what Mr. Maguire says:

The reverend gentleman saw fit to use my name in connection with my refusal to send my child to the parochial school, and also notified those of his congregation present that I was formally excommunicated for this refusal; but he wisely took good care not to state the reason for my refusal to have the boy longer educated at the parish school. I took the boy away because, in my judgment, the school was far inferior to the public schools of West Chester, and because the penalty for missing a lesson in catechism was a severe whipping. When I inquired, through a letter, about the severity of the lesson, and the punishment inflicted, I received, in reply, a letter from his reverence telling me to mind my own business, and that he would not tolerate interference from me. I replied in a letter, which was answered with a notice that my boy was turned out of the Sunday-school because I would not send him to the parish school; and, later on, the priest met me on the street, and in the most overbearing way threatened that he would deny the child the sacraments of the Church. Nine tenths of the parents sending their children to the parish school do so rather from a sense of fear than an understanding that it is good for them to do so. Many of them have told me of their troubles, and of the bad discipline in the school, and of the poor progress their children make. There is a great deal of smothered dissatisfaction.

THE BOSTON SCHOOL TROUBLE.

On the 8th of May, 1888, Rev. Theodore A. Metcalf, rector of the Gate of Heaven Roman Catholic Church, South Boston, complained to the Boston School Board that Charles B. Travis, a teacher in the English High School, in the course of his instruction in history, had made offensive statements in regard to the Roman Catholic doctrine and practice of indulgences, and asked for a remedy. After investigation, the committee concluded that the complaint of the Roman Catholic priest was, in their judgment, well founded, and that the book, *Swinton's Outlines of Modern History*, was also faulty, particularly in a foot-note explaining the doctrine and practice of the Romish Church, in the matter of indulgences. They therefore ordered Mr. Travis to be removed to another position in the school, and that *Swinton's History* be discontinued as a text-book.

This Roman Catholic interference aroused the citizens of Boston, and numerous public meetings were held during the summer and autumn, in the largest halls and churches, with immense audiences. Able speakers enlisted in the contest, and it was carried into other towns and cities in Eastern Massachusetts. Powerful addresses and appeals were made; and the interest in the school question was so great as to overtop the excitement incident to the State and national elections.

In Massachusetts women are allowed to be enrolled and vote on the election of school boards. Anticipating the annual city election, in December, there was a large registration of women in September, Protestant and Catholic women competing with each other, so that of the 23,000* women registered the two classes were supposed to be nearly equal in number.

It is impossible to give a full history of all the details of this great contest. Most Protestants claimed that the complaint against Mr. Travis was without good foundation; that it was an unwarranted meddling with our public schools, by Roman Catholic priests, and a part of their policy to rule and ruin the system; that the people must be aroused to resist the encroachments of Rome, etc. The agitation, now continued for about six months, has not yet abated in interest, and all phases of the Romish question have been freely discussed. In the meantime the Catholics have made few replies, but steadily pushed forward the erection of buildings for parochial schools in Boston, Waltham, Watertown, and other cities, and several thousand more of pupils were gathered into them when the autumn term opened. The election in December is awaited with great interest, and both parties are actively preparing for the contest. It now looks as though the greatest protest known for a long period will be made against the interference and aggressiveness of Rome in the affairs of our public institutions.

---

* In no previous year had more than 2,000 women registered.

118   ROMANISM vs. THE PUBLIC SCHOOL SYSTEM.

Similar movements against *Swinton's History* have been incepted by Roman Catholics in Lowell, Mass., and Troy, N. Y.

Much interest has also been excited within the past few months in Pittsburg, Pa., by the performances of the Catholic priests, in connection with parochial schools.

A year ago Father McTighe had himself elected principal by the school-directors of the Twenty-sixth Ward, a strong Roman Catholic ward, and undertook to establish a parochial school under the support of the city funds. This was found to be illegal, and aroused so much opposition that he was obliged to abandon his position in a month. Another experiment has followed, somewhat different, in the Fourth Ward. Rev. Father Sheedy opened a parochial school, on the 4th of September, in four rooms which he rented from the Ward School Board. Each room contained fifty pupils in charge of a nun. Professor Sullivan and his three lady teachers, who compose the public school staff in that ward, have only fifty-one pupils under their care, the two schools being separated by a narrow hallway.

The foregoing statement was sent through the country by the Associated Press. Inquiry* made in Pittsburg upon two points—whether the nuns were

---

* By the Editor of *The Christian Advocate*, New York city, N. Y.

paid from the public school funds, and whether the priest paid rent for the room—brought the following reply: The nuns are not paid from the public school funds, but belong to an unsalaried order of workers, supported by the Mother Superior, from contributions and endowments. The Roman Catholics pay the public school directors a stated sum of money, per month, as rent for the rooms.

Father Sheedy is represented as one of the most aggressive priests in the city, and it is conjectured that should his experiment succeed there are at least three other wards in the city, with a Catholic majority on the school boards, in which the experiment in Ward No. 4 will be repeated. The whole city is aroused upon the subject. The Protestant pulpits of Pittsburg are echoing with sermons on *Parochial vs. Public Schools*, and the whole country looks with interest to see the result.

SECTION VIII.

Statistical Exhibits of the Parochial Schools of Romanism in the United States.

THE data we are about to present have been collated from *Sadlier's Catholic Directory, Ordo and Almanac.* They will show the present magnitude of the movement, and in what sections of the country it is largest.

ROMAN CATHOLIC PAROCHIAL SCHOOLS IN THE UNITED STATES.

DIOCESES AND VICARATES.	Schools.	Pupils.	DIOCESES AND VICARATES.	Schools.	Pupils.
Baltimore	87	16,000	Columbus	35	6,649
Charleston	6	600	Covington	30	5,723
Richmond	33	1,993	Detroit	60	11,470
Savannah	4*	1,500*	Fort Wayne	70	8,696
St. Augustine	16	1,238	Grand Rapids	32	5,786
Wheeling	13	1,800	Louisville	60	9,100*
Wilmington	6*	530*	Vincennes	74*	14,000
North Carolina	3				
				568	108,972
	155	23,061	Milwaukee	118	8,000*
Boston	42	22,250	Green Bay	63	8,406
Burlington	17	3,981	La Crosse	48	5,000*
Hartford	68	13,282	Marquette	10	1,400
Manchester	26	5,600	St. Paul	73*	11,289*
Portland	14	3,671	N. Minnesota	20*	2,000*
Providence	17	9,000			
Springfield	21	7,330*		332	28,095
	205	65,114	New Orleans	40	11,000
			Galveston	8*	1,200*
Chicago	112	40,000	Little Rock	11	1,255
Alton	100	11,000	Mobile	18	1,200
Peoria	41	7,050	Natchez	25	2,107
			Natchitoches	4	300
	253	58,050	San Antonio	26	1,000*
			Brownsville	8	500*
Cincinnati	80	21,757			
Cleveland	127	25,791		140	18,562

STATISTICAL EXHIBITS.

ROMAN CATHOLIC PAROCHIAL SCHOOLS.—Continued.

DIOCESES AND VICARATES.	Schools.	Pupils.	DIOCESES AND VICARATES.	Schools.	Pupils.
New York	146	41,139	St. Louis	95	20,450
Albany	50	14,500	Cheyenne	2	175
Brooklyn	97	27,000	Concordia	4	345*
Buffalo	58	15,000	Davenport	34	3,940
Newark	75	23,404	Dubuque	54	6,676
Ogdensburg	15*	2,878	Kansas City	40	2,600*
Rochester	27*	8,000	Leavenworth	50	4,000
Syracuse	14*	4,590*	Lincoln	2	100
Trenton	24	5,800	Nashville	16	2,500
			Omaha	25	2,251
	506	142,311			
				322	43,037
Oregon	3	1,065*			
Helena	8	300*	San Francisco	13	8,000
Nesqually	19	155*	Los Angeles	15	
Vancouver's Isl'ds.			Sacramento	9	1,566
Idaho	2	68*	Utah	5	340
	32	1,538		42	9,906
			Sante Fé	13	2,000*
Philadelphia	68	25,000	Denver	21	4,250
Erie	58	5,837	Arizona	6	500*
Harrisburg	29	4,252	Indian Territory	8	165*
Pittsburg	71	21,000			
Scranton	18	4,490*		48	6,915
	244	60,579	Aggregate	2,847	567,740

* These being omitted in the *Year Book* for 1888, have been supplied from the *Year-Books* of 1886 and 1887.

The enrollment of public school children in the nation is about one fifth of the total population. If the Catholic children of school age bear the same proportion, they cannot be less than 1,500,000, leaving 932,260 not yet gathered into their schools. This is upon the basis of 7,500,000 Catholics in the United States when the *Year-Book* for 1888 was made up. If the larger estimates of 8,000,000 or 10,000,000 Catholics are true, then they have only about one third of their children in their parochial schools.

The revised statistics show the following summaries:

	Pupils.	Schools.		Pupils.	Schools.
In 1860	57,611	660	In 1880	427,230	2,288
In 1870	257,000	1,214	In 1888	567,740	2,847

The sections of the country in which these parochial schools are most numerous are as follows:

States.	Parochial Schools.	Pupils.
New England	205	65,114
New York	407	113,107
New Jersey	99	29,204
Pennsylvania	244	60,579
Maryland	87	16,000
Ohio	237	52,271
Indiana	144	22,696
Illinois	253	58,050
Total	1,676	417,021

There are outside of the above thirteen States 1,171 schools and 150,723 pupils; fifty-seven per cent. of the schools and seventy-three per cent. of the pupils are in thirteen States. This shows where the contest is likely to come soonest and sharpest.

For the purpose of conveying to the mind of the reader a more distinct idea of the parochial schools, the following exhibit is furnished of the number of the schools and pupils, and the religious brotherhoods and sisterhoods intrusted with the work of instruction, in two important dioceses, Cleveland and Newark, as reported in *Sadlier's Catholic Almanac* for 1881.

DIOCESE OF CLEVELAND.

Religious Orders in Charge of Parochial Schools.

BROTHERHOODS.

Brothers of Mary .... 9 brothers. ‖ Franciscan Brothers .... 3 brothers.

STATISTICAL EXHIBITS.

SISTERHOODS.

	Sisters.		Sisters.
Ursulines	52	Sisters of St. Joseph	14
Sisters of Notre Dame	67	Sisters of St. Francis (Tiffin)	6
Ladies of the Sacred Heart of Mary	30	Sisters of St. Francis (Joliet)	8
Sisters of the Humility of Mary	23		
Total		12 brothers, 200 sisters.	

Parochial Schools and Average Attendance of Pupils.

	Divisions.	Pupils.		Divisions.	Pupils.
Cleveland: St. John's Cath'l.	14	1,050	Galion: St. Joseph's	2	78
St. Augustine's	4	219	St. Patrick's*	2	73
St. Bridget's	4	186	Glandorf	7	300
Holy Family	5	300	Grafton	1	28
Immaculate Conception	4	271	Harrisburg	1	29
St. Joseph's	5	383	Hubbard	2	138
St. Malachi's	9	550	Kelley's Island	1	50
St. Mary's (Annunciation)	3	140	Kirby	1	50
St. Mary's (Assumption)	6	384	Landeck	2	90
St. Mary's (Holy Rosary)	8	529	Leetonia	3	280
St. Patrick's	10	558	Liberty	1	28
St. Peter's	6	385	Lima	4	260
St. Procop's	3	263	Liverpool	2	69
St. Stephen's	5	374	Louisville	3	138
St. Wenceslas	4	285	Mansfield	2	140
Akron: St. Bernard's	2	180	Massillon: St. Joseph's	2	92
St. Vincent de Paul's	2	146	St. Mary's*	4	357
Ashtabula*	2	105	Milan	1	37
Avon	1	30	Millersville	2	39
Bellevue	2	78	Monroeville	2	102
Berea: St. Adalbert's	2	85	Napoleon	2	90
St. Mary's	3	95	New Cleveland	3	100
Berwick	2	75	New Riegel	3	120
Bethlehem	1	54	New Washington	1	160
Big Springs	1	25	Niles	3	107
Brier Hill	2	100	North Ridge	1	30
Canal Fulton	2	127	Norwalk: St. Mary's	2	80
Canton: St. John Baptist	2	130	St. Paul's	3	162
St. Peter's (German)	4	255	St. Peter's	1	30
Carey	1	25	Ottawa	1	55
Chicago Junction	1	35	Ottoville	5	210
Collinwood	1	31	Painesville	3	146
Crawfordsville	1	45	Perrysburg	2	75
Crestline	3	113	Peru	2	76
Custer	1	40	Randolph	1	55
Defiance: St. John the Evan.	2	112	Ravenna	2	89
Delphos	9	270	Reed	1	26
Elyria	2	110	Ridgeville	1	39
Euclid	1	40	Rockport: St. Mary's	1	36
Findlay	1	66	St. Patrick's	1	43
Florence*	1	50	Rootstown	1	12
Fostoria	1	60	St. Patrick's Settlement	1	48
Fremont: St. Ann's*	2	100	St. Stephen's Settlement	1	32
St. Joseph's*	4	220	Sandusky City: St. Mary's	7	395
French Creek	2	80	SS. Peter and Paul	6	250

* Report of 1878.

Parochial Schools and Average Attendance.—Continued.

	Divisions	Pupils.		Divisions	Pupils.
Sandusky City: Holy Angels.	1	100	Toledo: St. Hedwig's	1	100
Sheffield	1	45	Immaculate Conception	5	315
Shelby Settlement	2	56	St. Joseph's	2	115
Sherman *	2	110	St. Mary's	8	619
Six-Mile Woods	2	100	St. Patrick's	8	483
South Toledo	2	115	St. Peter's	4	240
Strasburg	1	32	Upper Sandusky	2	115
Thompson's	3	130	Vienna	1	65
Tiffin: St. Joseph's	7	340	Wooster	2	103
St. Mary's	3	110	Youngstown:		
Toledo: St. Francis de Sales's	5	250	St. Columba's	9	600
Good Shepherd's	2	100	St. Joseph's	2	80

RECAPITULATION.

Churches.......................... 199
" building 6
Chapels............................ 20
Stations (without churches)...... 65
Secular priests.............. 137
Regulars.................... 31—
Total number of priests.......... 171
Seminarians 35
Seminary 1
Academies for girls 6
Number of girls attending academies and select schools,....... 668
Hospitals......................... 5
Orphan asylums 6
Reformatory for girls............ 1

Homes for the aged poor......... 3
Orphans......................... 683
Male religious communities...... 6
Female   "   "   21
Brothers........................ 39
Professed sisters, novices, and postulants..................... 662
Religious having charge of parochial schools.................. 212
Parochial schools 113
Parochial schools taught by religious........................ 64
Average number children attending parochial schools...about 21,000
Catholic population ......about 150,000

DIOCESE OF NEWARK.

Parochial Schools.

	Pupils.	Taught by
St. Patrick's Cathedral Schools, Newark	670	5 Brothers of Christian Schools; 6 Sisters of Charity.
St. John's, Newark	302	6 Sisters of St. Joseph and lay teacher.
St. Mary's, Newark	400	5 Sisters of St. Benedict and lay teach'r.
St. James's, Newark	1,100	7 Sisters of Charity ; 7 lay teachers.
St. Aloysius's, Newark	326	4 Sisters of Charity.
St. Peter's, Newark	700	10 Sisters of Notre Dame ; 1 lay teacher.
St. Joseph's, Newark	560	8 Sisters of Charity.
St. Benedict's, Newark	168	2 Sisters of St. Benedict.
St. Columba's, Newark	146	2 Sisters of Charity.
St. Augustine's, Newark	156	3 Sisters of Christian Charity.
St. Michael's, Newark	410	5 Sisters of Charity.
St. Pius's, East Newark	460	5 Sisters of Charity and 2 lay teachers.
St. Peter's, Belleville	217	3 Sisters of Charity.
St. Mary's, Bergen Point	425	6 Sisters of St. Joseph.
Sacred Heart, Bloomfield	191	3 Sisters of Charity.

* Report of 1878.

STATISTICAL EXHIBITS. 125

Parochial Schools.—Continued.

	Pupils.	Taught by
St. Mary's, Bordentown	207	5 Sisters of Mercy.
St. Paul's, Burlington	117	3 Sisters of St. Francis.
St. Mary's, Camden	350	7 Sisters of St. Joseph.
SS. Peter and Paul's, Camden	120	3 Sisters of Notre Dame.
St. Joseph's, Carlstadt	98	3 Sisters of St. Benedict.
St. Patrick's, Chatham	55	1 lay teacher.
St. Mary's, Elizabeth	320	5 Sisters of Charity and lay teacher.
St. Michael's, Elizabeth	168	2 Sisters of Christian Charity.
St. Patrick's, Elizabeth	1,110	8 Sisters of Charity and lay teachers.
St. Henry's, Elizabeth	188	4 Sisters of St. Benedict.
St. Cecelia's, Englewood	190	4 Sisters of Charity.
St. Mary's, Fort Lee	125	2 Sisters of Notre Dame.
St. Rose of Lima, Freehold	110	2 Franciscan Sisters.
St. Mary's, Gloucester	195	6 Sisters of St. Dominic.
St. Joseph's, Guttenberg	138	2 Sisters of St. Francis.
St. Joseph's Chr., High Bridge	65	1 lay teacher.
Our Lady, Hoboken	639	7 Sisters of Charity and 2 lay teachers.
St. Joseph's, Hoboken	150	3 Sisters of St. Francis.
St. Peter's, Jersey City	830	8 Sisters of Charity and 4 lay teachers.
St. Mary's, Jersey City	1,200	4 Brothers Christian Schools and 8 Sisters of Charity.
St. Joseph's, Jersey City	510	8 Sisters of Charity and 1 lay teacher.
St. Boniface's, Jersey City	175	5 Sisters of St. Dominic.
St. Michael's, Jersey City	668	8 Sisters of Charity and 2 lay teachers.
St. Bridget's, Jersey City	600	6 Sisters of Charity and lay teacher.
St. Paul of the Cross, Jersey City	340	5 Sisters of Charity and lay teacher.
St. Paul's, Jersey City	92	4 Sisters of St. Dominic.
St. Joseph's, Keyport	30	1 lay teacher.
St. John's, Lambertville	275	Lay teachers.
St. Vincent's, Madison	135	2 Sisters of Charity and lay teacher.
St. Rose's, Milburn	85	3 Sisters of Notre Dame.
Our Lady's, Morristown	250	2 Sisters of Charity and lay teacher.
St. Mary Magdalen, Millville	37	1 lay teacher.
St. Bernard's, Mount Hope	75	3 Sisters of Charity.
St. Peter's, New Brunswick	750	6 Sisters of Charity and 3 lay teachers.
St. John the Baptist's, New Brunswick	81	2 Sisters of Christian Charity.
St. Ann's, New Hampton	50	1 lay teacher.
St. John's, Orange	685	5 Sisters of Charity and 2 lay teachers.
Our Lady, Orange Valley	300	2 Christian Brothers and 4 lay teachers.
St. Rose of Lima's, Oxford Furnace	80	1 lay teacher.
St. Nicholas's, Passaic	225	3 Sisters of Charity.
St. John the Baptist's, Paterson	582	8 Sisters of Charity.
St. Joseph's, Paterson	242	3 Sisters of Charity.
St. Mary's, Totawa, Paterson	120	5 Sisters of St. Dominic.
St. Joseph's Hospital School	50	1 Sister of Charity.
St. Boniface's, Paterson	220	3 Sisters of St. Dominic and 3 Brothers of Mary.
St. Bonaventure's, Paterson	100	2 Brothers of Mary.
St. Mary's, Perth Amboy	125	3 lay teachers.
St. Paul's, Princeton	225	4 Sisters of Mercy.
St. Mary's, Rahway	87	2 Sisters of Charity.
St. James's, Red Bank	100	Lay teacher.
St. Peter's, Riverside	106	2 Sisters of St. Francis.
St. Mary's, Salem	50	1 lay teacher.

Parochial Schools.—Continued.

	Pupils.	Taught by
Sacred Heart, Shadyside	152	2 Sisters of St. Francis.
St. Mary's, South Amboy	40	1 lay teacher.
Our Lady, South Orange	130	2 Sisters of Charity.
St. Teresa's, Summit	70	1 lay teacher.
Our Lady of Mt. Carmel, Tenatly	95	Sister of Charity.
St. John the Baptist's, Trenton	610	7 Sisters of Charity and 4 Brothers Holy Cross.
St. Mary's, Trenton	517	4 Sisters of Charity and lay teacher.
St. Francis's, Trenton	150	4 Sisters of St. Francis.
Our Lady of Lourdes, Trenton	122	2 Sisters of St. Francis.
Holy Family, Union Hill	109	3 Sisters of St. Francis.
Holy Family, Waterford	50	3 Sisters of Charity.
Our Lady, West Hoboken	360	5 Sisters of Charity and 4 Christian Brothers.
Our Lady, Whippany	42	1 lay teacher.
St. Mary's, Plainfield	...	Being remodelled.

A new diocese (Trenton) now takes a part of the foregoing.

GENERAL STATISTICS OF NEWARK DIOCESE (YEAR-BOOK, 1888).

	No.			No.
Priests: Regular	55	} 180	Churches	103
Secular	125		Stations visited	15
Brothers	23	} 977	Monasteries	3
Sisters	954		Convents	9
Ecclesiastical Students in seminary	25		Seminary	1

	No.	Pupils.
Colleges (Boys)	3	288
Academies (Young Ladies)	18	1,420
Parochial schools	72	23,214
Industrial schools and reformatories	3	190
Total		25,112

	No.	Inmates.
Orphanages	5	627
Hospitals, cases treated during the year	4	4,536
Asylums	4	380
Total		5,543
Catholic population of diocese by recent census, about		160,000

DIOCESE OF BOSTON.

	1888.	1877.	Increase.
Parochial schools	42	18	24
Teachers:			
Sisters	370	166	..
Lay	31	11	..
Brothers	10	..	..
Total teachers	411	177	234
Pupils	22,250	7,296	14,954

STATISTICAL EXHIBITS.

CITY OF BOSTON.

	1888.	1877.	Increase.
Parochial schools	16	11	5
Teachers:			
Sisters	116	94	..
Lay	18	11	..
Brothers	..	..	..
Total teachers	134	105	29
Pupils	7,169	5,086	2,083

CHILDREN IN BOSTON.

	1885.	1875.	Increase.
Between 5 and 15 years, inclusive	75,988	71,195	4,793
Foreign in first or second degree			50,000
In parochial schools			1 in 7

Of the parochial schools in the diocese of Boston 16 are in Boston and 12 more in Salem, Lowell, Lawrence, and Haverhill—28 in 5 cities, leaving 14 in the diocese outside of 5 cities. But there are 105 towns and cities in the diocese, 100 of which have only 14 parochial schools; they are now being rapidly organized in other towns and cities.

CITY OF NEW YORK.

	No.		No.
Parochial schools	65	Colleges (two Jesuit)	4
Teachers (sisters and brothers)	550	Teachers	110
Pupils	29,149	Pupils	996
Select schools	19	Homes, asylums, etc., for children	11
Teachers (sisters and brothers)	116	Teachers	426
Pupils	1,673	Pupils	2,331

CITY OF ST. LOUIS.

	No.		No.
Parochial schools	46	Colleges (one Jesuit)	2
Teachers (sisters and brethren)	251	Teachers	22
Pupils	14,522	Pupils	699
Select schools	7	Homes, asylums, etc., for children	9
Teachers (sisters and brethren)	294	Teachers	227
Pupils	935	Pupils	1,045

The *Catholic Citizen*, of Milwaukee, gives the following census of the pupils in the Catholic schools in that city:

1882—Total Catholic school enrollment	5,180
1883— " " " " "	5,870
1884— " " " " "	6,520
1885— " " " " "	7,118
1886— " " " " "	7,797
1887— " " " " "	8,457
1888— " " " " "	9,096

It will be noted that the increase per year has varied from eight to ten per cent. This increase is in keeping with the increase in population. During the past year five new Catholic schools were opened in the city, four of which are located on the south side. The present number of Catholic schools in Milwaukee is 24.

THE HIGHER EDUCATIONAL INSTITUTIONS Of Romanism in the United States are as follows:

	Institutions.	Students of all grades.
Jesuit colleges	26	5,258
Other colleges	60	8,749
Theological seminaries	19	3,645
Female colleges	19	1,214
Total	124	18,866

Of the 86 colleges many are but little more than foundations for colleges, in an exceedingly undeveloped condition, and the students comprise those in the academic or preparatory course, their plan of college studies comprising seven years. The better class of their colleges numbers little more than 50, and the students in the course for the degree A.B., as near as can be ascertained, are 4,647. The non-Roman Catholic denominational colleges in the United States are 252, with 21,301 students in the course for A.B. In addition are the undenominational colleges, numbering 61, with 6,819 students.*

---

* For fuller information see *Christianity in the United States*, by the author of this volume. Phillips & Hunt, 805 Broadway, New York city, N. Y. Pp. 604-609, 611-613, 726.

STATISTICAL EXHIBITS. 129

But the curriculum of studies in the Catholic colleges is much inferior to that of most Protestant colleges. (See Part II, Chapter IX.)

That the reader may see the relative situation, the colleges and students of three other denominations are given in comparison:

	Colleges.	Students for A.B.
Roman Catholics	57	4,647
Methodists (all kinds)	67	4,938
Presbyterians (all kinds)	46	4,060
Baptists (all kinds)	45	3,728

To aid in the work of education, as well as asylums, etc., the Romish Church has already in this country 24 orders of priests, 11 orders of brothers, and 77 orders of sisters—112 in all.

GROWTH.

The increase* of the Roman Catholic Church in this country is one of the striking religious phenomena of this century. Conceding heavy losses in Europe, it has been their habit to boast of large gains in the United States. Its churches, schools, convents, ecclesiastics and adherents have increased many fold, and it has become a conspicuous factor in the main centers of the population. It exerts a large and, in some localities, a controlling influence in politics. Never was it plotting more deeply and determinedly than now, and some persons have grave fears for the safety of our free institutions. Let us be wisely active.

---
* By immigration; but smaller relative increase since 1870 than before.

GENERAL STATISTICS.

The church edifices of Romanism in the United States, as given in the United States census reports, were: 1850, 1,222; in 1860, 2,550; in 1870, 3,806. Estimated value in 1870, $60,985,506. The census of 1880 did not give ecclesiastical statistics. The following table contains the leading items of statistics for 113 years.

	1775.	1800.	1840.	1845.	1850.	1860.	1870.	1880.	1886.	1887.‡
Dioceses, Vicar Apostolics		1	9	23	29	48	78	69	76	78
Churches	52			675	1,245	2,519	3,912	5,816	6,910	6,829
Chapels, stations			232	592	585	1,278	1,480	2,684	3,281	3,067
Priests	26	50		707	1,302	2,316	3,966	6,402	7,678	7,706
Ecclesiastical students				250	322	499	1,015	1,170	1,630	1,954
*Male religious houses					35	109	115			
†Female religious houses				28	65	173	297			
Educational institutions for young men and ladies		4		89	123		167	759	681	709
Parochial schools						660	1,214	2,389	2,697	2,817
Pupils in Parochial schools						57,611	255,600	427,390	537,725	566,740
Hospitals, Asylums				94	108		295	284	465	472
Estimated Catholic population	100,000	500,000		1,071,800	1,614,000	2,789,000	4,000,000	6,367,330	7,200,000	7,350,000

NOTE.—The above statistics, from 1830 to 1887, have been collated from the *Metropolitan Catholic Almanac* and *Sadlier's Catholic Directory*. They do not entirely agree with Father Hecker's table in the *Catholic World*, June, 1879. We prefer to rely upon the Year-Books of the Church as far as we can. The rule observed throughout this table is to take the data given in each Year-Book as the figures for the preceding year. For example, those in the columns for 1886 and 1887 are from the Year-Books for 1887 and 1888.

* Monasteries. † Convents. ‡ Four items in this column show a decrease. ‖ See page 121 (foot-note).

PART II.

QUESTIONS INVOLVED IN THE CONTEST.

PART II.
QUESTIONS INVOLVED IN THE CONTEST.

IN discussing the vital questions involved in the Catholic school contest, and in the form in which the writer apprehends they are likely to be developed in the near future, it will be noticed that the subject revolves around the following points :

The Roman Catholics claim—

1. That all education, secular and religious, is the exclusive function of the Church (the Papal Church), to be administered in parochial schools under the sole direction and supervision of the Church, and that, in a free republic like ours, the Church has a right to establish and maintain such schools.

2. Roman Catholics contend that they have a right to a share of the public school moneys, and demand that the funds be divided, and their portion appropriated for their schools.

3. And that, so long as the public schools exist on their present basis, no sectarian text-books or instruction should be allowed in them.

Protestants claim—

1. That secular instruction is the function of the State, and that religious instruction belongs to religious institutions and the home. We allow the right, to all denominations who desire to do so, to establish and maintain church schools, seminaries, and colleges at their own expense; but we do not consider it either wise or equitable, or consistent with true loyalty to the republic, for any denomination to maintain schools in which supreme allegiance to a foreign pontiff is daily and prominently inculcated, or hierarchical dogmas taught.

2. We also claim that no sectarian, parochial, or denominational school is entitled to the moneys raised or funded for the public schools; and that to divide and appropriate a portion of those moneys to sectarian schools would be fatal to the integrity of the public school system and the welfare of the republic.

3. We furthermore protest against the introduction into the public schools of sectarian text-books, or books showing a sectarian bias, or the impartation of sectarian instruction, or the employment, as teachers in the public schools, of members of religious brotherhoods or sisterhoods* wearing the costume or any insignia of any church; and also insist that there shall be no sectarian interference with the administration.

Such are the leading points of difference between Roman Catholics and Protestants on the school question.

---

* This has been done in some instances.

QUESTION I.

As to the Right and Duty of the State to Educate.

AT this point, so vital to the republic, the Roman Catholic Church squarely joins issue with the educational policy of this country. In the preceding pages the attitude of that Church has been seen; but a few more official utterances will help some minds to more clearly apprehend the unmistakable policy of Rome.

In his famous Encyclical Letter, before quoted, issued December 8, 1864, the pope specified certain "errors" which he officially condemned, among which were the following, bearing directly on this question:

The entire direction of public schools in which the youth of Christian States are educated may and must appertain to the civil power, and belong to it so far that no other authority shall be recognized as having any right to interfere in the discipline of the schools, the arrangement of the studies, etc.

The most advantageous conditions of civil society require that popular schools, opened without distinction to all children of the people, and public establishments designed to teach young people letters and good discipline and to impart to them education, should be freed from all ecclesiastical authority and interference, and should be fully subjected to the civil and political powers for the teaching of matters and opinions common to the times.

The *Catholic World* * said:

As there is for us Catholics only one Church, there is and can be no proper education for us not given by or under the direction and control of the Catholic Church.

A writer in the *Catholic World* † said:

The superintendence and direction of the public schools, as well as those wherein the mass of the people are instructed in the rudiments of human knowledge and those wherein secondary and higher instruction are given, is the right of the Catholic Church. She alone has the right of watching over the moral character of those schools, of approving the masters who instruct the youth therein, of controlling their teaching, and dismissing without appeal to any other authority those whose doctrines or manners are contrary to the purity of the Christian doctrine.

In a public address ‡ Chancellor Rev. Thomas S. Preston, Vicar-General of the Diocese of New York, said:

I will state, briefly, the position in which the Catholics stand in regard to elementary and popular instruction. We have been misunderstood, and often intentionally so, for our explanations have not been received with candor or considered with justice. We only de-

---
* April, 1871. † September, 1875.
‡ Before the " Young Men's Local Catholic Union " of New York city, November, 1876.

sire to practice our religion, and we defy any man to call us in question for our love for our country. . . .

We cannot approve the divorce of education and religion, and, so far as our children are concerned, we must teach them, with secular knowledge, the truths of revelation and the mysteries of our faith. [Great applause.] Because we do this do we prevent our neighbors from doing it likewise, or from not doing it at all, as they please? No. We interfere not with their rights, and surely they, in justice and in reason, ought not to interfere with ours. [Applause.] So far as the common schools are concerned, it is a calumny often repeated, and no doubt to be repeated still, that we are opposed to schools for those who want them. It is not true. We are not opposed to the common schools for our Protestant friends, if they want them, but they will not answer for us, for the schools we want are those in which our children shall be taught the mysteries of their faith.

The Catholic Theory Stated.

One of the latest and fullest utterances of the Roman Catholic Church on this subject was by Rev. F. T. McCarthy, S. J., of Boston. This gentleman's statement and vindication will be given at considerable length, that the subject may be brought more fully and intelligently before our readers. He said:*

There is no State that has ever received the commission to educate. God never gave a commission to the State to educate. The function of the State

---

* December 22, 1887, in the Church of our Lady of Perpetual Help, Boston Highlands. The extracts are from the *Boston Herald*, December 23, 1887.

with regard to education is simply this—to protect the citizen in natural and acquired rights, and to further and to promote the temporal welfare of the citizen.

A word now with regard to the origin of civil society. This will throw more light upon the subject. In the beginning, when there was but one family— Adam and Eve and the children immediately born to them—that was all the civil society that existed. Adam was the head. By the law of nature he was the head. By divine ordinance he was the head. In the family his will was law, so long as that will was not in opposition to the will of God. But they begat more and more children, and their children married, and they multiplied, and they covered the earth. Now, it was discovered that there was need of some public authority, some one chosen to administer the government. There were felt certain wants. Those wants could be best supplied by association, and accordingly they entered into association. The individual surrendered a certain amount of his individual right, in exchange for certain protection that he received from the government of civil society. And this is the origin of civil society. Civil society is created by individual men, and the cession of the rights of individual men was only in as far as the cession of those rights was for the common weal. Hence we hear people talking now about the Commonwealth of Massachusetts—common weal; common welfare. That is what it means, the common welfare, and the common welfare is best secured by the yielding up by the individual of certain rights. But the Government is not to take rights, to usurp those that the individual has never given up, and the individual has certain inalienable rights that he cannot give up. And one of the rights that the individual and the parent cannot surrender, is the right to educate the children that are born.

How, then, does the State come to possess this right? Does it belong to the protective function of the State? But it is supposed that the parent, in educating, is in his right; therefore there is no question of the State protecting his right. Does it belong to that function which is promotive of the welfare of the individual and of the family? No. It is not to the interest of the individual or of the family to have the State as the educator. Let us suppose that the State is atheistical. Let us suppose that the State is hostile to religion. Let us suppose— and the fact exists in a great many places—that the State is hostile to the Catholic Church and to those who profess Catholic doctrine and submission to Catholic authority. I have already said that any body that undertakes to teach teaches by the choice of the parent, and according to the mind and according to the conscientious convictions of the parents; but how is a State that is atheistical, how is a State that is opposed to Catholicity to teach Catholic children, to fill the place of Catholic parents with regard to such children, to bring them up as the parent would have them brought up, and as the parent is bound in conscience to have them brought up? How can the State do that? The State cannot do it. But the State has not the right to do it, and when the State steps in and assumes the rôle of the school teacher then there is the invasion of the individual right, the invasion of the domestic right, the invasion of the rights of the Church, and the invasion of divine rights. But is there no circumstance under which the State is allowed to teach? No. There may be circumstances when the State may look after the education of children that are neglected, evidently, by those who have the lawful right to teach them. Orphans, for example, foundlings, paupers—they are to be taught. By the State? No. If the Church or if private charity does not attend to it the State must do it; but the State does not become the teacher. The State is simply to see that that child, thus abandoned, has the education that it has a right to. But that does not make the State the school-teacher.

The State Theory Vindicated.

Here is a full statement and defense of the theory of the Roman Catholic Church in regard to education. A close observer will detect the fallacies in Father McCarthy's reasoning. He says that "God never gave a commission to the State to educate." After referring to the first family, with Adam as its head, he says, where families multiplied there was some need of public authority, some one chosen to administer government. There were "certain felt wants, which could be best supplied by *association*, and accordingly they entered into association. The individual surrendered a certain amount of his individual right, in exchange for certain protection he received from the government of civil society. This is the origin of civil society." Hence the term "Commonwealth, Common Weal, Common Welfare."

Father McCarthy thus far states very well the logical basis of free republics. This is the basis on

DUTY OF THE STATE TO EDUCATE. 141

which the Commonwealth of Massachusetts was organized. The "Bill of Rights" says:

The body politic is formed by a voluntary association of individuals; it is a social compact, by which the whole people covenants with each citizen, and each citizen with the whole people, that all shall be governed by certain laws for the common good.

When the individual citizens of Massachusetts "associated" themselves for the purpose of forming "civil society" or the Commonwealth, by "surrendering" "a certain amount of individual rights," etc., and defined and fixed the limits of that surrender, in the Constitution of the State, and adopted the Constitution by the votes of the individual citizens, to whom it was submitted, they specified the education of the young according to the system then in use, particularly mentioning * "public schools and grammar schools in the towns"—a clear recognition of our public school system. They assigned as the reason, that "wisdom and knowledge, as well as virtue, diffused generally among the body of the people, being necessary for the preservation of their rights and liberties; and as these depend on spreading the opportunities and advantages of education," etc.

Something similar is found in the history of all the United States. The people have relinquished the

---
* See Constitution of Massachusetts, chapter v, section ii.

right and duty of secular education to the States. The States hold it as committed to them by the people—a fundamental principle in our republic. Hence, however Father McCarthy's theory may apply to monarchical governments, and even republics differently constituted, it does not apply to this republic, for the parents, as citizens, at the outset, relinquished the right and duty of secular education to the State.

Does Father McCarthy reply that the people, under God, have no right to thus relinquish the work of education to the State? Does he state this as an assumption? Where is the authority which condemns the relinquishment? If scriptural, where is the text to be found? If his answer is that the Roman Catholic Church holds to that doctrine, that may satisfy him, but non-Catholics ask for some other proof.

But, says Father McCarthy, suppose the State is "atheistical" or "hostile to religion," "would it be for the interest of the individual or the family to have the State as the educator?" That is a supposition which does not apply in this republic, and must, therefore, be ruled out of this argument.

But again he says, "Let us suppose—and the fact exists in a great many places—that the State is hostile to the Catholic Church, and to those who profess Catholic doctrine and submission to Catholic authority." We answer, that is not the case in this republic or in any individual State of this republic. Our national Constitution forbids any " law respecting an establishment of religion or prohibiting the free exercise thereof." The Constitution of Massachusetts says:

No subject shall be hurt, molested, or restrained in his person, liberty, or estate, for worshiping God in the manner and season most agreeable to the dictates of his own conscience, or for his religious profession or sentiments, provided he does not disturb the public peace or obstruct others in their religious worship.

Similar provisions are in the Constitutions of all the States.

THE CATHOLIC ASSUMPTION.

But the point underlying the whole is the Roman Catholic assumption that religion and secular education must be taught together; should never be separated. But may not the parents, the citizens, in a free republic, where there exist diverse forms of religion, which complicate and make impossible the teaching of religion in the public schools, agree to relinquish to the State the right and duty of teaching secular education, and reserve to themselves and to the Churches the work of imparting religious instruction? May they not do this as a wise arrangement, in the interest of harmony? This is what we understand has been done, to afford our Roman Catholic fellow citizens, and others, the privileges of our school system.

But the hierarchy steps in—not the mass of the Roman Catholic laity—and says "No; the exclusive function of all education, secular and religious, is in my hands—there must be no separation." This is a part of the absolutism of the papal Church. She claims absolute supremacy in all things: in education, in legislation, in government; that the State and the Church should be united; that the Church should control the State; that all legislation should be subject to her dictation. This is the logical basis of the papacy, and she carries out the lines of her policy wherever she can, and varies from it only where she cannot help herself. Her demand wholly to control education, secular and religious, is a part of her absolutism, the "thin edge of the wedge" which the Church of Rome is driving into our republican institutions for the purpose of splitting the republic. This, at least, is the logical trend of her movement.

This imperious hierarchy comes into our republic, knowing what it is, its government and usages, and asserts unblushingly these demands of an absolutism engendered amid the darkness and mold of the Middle Ages, demanding that which must ruin our

Duty of the State to Educate. 145

most valued institutions. Then, if not gratified, they twit us of the falsity of our boasted liberty, as though freedom were unbounded license. Said one prominent papal ecclesiastic in New York city:

Now, in this country, that boasts its freedom, shall a man rise and tell me, "All this is very well, but you shall support the common schools, no matter whether you like them or not; and if you don't wish to send your children to them, we are in the majority and you shall pay anyway?" Is this in accordance with righteousness and justice? Is this a free country, or is it not?

Strange are the fallacies resorted to to overturn our institutions. Papists fail to appreciate the genius of a free country. They live in the atmosphere of ecclesiastical absolutism. Absolutism is the warp and woof of the system in which they have been reared. They overlook entirely that it is the prime duty of a popular government to perpetuate itself by adopting measures promotive of the greatest freedom and the highest good of all. To accomplish this, restraints and requirements must be imposed upon its inhabitants. The "free country" the Romanists talk about does not recognize such necessities. The imposition of taxes, laws for restraining the vicious, and laws requiring men to do what they do not like to do, are, in their estimation, incompatible with the gloriously "free country" upon which they discourse. The logical result of such freedom is anarchy. The American people are not anarchists.

We cannot too distinctly emphasize the principle that self-preservation is the primal law of governments as well as of nature. What does history show to have been the bane of past republics, and the cause of their overthrow, but ignorance? Of necessity the State must devote primary attention to elementary education, compelling its children to have such instruction as will prevent their becoming instruments of danger. To accomplish this, schools must be supported at necessary expense, and in the least conflict with the rights and ideas of the parents. Said

Hon. Theodore Roosevelt:

There is but one point in reference to which any feelings of alarm are in the smallest degree justifiable— this is the public school system. We could suffer no national calamity more far-reaching in its effects than would be implied in the abandonment of our system of non-sectarian common schools; and it is a very unfortunate thing for any man, or body of men, to be identified with opposition thereto. But it must be borne in mind that hostility to the public schools is not really a question of sects at all; it is merely an illustration of the survival or importation here of the utterly un-American and thoroughly Old-World idea of the subordination of the layman to the priest. Not a few Protestant clergymen oppose our public schools on the one hand, and an ever-increasing number of Catholic laymen support them on the other. At my own home on Long Island, for instance, the chief opponent of the public schools is not the Catholic priest, but the Episcopalian clergyman; and he re-enforces his slender stock of tritely foolish arguments by liberal quotations from the work of a Presbyterian theologian.

The fight is not one between creeds; it is an issue between intelligent American laymen of every faith, on the one hand, and ambitious, foolish, or misguided supporters of a worn-out system of clerical government on the other—these supporters including Episcopalians and Presbyterians as well as Catholics. Our public school system is here to stay; it cannot be overturned; wherever hurt, even, it is only at the much greater cost of the person hurting it. The boy brought up in the parochial school is not only less qualified to be a good American citizen, but he is also at a distinct disadvantage in the race of life, compared to the boy brought up in the public schools.

The theory that the entire work of education is the exclusive function of the Church is a sequence of the old mediæval papal dogma that the Church is the prime, supreme, and all-embracing source of authority—that the offices of the State are subordinate to and dependent upon the supreme will of the Church, and that all functions, religious, civil, and social, must be administered under her direction and dictation. It does not require great logical insight to see that such a theory cannot be worked in the American republic. For the proper discharge of the functions of American citizenship there must be an American education.

A Plain Necessity.

It is a plain necessity that in a republic every boy should be educated to understand something of the polity of the Government, its structure and aims, instead of being educated to ideas and methods of absolutism, as in the parochial schools of Romanism. He should know something of business relations and trade; something in relation to criminal enterprises and moral enterprises, and trained to use his knowledge honestly for the good of his country. It is easy to show that where the education of the child is left wholly to the parent and to the Roman Catholic Church, as in Italy, Spain, etc., large masses grow up uneducated. In the hands of such people free institutions cannot safely rest. They cannot intelligently exercise the franchise. On that account the free State is in duty bound to educate its youth. To educate a large body of children outside of the institutions which educate the masses, as, for instance, in the Catholic parochial schools, is to build up classes and castes in our midst.

Confessedly it is the function of the State to correlate human forces, all the varied elements of society, so far as they need to be adjusted. There are necessities of the adult population for which the State must care, not merely as charities, but as acts of justice.

Many are the equalizing tasks of civil government. Certain obligations must be made to rest mutually upon the rich and the poor—upon nobles and peasants, upon willing and reluctant parents. The State is the aggregate, unified personality, in a representative way, particularly in a republic, correlating and administering whatever might otherwise remain unorganized and become disintegrating and ruinous. The children of the State, brought into existence without ability or wisdom to care for themselves, with parents often unfitted to wisely direct their education, and often utterly indifferent to it, must be conserved and provided for by the civil power. In a republic, requiring intelligence in order to the performance of the duties of citizenship, it is an imperative necessity that the State should provide for the education of the whole body. It must not be left to chance.

QUESTION II.

As to Religious Instruction in the Public Schools.

IN the early period of the New England colonies, when the Church and State were united and there was only one * denomination, the Catechism was generally taught in the public schools; not every day, but more or less every week, and often by the parish minister. The appointment of teachers very generally depended upon the approval of the local minister. In those days the first officers of the Ancient and Honorable Artillery Company were not appointed until they had passed a satisfactory examination in the doctrines of justification by faith, the office-work of the Holy Ghost, etc. But that time has passed away.

No one can believe more sincerely and strongly than the writer of this volume that a complete education must comprise religious instruction and training; that the religious faculty must be cultivated; and that instruction in religious truth is an absolute necessity. But this is not the work of the public

---

* There were very few churches of other denominations than the Congregational down to the Revolution.

school system. Teachers are not selected with reference to any particular kind of Christian faith. The course of study is secular. The home and the Church are the places for distinctively religious instruction.

The course of the Roman Catholic Church, in the early part of this school contest, impresses us as having been false and insincere, or, at least, the course of many of those who, in her own name, championed her cause. The objective point in many cases, and for a considerable time, was that the public schools were "sectarian," because of the use of the Bible in them. After the school boards had yielded, in many places, and withdrawn the Bible, or closely circumscribed it, then the Romanists declared they were not satisfied. The *Tablet* said: "This action does not meet, nor in any degree lessen, our objection to the public school system." The *Catholic World* said, "Exclude your Protestant Bible and all direct and indirect religious instruction from your public schools, and you will not render them a whit less objectionable than they now are; for we object not less to purely secular schools than we do to sectarian schools." Then came the cry that our schools were "godless," and the plea, "We hold education to be the function of the Church, and not the State," which has become the point since emphasized.

What a Romanist said:

A candid Romanist, in a letter to a New York secular paper, gave these reasons for protesting against reading the Bible in the public schools:

The Bible is the chief and sole source of Protestant beliefs; it is the potent weapon of the Protestant power. The most powerful engine of Protestantism is the Bible. The Bible, the whole Bible, and nothing but the Bible is the slogan and watchword of the Protestant chieftains. In this Bible is the foundation, the superstructure, the inside and outside, the length, width, height, and depth of the Protestant system. Now you have put this tremendous instrumentality, this chiefest thing in your religious system, into the public schools. By so doing you have Protestantized them; you have put them in specific opposition to Catholic principles.

When, early in July, 1888, Rev. Dr. McGlynn was interviewed by a correspondent of the *Christian Union*, and the fact was referred to that the chief objection recently heard from Catholic priests against the public schools was not that they taught the Protestant religion, but that they taught no religion at all, Dr. McGlynn said:

Yes, that is the point which they are urging now, but this is merely to keep in accord with the demand that all the children must have a religious education. The earlier Councils never objected to any thing in the public school system, except the giving of instruction antagonistic to their religion, and the conducting of religious exercises and the using of forms of prayer unfamiliar to Catholic children, if not forbidden them.

The object of the Roman Catholic crusade has been, first, to bring the public schools into contempt and suspicion, as irreligious and ungodly, and then to build up Roman Catholic schools on their ruins. They have complained that they were taxed to support "sectarian" schools. Now they want our school money to support their sectarian schools. When interviewed on this question, in 1875, Rev. Bishop McQuaid, of Rochester, said:

Archbishop Hughes did agree to some compromise on the exclusion of the Bible, but long before his death he saw the error of such a step. I was brought up very religiously, and remember being on my knees ten minutes each day while the New Testament was read to us. I do not want the Bible excluded from schools not frequented by Catholics; in fact, I think the teaching of any religion is better than none at all. No man could be more surprised than I was, when the Board of Education of Rochester voted the Bible out of their city schools.

In 1858 Archbishop Hughes, in a public lecture in New York city, made extraordinary allegations against the public school system, as not only "godless," but a powerful promoter of crime, because religious instruction was not imparted in connection with secular knowledge and training. He said:

The public schools of New York, under the pretense of bestowing the blessings and benefits of education upon the children of the metropolis, in fact communicate to them the rudiments of knowledge, accompanied with just so much intellectual skill and sagacity as to enable them to prey with more success and greater impunity upon the community; to become more finished and accomplished scoundrels, more ingenious forgers and counterfeiters, more polished murderers and assassins.

The public school system is a disgrace to the civilization of the nineteenth century; and I hope to live to see the day when the citizens of New York will look back upon it with shame and horror that such a gross and miserable delusion could ever have been suffered to take possession of the public mind.

. . . .

The teacher in the utmost exercise of his authority can only appeal to the intellectual faculties of his pupils; and if those faculties, sharpened by incessant and skillful use, choose to look upon dishonesty, fraud, or crime as innocent and commendable, the case is taken at once beyond the jurisdiction of the teacher, who is restrained, by the positive enactment of law, from appealing to any higher standard of religion or morality than the intellect alone can compass. The legitimate consequences of this state of things, thus induced, are frightfully apparent in the alarming increase of vice and crime which now stares us in the face; the burglars, the robbers, the incendiaries, the murderers, assassins, garroters, and rioters, who infest our streets and alleys, rendering property and person alike insecure, and threatening to deluge our streets with blood, and convert our boasted civilization into the most fearful anarchy, are but the matured graduates of the public schools, the representatives of its morality, the finished specimens of its powers.

A most astounding indictment! Bishop Hughes was capable of making bolder and balder statements than any other papal ecclesiastic, and those just quoted are a grave affront to American citizens. It requires so little acuteness to answer his allegations that it is hardly worth while to dwell upon them; yet we cannot let the bishop's statements pass unnoticed. More frank was the pastoral letter of the Second Plenary Council at Baltimore, in 1866, addressed to the Roman Catholic clergy and laity of this country:

It is a melancholy fact, and a very humiliating avowal for us to make, that a very large proportion of the idle and vicious youth of our principal cities are the children of Catholic parents.

Cardinal Antonelli is quoted as saying: "*The catechism alone is essential for the education of the people.*"

The process pursued in the Catholic schools dwarfs the intellect of the pupils, fitting them for the coarser occupations of life. Many Catholic parents have seen this, and removed their children from the Church schools. When threatened by the priests, they have answered, "My children have been in your schools three years, and have learned little besides the catechism; I prefer to send them to the public schools, where they will learn how to get a living in this world, since they must spend their lives here."

Dexter A. Hawkins, Esq.,* has demonstrated that so far does the training in the priests' schools fall short of fitting pupils to earn an honest living, that the Irish, who have largely attended these schools in New York city, in a term of years furnished more than three times as many paupers and criminals, according to their number, as the Americans, who, as a body, attend the public schools. In the city of New York, from 1871 to 1875, inclusive, the Department of Charities and Corrections cared for the following paupers:

		Ratio.
Americans	63,178	1.00
Irish	98,787	3.50
Germans	24,273	1.33
All others	17,563	1.50

The Roman Catholic parochial school sends forth its pupils with three and a half times the chances of becoming paupers which they would have if they had attended the public schools.

Mr. Hawkins continues:

But, says the Romish priest, in answer to the remonstrance of the parent, "If the catechism and the dogmas and practices of the Church taught in the

---

* See pamphlet, *The Roman Catholic Church in New York City and Public Land and Public Money.* By Dexter A. Hawkins, 1887, pp. 12, 13

parochial school don't enable the children to earn their living as well as does the course of instruction in the public schools, they at least correct their morals, and so make them better members of society."

This is a great mistake, for the facts show just the opposite.

In this city, in fifteen years and four months, ending December 31, 1875, the record of arrests gives the following:

                Number of Irish arrested................ 571,497
                Number of Americans arrested........... 387,154
                Number of Germans arrested............. 119,659
                Number from all other races arrested.... 92,934

And the names of those arrested show that a large percentage of those classed as Americans in the above table are of Irish parentage, and hence, to a large extent, attended the parochial schools. But taking the table just as it stands, and reducing the figures to a comparative ratio, based on the number of each race in this city, as fixed by the last United States census, and adopting the American as the unit, gives the following:

                Americans............ 1.00 | Germans............. 1.07
                Irish................ 3.28 | All other races 1.27

In other words, *a child trained in the parochial schools of the Roman Catholic Church is more than three and a quarter times as likely to get into jail as the child trained in the free public school.*

The above tables are the outcome of so large a generalization, running through so many years, that they are safe and sure indications of the tendency of the two systems.

Parents desire the welfare of their offspring; they see plainly the difference between the parochial school boy and the public school boy; hence it requires the constant application of the spiritual, and often of the corporeal lash of the priest, to compel them to withdraw their children from the feast of knowledge offered free at the public schools, and to send them to meager and mediaeval diet of daily catechism doled out in the parochial schools.

Pauperism and crime are the two most troublesome evils that infest and afflict society. This Church has raised mendicity from a vice to the dignity of a virtue; and its more ignorant followers believe that through the confessional and penance its priests have the power to pronounce absolution of crime; hence its failure to repress these two evils.

Such is the failure of the Roman Catholic system of religious education for which the priests plead in behalf of their parochial schools.

What has been the state of morals in those countries where all the popular education that existed was in the parochial schools of Romanism, or where the people, if uneducated, have been under her almost exclusive care? We give statistics based upon official censuses: *

COMMITTALS FOR MURDER FOR EACH MILLION OF THE POPULATION.

Protestant England............................	4 to 1,000,000.
Roman Catholic Belgium...................	18 " "
Roman Catholic Ireland.....................	19 " "
Roman Catholic Sardinia....................	20 " "
Roman Catholic France......................	31 " "
Roman Catholic Austria.....................	36 " "
Roman Catholic Lombardy.................	45 " "
Roman Catholic Tuscany....................	56 " "
Roman Catholic Bavaria.....................	68 " "
Roman Catholic Sicily........................	90 " "
Roman Catholic Papal States..............	113 " "
Roman Catholic Naples......................	174 " "

* Collated by Rev. M. Hobart Spencer, a clergyman of the Church of England. Censuses next preceding 1854.

Rev. Mr. Seymour, to whom we are indebted for the above statistics, says:

Name any Protestant country or city in Europe, and let its depths of vice and immorality be measured and named, and I will name a Roman Catholic country or city whose depths of vice and immorality are lower still.

Stockholm was said, a few years ago, to rank the lowest, in respect to illegitimacy, of any Protestant city in Europe—namely, twenty-nine per cent. of all the births. But the following Roman Catholic cities outrank this, the worst of all Protestant cities: Paris, 33 per cent.; Brussels, 35 per cent.; Munich, 48 per cent.; Vienna, 51 per cent.; Laibach, 88 per cent.; Brunn, 42 per cent.; Lintz, 46 per cent.; Prague, 47 per cent.; Lemberg, 47 per cent.; Klagenfort, 56 per cent.; Gratz, 65 per cent.

ILLEGITIMATE BIRTHS FOR EVERY 1,000 BIRTHS.*

Protestant Countries.		Roman Catholic Countries.	
Denmark	110	Baden	162
England, Scotland, and Wales.	67	Bavaria	225
Holland (35 per cent. Roman Catholic)	40	Belgium	72
		France	75
Prussia, with Saxony, and Hanover	83	German Austria	181
Sweden and Norway	96	Average	143
Average	79		

A few years ago Roman Catholic Dublin contained one prostitute for 301 inhabitants, and Lon-

* *New Englander*, January, 1870.

don one to 579. The Roman Catholic chaplain of the jail in Liverpool reported 1,812 Protestant women committed and 3,083 Roman Catholic women committed in the year 1864.*

The following † shows where the criminals belong ecclesiastically:

In the penitentiary at Joliet, Ill., July 22, 1888, fifty convicts were confirmed by Bishop Spalding, of the Catholic Church. They had been receiving special instruction for a month, so that they might be prepared to receive the rite. Confirmation, it will be remembered, is one of the seven sacraments of the Catholic Church, and it admits the recipient into full relations with the Church. Two years ago, at the same prison, one hundred and seventeen convicts were confirmed by Archbishop Feehan of Chicago.

Bishop Hughes had passed away before the astounding defalcations of Bishop Purcell, in Cincinnati, and the Augustinian fathers, in Lawrence, had come to public notice, involving the ruin of many households ‡ who had confided their funds to priestly hands. But why pursue this subject any further? Such are the facts in regard to the character of the people Rome has had under her training. How do her pretensions of great concern for the religious education of the young appear in this light? Can the young be trusted to her influence?

---
* *New Englander*, January, 1870.
† An item of current news in the newspapers.
‡ It is stated on good authority that the losers by Archbishop Purcell were all persons of the poorer class, no rich man being involved.

RELIGIOUS INSTRUCTION. 161

How to Supplement the Schools.

Bare secular instruction, unattended by religion, is sometimes declared to engender worldliness, forgetfulness of God and moral relations, and to lead to agnosticism. Some leading minds have pronounced such culture one-sided and mischievous. The moral sense, it is claimed, should be cultivated while the intellectual faculties are trained. Guizot, Portalis and Cousin have been quoted in support of this view. How to meet this question in non-sectarian schools is the problem. Non-sectarian the schools must certainly be, in a free republic, composed of such diverse religionists and nationalities.

Surrounded by Sunday-schools, churches, and Christian families, it is morally certain that few children will be left wholly without religious instruction, even if there are no religious exercises in the public schools. The sentiment is gaining ground that religious instruction is the function of the parent and the Church, and the extension of city missions and mission Sunday-schools, and the multiplication of religious agencies of many kinds is bringing the masses of children and youth more and more under some measure of religious instruction. But the moral wastes are still many, large, and alarming.

Within a few years many have felt that much

more should be done, and that something can be done, in inculcating morality in the public schools. The Presbyterian Synod* of New York four years ago adopted a resolution urging the incorporation into State and secular education, of moral and religious truth founded on the following basal propositions: a personal God; individual responsibility to him; immortality; a future judgment; and the Ten Commandments, as interpreted by the Sermon on the Mount. The Synod appointed a committee to inquire as to the practicability of securing a union of different denominations on such a basis. Rabbi F. de Sola Mendez, representing the Orthodox Jews, indorsed the plan heartily, with the exception of the last proposition, which he thought might be open to misapprehension in that form. Rabbi Gottheil, representing the radical Jews, took substantially the same position.

The Archbishop of New York was interviewed, and responded as follows, through his Vicar-General:

ARCHBISHOPRIC OF NEW YORK,
CHANCERY OFFICE, 266 MULBERRY STREET,
NEW YORK, *Dec.* 12, 1885.

REV. DEAR SIR: The most reverend apostle desires me, in his name, to say, in response to your letter, that the Catholic Church has always insisted,

---

* The Evangelical Alliance of Boston Ministers has agitated the question of a book on morals for schools.

and must always insist, upon the teaching of religion with education. For this reason we cannot patronize the public schools, and are forced to establish our own parochial schools. The question of religion, where there are many different denominations, each with its own creed, is a difficult one to settle. We could be satisfied with nothing less than teaching our whole faith. Protestant denominations, if they value their own creeds, ought to feel as we do. Denominational schools are, to our mind, the only solution of the question. This plan should satisfy every one, and would save the State a vast outlay of expense.

The points you propose, while better than nothing, would never satisfy us, and we think they ought not to satisfy many of the Protestant Churches; while the infidels, who are now very numerous, would certainly reject them.

We believe that the country will yet see the ruinous effects of an education from which religion has been excluded.

With sincere respect, on the part of the archbishop and myself,   Yours very truly,
                                T. S. PRESTON, V. G.
REV. GEO. PAYSON, Ch., etc.

It is plain that no compromise is possible with Roman Catholics. Still the question remains.

Judge Robert C. Pitman,[*] of Massachusetts, speaks in a manner showing close, clear discrimination, worthy of much attention.

Can we teach ethics without religion? Probably. I say probably because there is not much experi-

---

[*] *Forum*, May, 1888.

mental proof. We hear more than we see of that kind of teaching. But we cannot teach with authority; we cannot teach with impressiveness, without thought of Him who is the Absolute Right. The peculiarity of Christianity itself is not in the revelation of new ethical truth, but in bringing to us that new sense of God, and of our relation to him, which makes the idea of duty regnant in the heart. Matthew Arnold very inadequately defines religion as "morality touched with emotion." But, although it is much more, it is that; and without religion morality has neither emotion nor motion. It will stay in the text-book.

And so, coming to the heart of the problem, I say that I would have religion taught as a part of our public education. What religion? The only religion that is a part of the common law, the only religion that permeates our literature, and the religion that is related to all our modern civilization—Christianity. But it should be the Christianity of Christ, not that of sects; the Christianity which, in its practical aspects, is fitted to be the universal religion of mankind; which appeals, as did the Master, for its test to the common judgment of what is right. Can the public school teach such a common Christianity? It were indeed a scandal to our religion, if there were no ground upon which its nominal adherents could stand together. Can it be that our schools must be left pagan because we are sectarian? Such a conclusion is repulsive to the common sense of the community. All the tendencies of the age are toward breadth and unity. I think there are but very few who call themselves Christians, who would prefer that our schools should be godless, rather than that they should confine themselves to the Lord's Prayer as their liturgy, the two great commandments as the rule of holy living, and the doctrines of the Sermon on the Mount as the inspiration and comfort of the soul.

Rev. Drs. Seelye, of Amherst College, Bartol, of Boston, and others, hold similar views. In regard to this proposition *The Pilot* (R. C.) editorially says:

As to the Catholics, they would, at least, have no new grievance, and many of them would see a distinct gain in removing from the public schools the reproach of godlessness. But should they still object—as assuredly they would—to availing themselves of the public schools, Judge Pitman would favor handing over "these departments for the instruction of their children to teachers of their own faith, under such arrangements as should insure an intelligent, systematic, and faithful performance of that duty." In other words, the writer would have Catholic teachers visit the public schools, at fixed times, for the special religious and moral instruction of the Catholic pupils. This, however, should be not in recognition of a right, but merely as a concession, creating no claim for compensation, since the State had already provided, according to its best judgment, for the religious instruction of all.

But why this awkward and unsatisfactory compromise—which means, in effect, to set up a State religion in the schools at the expense of all the tax-payers, and discriminate against the Catholic tax-payers, because they cannot in conscience accept it—when a simple and well-tested solution of the difficulty is offered by the denominational system. Still, every word that deepens the growing sentiment in favor of religion in popular education is a distinct gain; and Catholics have no fear but that, once the American mind is thoroughly convinced on this important question, it will find an equitable settlement for it.

Judge Pitman's plan, therefore, will not be accepted by Roman Catholics nor by the Jews, and it remains a delicate matter to introduce any religious instruction into the public schools. A common method, in Massachusetts and other New England States, is for the teacher, at the opening of the school, to read a few devotional passages from the Psalms and offer the Lord's Prayer, those of the pupils joining who choose to do so, and those who prefer remaining outside until the close of this brief exercise. This plan generally works without friction.

The provisions of the national and State Constitutions are such that the matter of religious exercises in the public schools is restricted within very narrow limits, specific instruction being ruled out.

The Constitution of the United States says:

Congress shall make no law respecting an establishment of religion or prohibiting the free exercise thereof.

Massachusetts says: "No subject shall be hurt, molested, or restrained in his person, liberty, or estate, for worshiping God in the manner most agreeable to the dictates of his own conscience, or for his religious profession or sentiment."

Its Bill of Rights says also: "All religious sects and denominations demeaning themselves peaceably and as good citizens of the Commonwealth shall be equally under the protection of the law; and no subordination of any one sect or denomination to another shall ever be established by law."

A statute, in the same spirit, forbids the introduction of any text-book "favoring the tenet of any particular sect of Christians." These are in harmony with the act of the people which, in 1833, finally destroyed the power of towns or the State to tax the people for the support of churches.

An Able Discussion.

Said Rev. A. H. Quint, D.D.,* after quoting the foregoing:

These provisions declare a perfect equality of religious denominations, that no one shall be put in power by law, and that no tenet of any sect shall be favored. This necessarily rules out of the schools religious instruction, if it is consistently carried out. A Romanist cannot impose his tenets upon a Protestant child, and a Protestant teacher cannot impose his tenets upon a Catholic child. A Baptist teacher cannot teach immersion, and a Congregational teacher cannot teach endless punishment. Whether we like this or not, it is the fact. No "common law" even, no theory of some unwritten power in the State, can override the constitutional fetters which the American Revolution produced. No clearer authority is needed than that of Judge Story, in his opinion in the great Girard will case, where he declares this new limitation, and where he says, of the equality stated in the Pennsylvania Bill of Rights (like others), that "the language must have been intended to extend equally to

---

* *Congregationalist*, July 26, 1888.

all sects, whether they believe in Christianity or not, whether they were Jews or infidels."

It is not the spirit of American government for the State to select and pay, from public taxes, ministers of the Gospel to preach even sound doctrine, however much it might be for the public good. On the same principle it is not for the State to employ school-teachers at the expense of the taxpayers to teach the Gospel of Christ to children; and any religion less than that is not worth fighting over.

It has been said that the State has inherent right and duty to determine what the education of children shall be. There is much truth in this, but it needs very careful limitations. Did the Protestant world approve when the Catholic authorities in Italy (if I remember), seizing from his parents the Jewish boy Mortara, educated him in the Romanist faith? The truth is, the State must insist, for its own existence and welfare in a republic, on the instruction of children in all needed branches, and for the diffusion of general intelligence as against ignorance. This grand idea demands the school system; but let it stop when it interferes with religious faiths.

From these premises Dr. Quint reasons very conclusively that,

Any satisfactory religious instruction in public schools is absolutely impracticable, and we may as well acknowledge it. An avowedly secular system is far better for religion than a formal sham. We cannot teach the distinctive tenets of any Christian denomination. Then, without tenets, what is there to teach? Our own Churches cannot consent to the Romanist papal authority as a tenet on one hand, nor to the denial of Christ's divinity on the other; and neither of these will leave the field to us, nor to all the denominations combined, who hold the "doctrines commonly called evangelical." There is no possible common ground. Eliminate all except what all hold in common—Romanist, Protestant, indifferent, Jew, freethinker—and the remainder! Are majorities to rule? There is nothing more dangerous than majorities unfettered by constitutions.

It may be said that we have the Bible read in schools. A law of 1855 required it, and a law of 1880 forbade all "note or comment," and excused from it all pupils whose parents objected to it. How much Bible is that? One teacher reads of Moses in the bulrushes and of David and Goliath; and another reads colorless Psalms. Suppose the law be changed, and note and comment be made lawful—whose doctrine is to be taught by the teacher to our children?

No. The safest way, the wisest way, is to secularize the schools. It is simply asserting the American principle that no Church or anti-church shall use for its own purpose the public schools maintained by the taxation of the people. It makes them no more irreligious than a State blacksmith shop would be. It would teach the ordinary branches at the public expense and leave religious teaching to parents, where God himself placed it. God established the family; men established the public school system.

It must not be understood that secularizing the schools excludes teaching and training in the moral virtues. These lie at the basis of all beliefs or no beliefs. They enter necessarily into the government of every school and the daily intercourse of one pupil with all other pupils. They cannot by any possibility be put out of sight. They are proper subjects of direct instruction. The Massachusetts Constitution, which prohibits so plainly the tenets of every sect and denomination, expressly directs all teachers to "inculcate the principles of humanity and general benevolence, public and private charity, industry and frugality, honesty, and punctuality in their dealings; sincerity, good humor and all social affections and generous sentiments among the people." Nor is there any doubt that this subject should be emphasized even farther than it now is.

It is plain that if all classes are to use the public school there must be no specific religious instruction. It cannot be imparted consistently with the American system of government. If religious instruction is given, it will be almost certain to savor of some particular sect; and moneys raised by taxation upon the whole people cannot be rightfully used for that purpose. Religious education must be taught elsewhere —in the Church and the home. Neither the State, nor the Church, nor the home singly can do the whole work, the complete work, of education.

A writer in the *Catholic World*,* himself a Roman Catholic teacher, under the caption, "*Send the Whole Boy to School*," in asserting that the Church can impart complete education, makes the fatal assumption that the Church can annihilate the school, and even the home, assuming the prerogatives both of the parent and the State.

---

* August, 1883.

QUESTION III.

As to a Parochial School System for all Parties.

THIS inquiry is entertained, tentatively, by some persons as a possible alternative, hoping it may afford a safe and satisfactory solution of a difficult question. Nor is it strange that some should thus inquire. The Lutherans in this country, it is stated, have 150,000 pupils in parochial schools, and 1,621 teachers, with 500 more in training. These schools are in the non-English portion of the Lutheran churches, the object being to prepare their children for a transition to a new language and new customs. The Episcopalians have some parochial schools. About 1845 the O. S. Presbyterians undertook to form such schools—quite an extensive effort—but the plan did not succeed.

Until quite recently there was no public provision for education in England. Private or parochial schools were all, but subject to no State authority or control. In districts where such schools did not exist, and among classes outside of the influence of any religious denomination, there was no public provision for supplementing this deficiency. All elementary education, until the act of 1870, was dependent on voluntary enterprise or casual endowment.* The first approach to a public system of education was by means of grants in aid of private schools administered by a committee of the Privy Council. This system was not superseded by the act of 1870, but means were taken to insure the existence, in every school district, of a "sufficient amount of accommodation in public elementary schools." †

Under this parochial system—all the schools there were, for a time—there grew up a large uneducated class, not directly associated with any religious body; and it became necessary to establish what were called "rate schools," supported by taxes, etc., to meet the needs of this heretofore neglected class. The National Education League was formed, insisting that "all schools aided by local rates should be unsectarian." So England has been suffering from these diverse classes of schools—the unsectarian schools, the Roman Catholic schools, the Church of England schools, the Wesleyan schools, the Baptist schools, the Presbyterian schools, all educating the rising people differently, fostering class distinctions, with multiply-

---

* Scotland remained wholly under the parochial school system until 1872.
† See *Britannica*, article Education.

A Parochial School System. 173

ing and widening divergences, and with no broad, deep, unifying influences in the schools.

The English Government has found it necessary to adopt a non-sectarian secular system of State education in India. It is to be conducted by government institutions, in which British specialists will supervise and direct an enlarged system of technical education. Moral training will be provided for by a text-book based on natural religion. This means that the Government will endeavor to hold a neutral position between Mohammedanism, Buddhism, and Christianity —the great conflicting religions in her vast Eastern empire—and will inculcate morality based on such grounds as are common to all these forms of faith.

Three Prominent Testimonies.

Almost simultaneously, in the year 1871, three of the most prominent men of the time (see the *Christian World*, January, 1872,) proclaimed their views from widely different points of observation upon the public school question. The first was a voice from the Vatican, which the so called Ecumenical Council had declared infallible, and must be received by loyal Catholics as the voice of God. It pleads for sectarian or parochial schools. The pope, writing by Cardinal Antonelli, his secretary, to the Bishop of Nicaragua, printed in the Nicaragua *Gazette*, Jan. 1, 1870, says:

We have lately been informed here that an attempt has been made to change the order of things hitherto existing in that republic, by publishing a programme in which are enunciated "freedom of education" and of worship. Both these principles are not only contrary to the laws of God and of the Church, but are in contradiction with the Concordat established between the holy See and that republic. Although we doubt not that your most illustrious and reverend lordship will do all in your power against maxims so destructive to the Church and to society, still we deem it by no means superfluous to stimulate your well-known zeal to see that the clergy, and, above all, the curates, do their duty. G. CARDINAL ANTONELLI.

This language needs no explanation. "Freedom of education and worship are contrary to the laws of God and of the Church! . . . destructive to the Church and to society." Infallibility makes this declaration with respect to one American republic. Logically it holds equally with regard to all republics.

Next comes another utterance. It is from France, a Roman Catholic country which two hundred years ago drove out the Protestant Huguenots with the rack and sword. It was her most prominent statesman, Gambetta, who spoke in an address, Nov. 15, 1871 (in St. Quentin), on the subject of a comprehensive measure of general education, as one of the most important means for improving the internal situation of France, the most pressing and urgent of all reforms. What system does he recommend? He knew all about the Roman Catholic parochial system. Does he recommend that? No. He wants to abolish all " class distinctions." He was for " absolutely gratuitous, obligatory, lay instruction." He was not only for the separation of Church and State, but for the entire separation of the schools from the Churches. He considered that not only a question of political, but of social order. He utterly denied the force of the objection that partisans of lay instruction wanted to breed up atheists. In his proposition, he said, there was nothing hostile to religion. But he strenuously denied the right and opposed the pretension of a dominant party in the Catholic Church to impose the innoculation of their peculiar faith or profession, as a necessary concomitant of the lay education of which all stood in need. " Let religious education," he said, " whether Catholic, Jewish, or Protestant, be given in religious temples, according to the choice of parents; but let not the Catholics, with their claims to exclusiveness, have any thing to do with that propagation of necessary knowledge which it is the State's duty to see imparted to every citizen."

It is not strange that France, after learning by her painful failures, under the old parish school system, and witnessing the success of the United States under her common school system, should borrow our system of education, and hope thereby to build up and sustain her republic.

Next we have the testimony of the oldest and most eminent statesman of Europe, at the time of its utterance, only five days from the time that Gambetta made his great educational deliverance. I refer to Lord John Russell. Writing to a member of the House of Commons, he commends his speech in favor of the "National Educational League," which insisted that "all schools aided by local rates should be unsectarian." He did not object to the reading of the Bible in an unsectarian way, but decidedly favored it, in the schools. He then proceeded to say, "My wish and hope is that the rising youth of England may be taught to adopt, not the Church of Rome, nor the Church of England, but the Church of Christ."

Noble words from a statesman of ripe wisdom, full of honors and fame. In an atmosphere of freedom, freedom of education and freedom of worship, Rome cannot succeed. How different this plan from molding the childhood of the race in the Roman Catholic machine! In view of these testimonies, an intelligent people will not long hesitate in deciding between the parochial and the public school system.

A Questionable Right.

It is often said that the Catholics have a *right* to their parochial schools if they want them, for this is a free country. Of course, under the Constitution, this is true. And yet, on certain ethical and prudential grounds, it is not wise policy for the children of a republic, in the plastic period of life, to be separated into class schools of a strongly sectarian character, where the lesson is taught that the highest civil and religious authority is a foreign potentate. The future welfare of the country depends upon making our diverse populations homogeneous. And the American public school is one of the chief factors for producing this result. Our government recently issued an order requiring that no instruction be imparted to the Indians, except in the English language. Why? Because this method of instruction would help to make them American citizens more quickly. For this reason objection might be made to juvenile schools in the French, German, and Scandinavian languages, because they would so far postpone and prevent the process of making these foreign elements homogeneous, and fitting them for enlightened harmonious American citizenship. So, too, the Roman Catholic parochial schools, calling off a large portion of our young population into class schools apart from the mass of the people, and then drilling them under a regimen essentially un-American and mediæval; instilling into their minds the theory of church supremacy over the State, with supreme reference to the will of a foreign pontiff; teaching them to believe that all persons not Catholics are continually in mortal sin, heretics and schismatics, whom the Roman Catholic Church is in duty bound to exterminate; such instruction stands directly in the way of the process of assimilation so necessary, in this country of diverse peoples, in order to make the homogeneous citizenship on which the future welfare of the country depends. For this reason we do object to the parochial school system, though we cannot deny it on the ground of abstract right to Roman Catholics.

To us it would appear to be wise legislation to forbid the gathering of children into private schools of any kind, Catholic, Jewish, Protestant, or any other, until they shall have reached their fourteenth year. If any denominations desire to maintain educational institutions for those who have passed that year, they might safely be allowed to do so. The law we would recommend would be entirely unsectarian. It would make attendance upon the public schools compulsory for all children under fourteen years of age, with no exceptions for any private schools.

Such legislation at first will seem to many radical and impossible; but it is just what Mexico and Chili have done, after a long experience with the parochial schools of Romanism. In Mexico "parochial schools are prohibited, and although the clergy still exercise a powerful influence among the common people, whose superstitious ignorance has not yet been reached by the free schools and the compulsory education law, in politics they are powerless." * In Chili the "Liberal Majority has established non-sectarian schools, and passed a compulsory education law, under which all citizens who send their children to the priests and nuns to be taught have to pay a tax or fine to the State." †

In an elaborate address ‡ delivered by Rev. Father T. J. Conaty, of Worcester, on the occasion of laying the corner-stone of a parochial school in Jamaica Plain (Boston), July 22, he said, "We are not in favor of Romanizing the public school, but we are in favor of Romanizing the education of our children." We claim that to the extent their education is Romanized, to that degree it will unfit them to make good American citizens.

A CATHOLIC TESTIMONY.

The necessary influence of the public school system in fitting the rising youth for American citizenship was well stated by a young Roman Catholic to a reporter of the *Boston Herald*. §

I was educated in the public schools of Boston, and was always a Roman Catholic. I am very free to tell you what I think of public as compared with parochial schools. I was educated in the former, and every step

---
* See *The Capitals of Spanish America*, by W. E. Curtis. Harper Brothers. 1888. Page. 4. † *Ibid.*, Page 494.
‡ *Boston Pilot*, July 28, 1888.
§ See *Boston Herald*, July 14, 1888.

of my schooling but endeared them to me and made me a warmer advocate of them. The studies were such as to make me tolerant. I became acquainted with children of all classes, under all conditions. I became filled with admiration for the institutions of my country. To this education I owe all I am or hope to be. To this education I attribute the individual scope which, as time progresses, I find broadens out into a love of fair play for all, and an antagonism toward every thing which tends to hedge in or prevent the fullest development of whatever in a man tends to further his interests, and makes him a good and obedient citizen of a free country. This is my opinion of what our public school system tends to do.

Now what benefit is to be derived from the parochial school as compared with the public school? I say that, in one case I grow up acquainted with the people of every degree of caste and of every nationality. I see what is good and what is bad in all. I become tolerant of faults incidental to the individual, and look upon him as a part of the people who have a common interest at stake. In the parochial system I should have seen only one side. My acquaintance would be only with those who are like myself, and who believe as I do. Say what you may, in a moral sense, I should be only disposed to look on those as right, and all as wrong who do not believe as I do. From the outset I should have been on the defensive and suspicious of others. I should look coldly upon them. I should become indifferent to their wants and grow up to despise them, simply because I did not know them. Much can be said, I will admit, on the side of the duty which the parent owes to the child, the child to the parent, and the parent to the State; but I look upon this republican form of government simply as a compact of all the people for a common good. Hence, it

A Parochial School System. 181

does not permit the education of the masses free from the control of the State. Since its security rests in the individual intelligence of the people, it must know that the tendency of education does not undermine the very foundation of its institutions. I mean, that an anarchist cannot be permitted to open a college free from State control, or to teach a doctrine which, if followed out, would end in confusion and disrespect for the laws.

The school question is simply, "Can I obtain a better education for my children, to fit them to go out into the world to fight the battles of life, from a public or a parochial school? I say, unhesitatingly, judging from my own experience, and from the history of the lives of my school-fellows, from the public school. That acquaints a child with every kind of people, and teaches, indirectly, love and respect for the doctrine that all are equal before the law, and have a right to individual opinion and the full enjoyment of freedom. For a republican form of government a public system of education must be kept up, no matter what other system is permitted. The State must always know the plan of education which is taught, and must, for its own safety, be the judge of what is right and best calculated to perpetuate its institutions and make its people peace-loving and loyal.

There is evidently a wise philosophy in what this Roman Catholic says. This is the reason why we cannot favor parochial schools.

Other Testimonies.

A writer in the *Popular Science Monthly* last July, in view of the corruption and the mismanagement connected with the administration of the School Board of New York city, expressed the opinion that it may yet be found better to resort to the voluntary methods, by the private or parochial systems. Referring to this article, an editorial writer in the Boston *Herald* * said :

This is flying in the face and eyes of the American system of education ; the system that lies at the basis of our government, the system that seems to be bound up with the development of a free people. It is certainly a step in socialism for the State to educate the youth at the public expense; but it is indispensable to the fair and proper working of our institutions, and it is one of the first principles of our national life. To break up this system and to go back to education through private parties, religious or secular, is to turn toward the sunset and to forget the conditions on which our institutions are to be maintained. The editor of the *Science Monthly* has a bee in his bonnet, if he thinks that the education of a great people like our own is to go back again into private hands, or if he thinks it would be possible to obtain anything like the results which are now reached, by depending upon the parents for the payment of the school rates for their children.

Mr. E. C. Carrigan,† of the Boston Public School Board, said : "I believe if a vote of the Irish-Americans of Massachusetts, especially Boston, was taken, nine tenths would give the public schools the first place. . . . I have never had any sympathy with

---

* August 1, 1888.   † Boston *Herald*, August 6, 1888.

any other school system than that established by the State and maintained by public taxation. In my opinion it is neither necessary nor desirable that private schools should be established, especially for children who are mentally and physically able to do the work of our public schools. I should be happy if the children of all classes were taught the common branches of learning prescribed by law in public schools, for these schools are good enough for every child in the State, and if they are not, then it is clearly our duty to make them so."

Two Hostile Camps.

The Roman Catholic theory of parochial schools separates the children into two nationalities, and almost into hostile camps. Several instances of hostile demonstrations, by hootings and even blows, by pupils of the Roman Catholic schools toward those of the public schools, have already occurred, greatly to the disturbance and embarrassment of the latter. There is no growing up of habits of increasing toleration and respect, but rather of suspicion and hatred. What a misfortune thus confronts the State! Not merely a variance in religious doctrines, but separation in sympathy, in types of life, in ideas of government, producing a divergence, widening from infancy to childhood, and through childhood to manhood.

Do Roman Catholics point to the sectarian schools of some Protestant denominations? We reply that in those schools these denominations teach no such distinctively sectarian dogmas, with radical hierarchical assumptions and supreme allegiance to a foreign potentate, etc., etc., as are taught in the parochial schools of the papal Church.

We cannot therefore look with favor upon the adoption of a system of parochial or church schools for all denominations as a possible alternative. The prime thing sought in the parochial schools of Romanism is ecclesiastical instruction. Separated from State control, the influences which mold the pupils are, first and last, sectarian. The Roman Catholic Church is ranked above the State and the country; but it is not the "seeking first the kingdom of God and his righteousness," which Christ enjoins upon all. It is rather the absolutism, and exclusiveness, and extreme functions of the Roman hierarchy which are distinctively inculcated. These things are to be taught by teachers for the most part foreign by birth and training, un-American in spirit and ideas, so that the Catholic parochial schools are sure to be un-American in character. If not purposely unpatriotic, nevertheless from the very fact of the avowed purpose as a papal institution, from the character of the teachers and the course of instruction, it is ill adapted

A PAROCHIAL SCHOOL SYSTEM. 185

to make intelligent and genuine American citizens. Its bias is positively against American institutions. Here lies one of the fatal defects of the parochial school. When it is considered that most of the children are of foreign-born parents, who especially need the patriotic and molding influences of the typical American public school, it is not difficult to see that the parochial school antagonizes the public school system, and that its phenomenally rapid growth, as an institution, is a menacing danger. We make no complaint against the parochial school on the ground that it teaches religion, but because it teaches the theories of a *politico-ecclesiastical* hierarchy directly and irreconcilably hostile to a republic, and rigidly drills those ideas into the minds of its pupils, by long-continued reiterations. Its crying defect is that its teaching is not only un-American but anti-American, and will remove every one of its pupils, in their ideals, far from a proper mental condition for American citizenship, and enhance the already too difficult task of making them good citizens of a republic. It is largely *political* instruction, in which the pope is the sovereign ruler whose dominion is not to be questioned.

To cramp and compress the mind, while young and plastic, in the rigid molds prepared in the Middle Ages is what Romanism means to do.

QUESTION IV.

As to Whether the Public School Funds can be Divided.

THIS question takes us into the heart of the problem. It is proposed by several classes of persons.

1. Some well-meaning but timid people, seeing the sharp feeling that exists, and desiring to avoid trouble, but who have not thought the question through, ask if we cannot let the Catholics have what they want, and thus end the matter.

2. Another class make this inquiry because they fear the disastrous effects upon our public school system if the school moneys should be divided, and they will be relieved, if they can be assured that there are legal or constitutional guarantees to prevent it.

3. The other class are Roman Catholics, who propound the inquiry in a more assertive form, and in a spirit which indicates a determination to get the money at all hazards.

The question, then, fully stated, is, Can the public school moneys be divided, and a portion be given to aid Roman Catholic parochial schools—that is, can it be done consistently with the spirit and letter of our national and State constitutions?

I will not pause to ask what may be done, under possible Catholic ascendency, in some localities, in defiance of law and constitutional guarantees. That would be a condition of anarchy from which we hope to be spared. In a time of anarchy there is no knowing what will happen. Let us notice briefly what are some of the provisions of the constitutions:

The Constitution of the United States says:

Congress shall make no law respecting an establishment of religion or prohibiting the free exercise thereof.

But to appropriate school fund moneys to Catholic parochial schools, which make so prominent in their course of study the distinctive inculcation of Roman Catholic dogmas, even the hierarchy, as we shall soon show, is a plain violation of this article of the Constitution of the United States. Such an appropriation of moneys would be an official act aiding in the establishment of religion—that is, the Roman Catholic religion. The *letter* of the article says: "Congress shall *make no law* respecting the establishment of religion." But the *spirit* of the article prohibits any thing which would help the establishment of religion.

The Constitution of Connecticut declares (Art. I, Sec. 4):

No preference shall be given by law to any Christian sect or mode of worship.

But if school moneys are appropriated to distinctively Roman Catholic schools, teaching the peculiar dogmas and ecclesiasticism of Rome, preference is thereby given to that Church.

In 1855 the Constitution of Massachusetts was so amended as that no money can be "appropriated to any religious sect for the maintenance, exclusively, of its own schools."

The Constitution of the State of New York (Art. I, Sec. 3) forbids "any discrimination or preference" for any "religious profession or worship." But to aid parochial schools, as they are conducted, and as the Third Plenary Council instructs that they shall be conducted, as we will soon show, is exercising "a discrimination or preference" for a particular "religious profession or worship."

In 1874 Pennsylvania, by the overwhelming majority of a popular vote, adopted an amendment to her Constitution which declares that "no money raised for the support of public schools shall be appropriated to or used for the support of any sectarian school." Said a writer recently, citing these sections in the *Christian Union:*

PUBLIC SCHOOL FUNDS. 189

I venture to suggest that, if the common schools of every State in the Union were as firmly intrenched and protected in the organic law of the respective States, the coming battle with the subtle enemies of free institutions would be virtually deferred for a hundred years to come, by which time the threatened crusade would be postponed indefinitely.

Such provisions simplify the problem, forestall and neutralize the friction of open controversy, and greatly discourage *sub rosa* plotting. In Section VI, Part I, other State constitutional provisions are cited, showing that in twenty of the States such a division and appropriation of public moneys is prohibited.

The kind of education for which Roman Catholics desire a division of the school money by the State involves the recognition of a particular religion by the State, and a discrimination in its favor which necessarily carries with it the converse right to discriminate against it.

CATHOLIC BOOKS.

The religious books used in the Catholic schools are not merely *religious*, treating upon practical religious matters, pertaining to the character and the common life, but they are *distinctively doctrinal* and *politico-ecclesiastical*, inculcating the fundamental tenets of the papal hierarchy—as clearly and distinctively sectarian and anti-republican as they can well be. For instance, these among others, and perhaps chiefly, are used: *A New Treatise on the Duty of a Christian Towards God;* * *The Doctrinal and Scriptural Catechism, or Instruction in the Principal Truths of the Christian Religion.* † These two books are full of the peculiar doctrines and practices of the Romish Church. The last is a minute and complete exhibit of the dogmas of the papacy. All the exclusiveness and absolute political supremacy of Rome is fully developed and inculcated. The child is taught that there is no salvation out of the papal Church; that there is no hope for what she calls "heretics" and "schismatics." Twenty-two pages are devoted to the subject of baptism, seven to confirmation, forty-seven to the eucharist, thirty to penance; in all of which the book descends to the usual explanations and subtle distinctions of the Roman Catholic theologians.

It is for the maintenance of such instruction in their parochial schools that the Roman Catholics ask the State to appropriate public school moneys. When the State does that, how far shall we be from having a union of Church and State—a Church supported and built up by funds appropriated by the State?

Bishop McQuaid avowed this strengthening of the Church as their object when he said in the Plenary Council, "Without these schools in a few generations

---

* By Rev. P. Collot.   † A Church Catechism.

our magnificent cathedrals and churches would remain as samples of monumental folly—of the unwisdom of a capitalist who consumes his fortune every year, without putting it out at interest or allowing it to increase. The Church has lost more in the past from the want of Catholic schools than from any other cause named by me this evening." *

After all this already ample evidence showing that the parochial schools are *distinctively* identified with the Roman Catholic hierarchy, and consequently so positively "sectarian" that, under the laws and Constitution of the United States and of the several States, the division or appropriation of public moneys for their benefit amounts to a "discrimination or preference" for a particular "religious profession or worship" equivalent to governmental action for "the establishment of religion," it may be claimed that these schools are *only constructively* identical with the Church in their teachings.

The Third Plenary Council.

We, therefore, now ask attention to still stronger and more direct proof, which shows that the Roman Catholic schools are *officially* and *organically* connected with and a *part* of the Roman Catholic *Hierachy*. We refer to the official action of the Third

---

* Memorial volume of the Third Plenary Council, p. 174.

Plenary Council, in 1884. The authority for the statements about to be made is official : *" Concillii Plenarii Baltimorensis III. Acta et Decreta,"* approved by the Supreme Pontiff, Leo XIII., on the 10th of September, 1885 ; recognized by the *Sacra Congregatio de Propaganda Fide* on the 21st of the same month. Published by John Murphy & Co. Baltimore, 1886.

This Council was held in Baltimore, November 9 to December 7, 1884, Archbishop Gibbons presiding as delegate apostolic. Associated as members of the Council were 14 archbishops, 56 bishops, 1 vicar-apostolic elect, 3 procurators, 1 archabbot, 6 abbots, and 1 superior-general. In addition to these the Council was attended by 31 superiors of religious orders, 11 heads of seminaries and 38 theologians—a total of 212 persons constituting the entire body, not including the protonotaries, etc. Cardinal McCloskey and six bishops were absent on account of sickness. These figures in this connection speak volumes, showing the prime rank and authority of the Council, but all subject to the pope, and its acts of no binding effect until approved by the pope and his associates in Italy.

In the Appendix to the Acts and Decrees of this Third Council we find the "*Instructio de Scholis Publicis ad Episcopos Americae Septentrionalis Foed-*

cratae," from which we take the following, which shows the animus and object of the parochial school movement:

Very often the Sacred Congregation for Propagating the Faith has been informed that the very gravest losses are impending over the Catholic youth in the United States of North America, from what they call there the public schools. This sad information caused the aforesaid Sacred Congregation to determine to propose to the bishops of that jurisdiction (*ditionis*) not a few questions, which looked, partly, to the causes why the faithful allow their children to frequent non-Catholic schools; partly, to the means by which youths can be more easily kept from schools of this description.

IT COMES FROM ROME.

This shows that the head of this opposition to our public schools is in Rome, and that foreign interference incepts and pushes the movement. This shows, too, that the chief concern is loss of Catholic youth from the Catholic Church. While, further on in this papal document, there is allusion to liability to corruption in morals, yet the chief emphasis is laid upon "loss on the side of faith," "perversion" from the Church. They say, "They (the schools) have seemed full of danger, *ex se*, and thoroughly averse to Catholicism." "The children neither learn the rudiments of the *faith* nor are interested in the precepts of the *Church*." They also complain of the public schools as "*disjointed from the authority of the Church*," with "teachers employed from every sect indiscriminately." This document closes with a menace to "contumacious parents who continue to patronize the public schools."

These are the reasons why that papal body, "The Sacred Congregation for Propagating the Faith," pressed this subject upon the bishops of the United States. Such is the official source and animus of the movement. It comes from the papal hierarchy in Rome.

Now we are ready to look at the specific instructions of the Plenary Council, as presented in their official "Acts and Decrees." Title VI reads, "*De Catholica Juventutis Institutione*" (concerning the Catholic institution for youth). This topic is divided into two chapters, on the parochial and the higher schools respectively. After citing the evils of a *mere secular* education, and such texts as, "No man can serve two masters," and "He that is not for me, is against me," they say (No. 196):

> Therefore we not only of our parental love exhort Catholic parents, but we even charge them by all the power we possess that they procure for their dearly beloved offspring, given to them by God, born again to Christ in baptism, and destined for heaven, an education truly Catholic and Christian; and that they defend their children during the whole period of infancy and boyhood from the dangers of *a merely sec-*

ular education; . . . and that for that purpose they send them to parochial or *other truly Catholic* schools, unless by chance the Ordinary judge that in a particular case something else can be permitted.

The second section of this chapter treats upon "the ways and means for promoting parish schools. (Section No. 201, fin.). "And first, as regards priests, we have determined that the candidates for holy orders now in the seminaries be sedulously taught that one of the chief duties of the priest, especially in these our times, is the Christian instruction of youth, and that that is *not possible* without *either parish schools* or *others truly Catholic.*" The priest must love his schools, "*sicut pupillas oculorum*" (as the apple of his eye), must visit them frequently, must teach history and the catechism himself, if possible, and must take care "that books compiled (*concinnati*, skillfully put together) by Catholic writers be always used in the school."

Section No. 202 instructs the laity that the school is *an integral part of the parish,* "without which *the very existence of the parish,* in the future, is endangered." The laity are to liberally support the schools, and to have certain rights and privileges in regard to the schools, to be more accurately defined hereafter by diocesan statutes—" saving *ecclesiastical* rights, as to appointing and dismissing teachers, as well as rewards, discipline, and direction of teaching (*doctrinæ*).*"

Section No. 203 provides that each bishop is to nominate a Diocesan Commission of Examination, to examine teachers and award a diploma, without which no teacher can be engaged in any parish school. This diploma is to be good five years, and in every parish. At the end of this period the teacher is to be re-examined. Section No. 204 provides that besides this Board of Examination, school commissioners are to be appointed, composed of *one or more priests*, for the inspection of schools, and such commissioners are to make full reports to the *bishop* of the diocese.

Section No. 207 says that these decrees must be " pondered and observed with religious zeal, that our parochial schools may more and more increase in number and worth, and daily stand forth not only as a *hope* and *pillar of the Church*, but also an honor and glory to the republic."

We have thus seen, on prime official authority—the Acts and Decrees of the Third Plenary Council of the Roman Catholic Church in the United States, and duly approved by the pope and cardinals—that the parochial schools are a distinctive part of the plan of the Roman Catholic hierarchy, designed to promote and build it up. The movement is pushed forward from Rome. The object is declared to be to save the Church from loss by lapses from the faith. The complaint against our public school system is that it is "disjointed from the authority of the Church." The Catholic schools are enjoined upon parents "by all the authority we (the Catholic hierarchy) possess." "None but Catholic books, skillfully put together (*concinnati*), shall be used in the schools." They declare that the school is an integral part of the parish, "without which the very existence of the parish, in the future, is endangered." The "examining, appointing, and dismissing of teachers, as well as rewards, discipline, and direction of teaching (*doctrinæ*)" are "ecclesiastical rights" not allowed the laity, but reserved for the hierarchy. And the desire is expressed that these schools may stand forth " as a hope and pillar of the Church."

The Question Involved.

Now to the point involved. If the public school funds are divided and appropriated in aid of the Catholic parochial schools the money will go directly to build up the Roman Catholic Church—not remotely or indirectly, but directly. And, moreover, that Church is very largely a political institution, a powerful combination of political and religious elements, and, as an acute Frenchman once remarked, "it is more of a political than a religious institution, and the instruction has a direct bearing upon political life."

It teaches that the Church and State are not to be separated; that the Church is rightfully superior to the State and to the government of all States; that this is the teaching of the infallible Church. Let the application of this doctrine to their conduct as citizens be made at some later period in life, and who can doubt, if they are "good Catholics," that they will decide that their first allegiance is due to the Catholic Church rather than to their country? Let the issue be distinctly made whether in these United States the Government shall control the Catholic Church or the Catholic Church shall control the Government; and every good Catholic is bound to do all in his power to subject the Government to the Catholic Church. This doctrine will find approbation at the polls; in city, town, state and national government; in legislative and congressional and judicial action; in all which relations the sons of Rome will seek to promote her interests—the logical consequences of her hierarchical assumptions.

Profoundly wise and full of deepest insight are the following words:

The movement of modern society is toward the winning of victories by the subtile arts of legislation rather than by the crude expedient of physical force;

and it is safe to say that since the Catholic Church was stripped of its temporal power and has been at liberty to devote more attention to the intellectual battles of legislation, it has gained more than it has lost through the carnal victories of its opponents. It is very busy and very successful in winning these victories, and we have only to open our eyes to what is going on about us to see that this is so. For testimony on this point, I will refer the reader to the Session Laws of the State of New York, where he will find that, by successive steps of legislation, the Catholic Church has it pretty well established that it is entitled to special legislation for the promotion of its interest. It is no longer content to have its members controlled by the general laws that apply to the body of citizens in general, but at every session of the Legislature bills are introduced, with reference to the Catholic Church or some of its institutions, by which the principle is recognized that this Church constitutes a body separate and apart from the rest of the community, and must be legislated for by itself. The ordinary course of legislation is not good enough for it; it must have better; and it gets it. Does any body doubt that by this process the Catholic Church is exalting itself above the State in this State of New York? Does any body doubt that the germ of its power for this end is found in its teaching of the doctrine of the infallibility of the Church in matters of "faith and morals?" Does any body doubt that the primary motive for the establishment of Catholic schools is that this and similar doctrines may be the better instilled into the mind of the young as a means toward the acquirement of power? Does the non-Catholic citizen think it would be a good thing to have these schools sustained by his money, taken from him by the arbitrary power of taxation?

This is the practical form in which the subject of Catholic schools presents itself to us, and it is by no means unimportant to know what is taught in them.*

Mistakes Made by States.

Is it asked, Has not the State sometimes appropriated funds to aid mixed educational and charitable institutions? Yes; and also to mixed religious and philanthropical institutions, to industrial protectorates, to Indian schools, etc. The moneys thus given, however, were not regular school funds. These appropriations have sometimes been made, in part, from considerations of convenience, because it seemed the easiest way to do something for a needy class. This system of charity-giving by the State has grown up, as many evil systems have developed, by a series of accretions, and possibly accidents, because it has been found easier to give money to institutions already existing than to found new institutions for such ends. But we are sure that it is a mistaken policy for the State to appropriate money to institutions and agencies not under the control of the State. "State and private enterprises, whether religious or non-religious, should not go into partnership, with the State, as a sleeping partner, furnishing in whole or in part the capital."

---

* Article in the *Christian Union*, July 26, 1888, by John Rockwell.

Notwithstanding what has been said is it still asked, Are not the Catholics entitled to their share of the school money, if they want it? An objection put in this form is very popular in a republic, and it is pressed with great effect on some minds. Again and again, in a variety of forms, we hear the reiteration that Catholics "are forced to pay tribute to the public school system, in which they do not believe." "The Catholic considers it unfair to tax him for the support of the public schools, to which he cannot send his children." "The Catholics protest against paying for the education of other than their own children."

Fallacy of the Plea for Exemption from Taxes.

But how is it with a large class of wealthy bachelors, who pay large taxes but have no children to educate? How many childless couples, also, there are, holding large property and paying large sums into the public treasury! And how many wealthy families send their children entirely to private schools, at large expense! In every large city there are many such schools, supported at great cost by parties who also pay immense taxes for the public schools. Moreover, there are not a few who theoretically do not believe in the public school system, but who, nevertheless, pay taxes for its support. The Baptists, Congregationalists, Methodists, Presbyterians, Episcopalians, etc., have numerous academies, seminaries, etc., which rank with the best high schools, which are supported entirely by those who choose to send their children to them, while at the same time they pay the taxes for public schools. If these unnumbered classes could be tabulated they would make a large body. Many of them have no choice in the matter, and some of them complain of injustice; but they excite no sympathy. Why? Because the public school system fosters the general intelligence, promotes public order, and contributes to the moral poise of our citizenship. In many ways it helps the general moral and social interests of the country and its material prosperity. All these classes get a full return for the taxes they pay. They can only complain of the compulsion exercised upon them, and that will be in vain until they find something better than a government by majorities.

The appropriation of money to the support of distinctively Roman Catholic schools would be very unjust to those citizens and taxpayers who conscientiously believe that the Roman Catholic system is wrong in itself, and injurious in its consequences to individuals and to communities. It would be such a union of Church and State as is forbidden by the spirit and tenor of American institutions. Protestants have political and civil rights as well as Roman Catholics, and the support of distinctively Roman Catholic schools, at public expense, would be a violation of those rights, just as the support of a distinctively Methodist, Episcopal, Baptist, or Congregational school, with money drawn from taxes upon the whole people, would be a violation of the rights of individuals not represented in the denomination receiving the funds.

QUESTION V.

As to whether, as a matter of comity, we ought not to find some way to divide the School Funds.

WITH great show of candor the inquiry is made, whether our Roman Catholic fellow-citizens, who make this demand, are not so large and respectable a minority that we ought to cease to tax them for the support of a system in which they do not believe, and which they feel they cannot patronize. Or, if still taxed, can we not find some way to give them their share of the school funds?

It must be admitted that in a republic like ours the majority ought to treat with deference a large and respectable minority, especially in matters upon which men are so sensitive as in respect to taxation and questions of conscience. Nevertheless, sometimes there are matters at stake too sacred to be surrendered to minorities, however large and respectable. We are ready to charitably entertain all alleged conscientious scruples; but when the conscience is the creature of a hierarchy, dependent upon the dictum of foreign ecclesiastics, and this minority is dragged and coerced into its attitude, the case is very different.

We cannot quite say with Dr. Lyman Abbott, in a recent number of the *Christian Union*, "If our Roman Catholic fellow-citizens objected to the American public school system, it would be very questionable whether we should have the right to put their children into the public schools, or even to do this indirectly, by taxing them . . . to support such schools." But we go on, with Dr. Abbott, to say, "Though great regard is to be paid to the opinions of a large and reputable minority in a republic, no such regard is due to the opinions of a close corporation under the control of a foreign potentate. And the decrees of the Plenary Council are the decrees of a close corporation under the control of a foreign potentate." We ought to respect the wishes of our German fellow-citizens. "But if a German Bund existed in America, all of whose officers were appointed by Bismarck, and were answerable for their action only to Bismarck, their opinions on public affairs would not be entitled to any political deference."

Hierarchy *vs.* Laity.

There is good reason to believe that the action of the Roman Catholic hierarchy in regard to the parochial schools does not represent the laity of that Church. The Catholic Church does not claim to be a representative body. The hierarchy does not speak *for* but *to* the laity. It does not express what the laity want, but tells them what they must take. The pope commands his children—does not consult them. The pope appoints the cardinals, and the cardinals elect the pope, and the pope and the cardinals control the Church. The Plenary Council was not a convention of representatives of Roman Catholic congregations, and all its doings, before becoming obligatory upon the priests and laity, had to be approved and confirmed by the pope and his associates in Italy. The Plenary Council at Baltimore represented, not American Catholic opinion, but Roman papal opinion, and is entitled to just so much weight as the opinion of any other foreign potentate, namely, according to his character. More than this, we have a right to resent his unlawful interference in our affairs.

So far from *representing* the sentiment of the American Catholics, we have reason to think that the Plenary Council and the hierarchy represent the *reverse* opinion. It is a familiar fact that more than once—many times—the priesthood has attacked the public schools, and yet against persuasions and commands, from the pulpit and in person, the laity have voted to sustain them, and have continued their

Shall the School Funds be Divided? 207

children in attendance upon them. Again and again have priests and bishops attempted to compel Roman Catholic parents, under threat of excommunication and privation of the sacraments, to withdraw their children from the common schools, and ever and again have the priestly commands and threats been disregarded.

Slow Growth of Parochial Schools.

It is to be presumed that the oldest parochial schools in the country are the best developed, namely, those of New York, Brooklyn, Boston, etc. But in neither of these cities is a majority of even Roman Catholic children found in the parochial schools. And yet how strenuous have been the endeavors of the priesthood, by coaxing and coercion, to bring them into their schools! In Boston there are probably 40,000 to 45,000 Roman Catholic children between the ages of five and fifteen inclusive; but only a little more than 7,000 are in the parochial schools.* All this notwithstanding this school contest has been going on from thirty to fifty years, in different parts of the country. How slow is the increase, too:

From 1860 to 1870 their pupils increased 200,000 †
From 1870 to 1880   "   "   "   169,000
From 1880 to 1886   "   "   "   140,510

---

* The number has been increased during this year.
† See Section VIII, Part I.

These are the statistics of *Sadlier's Catholic Year-Book.*

In July, 1888, Father McGlynn, of New York, said:

A large part of the fanatical clamor for church schools comes from foreign priests, who care more for their foreign language and foreign ideas than they care for the Church itself. They do not wish their people to be Americanized. Their opposition to the public school is disloyalty. National common schools are indispensable to a common nationality.

And a young Catholic layman, educated in the public schools in Boston, said to a reporter of the *Boston Herald:*

It is unquestionably true that a very large number of people educated in the Catholic faith—people, let me say, who are loyal to the teachings of the Church in which they have been raised—are unalterably opposed to any thing that savors of a change in the method of educating their children. They are not in favor of parochial schools, and have the courage of their convictions to such an extent that the advocates of parochial schools within the Church have quite all they can do to answer the objections offered by this class to which I refer. How foolish it is, then, to alienate these people and force them, by ungenerous and bigoted attacks upon the Church which, from their youth, they have been taught to regard with reverence, to go over to the side of the more intolerant! My belief is, and it is shared by a majority of those who were educated in the public schools, that religious teaching should have no part in the **public** school system of education. I do not want my children taught any thing but what strictly belongs to secular education.

What stronger evidence that their people are most obstinately holding back from the Catholic schools and tenaciously holding on to the public school system? Why? Because they do not believe in the Catholic school system.

The specious plea, therefore, that we ought to respect the sentiments of a large mass of Roman Catholics, the majority of their laity, is not well founded, either in fact or in principle. And the hierarchy, which has presumed to speak for the Church, only represents a foreign, self-assuming, imperious corporation. We do not ask them what is for the good of this republic. The great mass of Roman Catholic people favor the perpetuation of our American common school system.

As to the question of tolerance, we ask, Who is the intolerant party? It looks as though either Catholic consciences or Protestant consciences must be hurt. We see no third alternative. The Catholic conscience, however, in this matter is not the conscience of the masses of Catholics, who do not object to the public school system, but rather favor it, but that artificial ecclesiastical conscience which the foreign hierarchy has produced. And those representing this kind of conscience are a very small minority, whom it is better to hurt, in this extreme case, than to hurt the consciences of the overwhelming majority of the nation. The nation has rights of conscience as well as irreconcilable minorities. It is as intolerant that a small hierarchical minority should dictate our national policy, as for the Orange Lodges of Ulster to attempt to rule all Ireland. A part can never be greater than the whole. The rights of a minority pushed to an extreme become the wrongs of the majority.

It is a self-delusion to say, "You must not take my money in public taxes, and then use it for any object of which my conscience disapproves." What nonsense! No civilized government could be administered on such a basis. The Quaker disapproves of war, but he must pay the war-tax all the same. Government could not be carried on a single day if this principle were observed. "The conscience of the minority can never be allowed to become the tyrant autocrat of the nation."

In a New England city, some intelligent Catholics desiring to liberalize some of their church matters asked the bishop if it could not be done if the majority of the parish favored it. Straightening up into a lordly attitude the bishop answered, "*I am the majority!*"

QUESTION VI.

Is a Compromise Possible?

IS it possible to harmoniously adjust the differences involved in this great controversy? I think I voice the sentiments of the mass of American citizens when I say a settlement would be hailed with delight, if placed upon an honorable basis, and if it could give security for the integrity and welfare of our civil institutions. I am sure none of us desire to take advantage of our majority in the popular vote. We do not wish to *force* the question against the Roman Catholics. It is chiefly a question of self-preservation—preserving the integrity of our institutions.

What are some of the plans for a compromise?

The one which meets us first is the old proposition we have been combating—namely, to divide the school funds; giving to Roman Catholics their share, and to Protestants their share. This proposition keeps re-appearing like Banquo's ghost. But it is no compromise. It is the ultimate demand of the Catholics, with no concession whatever.

But Protestant Churches do not want their part of

the funds divided off to them, for they do not want to set up parochial schools. They prefer State schools for their children and for the masses outside of all denominational relations. They think the best interests of the republic require the public school system, and that the welfare of the whole country should be considered rather than the wishes of a single denomination, and especially when the demands of that denomination are stimulated by the dictation of a foreign hierarchy. Who are most entitled to be considered, in a republic like ours: the Roman Catholics, who constitute only about $12\frac{1}{2}$ per cent., or the non-Catholics, who constitute $87\frac{1}{2}$ per cent. of the total population? We need not press an answer. The Protestants do not want a share of the school funds divided to them. They do not want the school system dismembered; and, more than this, we have before shown that we have good reason to think the *majority* of Roman Catholics are opposed to such a division.

THE REAL POINT.

The issue is not between Roman Catholic *education* and Protestant *education* as such; if it were there might be some plausibility in the demand. But the question is whether we will make our national education *ecclesiastical*, as would be the case if the

Is a Compromise Possible? 213

funds were divided and distributed among the denominations. We are not ready for this. We object to education controlled by the various Protestant denominations as truly as we do to education controlled by Roman Catholics. "There is, indeed, a difference, and an important one," as has been well stated; * "the former would be ruled by Americans, and in the interest of America; the latter by the pope, and in the interest of the papacy; the former by a body of men themselves ruled by the public sentiment of their nation; the latter by a foreign potentate, having no interest in American well-being, and not amenable to American public opinion, nor even to American law. But *both would be ecclesiastical.* And it is to ecclesiastical, not merely to Romish ecclesiastical, control of our systems of education that we object." It is in the interest of *religion*, and of *education*, and of the *republic* that we make this protest.

Another proposition † is, "To leave all the schools under the control of the State, to allow the State to build the school-houses, to select the text-books, to adjust the curriculum, and even conduct the examinations, provided the Church of Rome may select and appoint the teachers." Rev. Bishop McQuaid ‡ de-

---
* *Christian Union*, May 31, 1883. † *Christian Union*, May 31, 1883.
‡ In an interview in December, 1875.

scribed the working of this plan in Lima and Poughkeepsie, N. Y.:

REPORTER. How was the parochial school incorporated at Lima?

BISHOP. They had no room for all the pupils who wished to attend the district school, and therefore proposed to the Catholics that the latter should reopen theirs, which had been closed. This was done, and at first lay teachers gave instruction at the parochial school, the authorities paying all expenses. On the 1st of January we said: "Will you pay sisters as well as lay teachers?" And they consented, provided the sisters could pass the necessary examination. I was asked if the sisters should submit to such a test, and replied, "Certainly. We want no teachers who are unable to show abundant familiarity with the ordinary studies required." The superintendent of Livingston County appointed a day for the examination, which was to take place at Livonia, and two sisters were sent there. But, unfortunately, the poor sisters in some way missed the train, and, not wishing to fail in the appointment, hired a carriage and rode the entire distance of twenty-six miles on as cold a day as we had last winter. The examination lasted two hours and proved satisfactory. The school is still in active operation. No religious instruction is given during ordinary school-hours, and any body can come to see that there is no violation of this rule. The school authorities pay the salaries of two sisters, but a third is paid for by the parents. Catholic children outside of the village attend school and pay a rate therefor. There is a parochial school at Corning conducted on the same plan. In Poughkeepsie the plan has been in successful operation for two years. All Catholic pupils attend a single school in which no religious instruction is given during ordinary school-hours, but the teachers are selected by the authorities and paid by the city school authorities.

It is believed that this plan has not worked satisfactorily to either party; for, as has been well said, "whoever controls the teachers really controls the school. For the school is a teaching institution, and to control the teachers is to control the quality, and character, and spirit of the teaching. Let who will determine the creed of the Church; he who chooses its ministry shapes its future. The power of the school is the personal power of the teacher; whoever exercises that power exercises the real control over the school. Compromises should be equal. What would the hierarchy say to the proposition that the Church should fix the curriculum, and the State select the teachers? A skillful Protestant could so teach the Roman Catholic catechism as to turn half her pupils out, at the end of the year, impregnated with Protestantism." *

Another proposition which has been considered is to leave the school-houses in control of the State, and allow the ministers of religion to teach religion before and after the session of the school. Rev. Bishop McQuaid, in the interview just referred to, said:

---

*_Christian Union_, May 31, 1880.

The State cannot reach all these children, but we can, and we do not ask the State to pay for the religious influences we throw around these children, but simply for the secular teachings they receive. We erect the buildings, provide the teachers, who shall, however, be subject to the examinations required by the State; and then for a nominal rental we allow the State full control of these schools, during the ordinary school-hours, in which time only secular instruction shall be given. Before and after such hours we propose to give the pupils such religious teaching as we deem essential in the education of youth. The plan is already in practical operation at Corning, Elmira, and Lima, and by the co-operation of Republicans, and still more markedly in the schools of the Children's Aid Society in New York. The same principle is carried out in most of the public schools of the State, in which, before and after school-hours, religious exercises in harmony with the convictions of the parents are commonly held, where they are not as a rule the practice during school-hours.

But the hierarchy has rejected this plan, and that wisely, for, as Dr. Abbott has said, "Religion cannot be done up in a separate parcel and handed out to the pupil after school is over. Religion is not a fringe that can be tacked on or left off a garment. It is a dye impregnating every thread of the pattern."

Another Scheme

has just come to public attention. A large influential journal* gives the following fact:

---

* *Boston Journal*, October 27, 1888.

Is a Compromise Possible? 217

The report of the Superintendent of Public Instruction for the State of New York for the current year contains an interesting account of a Catholic school experiment. For twenty years St. Raphael's Catholic Church in Suspension Bridge has had a parish school. In 1885 the church asked the local Board of Education to take this school under its care and maintenance and to allow the sisters in charge to remain as teachers. This was done. The school was continued as before, under sisters in their garb, but at the public expense, the board leasing the building from the church at a rental of a dollar a year. In 1886 the acting State Superintendent decided that this arrangement was an illegal discrimination in favor of a certain class, and void. Some minor change was then made, and the lease continued for five years. The matter was again appealed to the State Superintendent, and he concluded that a decided discrimination was made in favor of the Catholic Church in employing sisters who dressed in the garb of their order, with beads and crucifix, and were addressed as "Sister Mary," "Sister Martha," etc. The Superintendent says:

> The conclusion is irresistible that these things may constitute a much stronger sectarian or denominational influence over the minds of children, than the repetition of the Lord's Prayer or the reading of the Scriptures at the opening of the schools; and yet these things have been prohibited, whenever objection has

been offered; by the rulings of this department from the earliest days, because of the purpose enshrined in the hearts of the people, and embedded in the fundamental law of the State, that the public school system shall be kept altogether free from matters not essential to its primary purpose and dangerous to its harmony and efficiency.

The Superintendent directed that the sisters, within fifteen days, should put off their religious costume, and should be addressed by their names, as Miss So-and-so. As they would not do so the connection of the school with the public schools ceased.

In November, 1876, Rev. Father Preston, Vicar-General of the New York Diocese, attempted to state

Two Possible Solutions:

There are only two solutions to this difficulty— either exempt from taxation those who do not desire to send their children to common schools, or else give to every private denominational school its proportion of the taxes generally raised. Where is the difficulty in the way? Where the objection to either solution? There can justly be none. If you can exempt us from taxation, then of course we shall have nothing to complain of. Let those who want schools have them; but if the State thinks it best and most expedient to impose a tax for the support of education, then let it divide the sums so raised by taxation in a manner agreeable to itself among all classes of its citizens.

It is urged as an objection that it would be difficult for us to establish a system on which taxation should

Is a Compromise Possible? 219

be divided, as there are many poor Catholics who have children to be educated but no taxable property, personal or real estate. Well, we only ask what is just. We are not begging for a donation. But I know of poor Catholics who have to help to support the common schools for rich Protestants' sons, and have to help build and support Catholic schools besides.

These propositions are only slightly different from others. But at the risk of repeating somewhat, they will be noticed. It requires but a moment's consideration to see that Father Preston's arguments, however plausible they may have seemed to the Catholic audience to whom they were addressed, overlook the prime duty of popular government to perpetuate itself, and that in consulting in regard to securing the greatest freedom it must also consult the greatest welfare of all. To accomplish this some restraints and requirements must be imposed upon the inhabitants. If Catholics are to be relieved from taxation because they do not believe in the policy of non-sectarian schools, the Methodists, Baptists, and all other denominations may make the same demands. So may those who pay the largest tax, and send no children to the schools, inquire if this is a free country. The result of this proposition would be, that there would be nobody left to be taxed to support schools for the great mass of children whose parents are too poor to educate them at their own expense, and could not pay taxes necessary to support the proper schools.

The other proposition is no less mischievous. Suppose the Catholics to be allowed their portion of the school money, could other denominations be denied the privilege, should they demand it? If this were done would not the whole school fund be frittered away, while there yet remained a large class of children, most needing schools, for whom no adequate provision could be made? Besides, what manner of teaching could we expect in schools exclusively sectarian?

The Separate Schools Act,

adopted in the Province of Ontario, Canada, is another plan of compromise. It provides that a given number of Roman Catholic or Protestant or colored "rate-payers" petitioning to be permitted to set up "separate schools," will be allowed to do so. They may then produce certificates showing that they are tax-payers, and be excused from the payment of their portion of the public taxes which goes to support the public schools. The schools which they shall thus set up are to report their registers to the Public School Board, etc.

This system is a residuum from a prior system under the old Legislative Union (1841–1867), and perpetuated under the British North-American Act. But we are informed that even this system does not relieve the public school system of the province from Romish interference and maneuvering. The priests bring their influence to bear upon the public school system, and endeavor to promote their interests in ways often very irritating.

Radical Antagonism.

The antagonism between the two systems is so radical that they cannot be compromised without the destruction of one or both. "It is a question of supreme control,* and who can show how supreme control can be divided? The American theory is that the public school system, supported by the State, must be controlled by the State, and that such management is necessary to the maintenance of republican institutions. The papal hierarchy claims that the *Church* holds the exclusive function of directing and controlling education. Americans claim that education must be American in its ideas and spirit, that it must be controlled by Americans, and administered to make loyal citizens of America. The hierarchy claim that it must be Roman Catholic— controlled by Rome and administered to make loyal children of Rome." * How can such contrary issues

---

* See editorial in *Christian Union*, May 31, 1888, p. 675.

be harmonized? They must be settled one way or the other. There seems to be no middle ground. The hierarchy will not be satisfied unless we concede its claims—a question of absolute self-surrender—involving, in its sequence, the surrender of our republican institutions. Most effectively and powerfully is this question put in the *Christian Union*:*

"The real question at issue between the republic and the hierarchy is not, What shall be *taught?* nor who shall *teach?* but in what spirit and to what end shall the teaching be conducted? The Roman Catholic hierarchy declares that our free school system is Protestant; and it is more than half right. The object of the hierarchy is to teach submission; the object of our free school system is to teach independence. The one forbids questioning; the other stimulates it. The one conducts every inquirer to an infallible Church; the other throws him back upon himself. The one bids him listen and obey; the other bids him investigate and learn. The one teaches him to submit; the other teaches him to think. The one drills him to be a private in a magnificent army; the other invests him with power of self-command in a self-governed community. The one, as we have already said, makes him an obedient child of Rome; the other an authoritative citizen

---

* May 31, 1888. Two articles, in successive numbers.

of a free republic. To him who asks for the truth Rome gives only authority; to him who asks for authority the republic gives only truth. These roads do not lead in the same direction, and cannot conduct to the same goal. Rome has never made an independent people; she never can. That independence which is our pride is her anathema. That individualism of judgment which we seek to create she seeks to destroy. It is idle to propose a compromise between two systems thus antagonistic, in their origin, their methods of administration, their spirit and scope, and the ends which they severally pursue. The American citizen must decide between the ecclesiastical and the non ecclesiastical systems of education—between the system which has produced Italy, Spain, France, and Ireland, and the system which has produced the northern half of the United States. He cannot combine them. Neither compromise nor alliance is possible."

The conditions demanded by the papacy involve the certain destruction of the public school system.

QUESTION VII.

Can both parties patronize the Public Schools harmoniously, and on what basis?

THE answer to this question is found in the plain, familiar facts of our public school history. This is what has been done all along, for many years, with very little irritation, only occasional disturbance, and that not amounting to much, except under these recent demands by the hierarchy for a division of the school funds. And even now, notwithstanding these demands, so far as the administration of the work of the schools and the scholarly drill and improvement of the pupils are concerned, and these are the chief things, the schools are doing well, quite as well as ever. The exceptions, if any, are exceedingly rare.

Almost all parties seem to be well impressed with the importance of harmonizing the administration of the public schools, so that Catholics and Protestants and the diverse nationalities may pursue their studies together without embarrassment. In a republic like ours all classes must be mingled together, and taught to work together, in every possible way, from childhood upward. It is the only way to make them homogeneous, especially while receiving such large immigration. The earlier in life this fusing of diverse nationalities is begun the better, for it is comparatively difficult in advanced years. The public schools can undoubtedly be harmoniously conducted on the plan of making American citizens, not Romanists or Protestants, if both parties will treat each other equitably. Civil and religious liberty must be held inviolable. Any attempt at intolerance, in the working of either our political or educational system, by Catholics against Protestants, or by Protestants against Catholics, will hinder the working of the assimilating process, so necessary to make a homogeneous people, and imperil our institutions.

ULTRAISM.

In times of excitement it is natural that some persons will give utterance to ultra and unreasonable views. I call attention to two specimens—one by a Roman Catholic periodical and the other by a Protestant mass-meeting, and both quite recent:

Within a few weeks the *Catholic Review* made a very ultra utterance. It said:* "It is impossible to teach modern history in a mixed school. Every inch

---
* July, 1888.

of it (modern history) is contested ground, and especially have the annals of the last four centuries been covered and swamped by swarms of malignant falsifiers, and twisted into fantastic shapes in the heat of fierce controversies. No teacher can teach this history to a child of a different faith without wounding the latter's feelings, and attacking her religion; and just in proportion to the person's earnestness of belief will be the harshness of the wound and the bitterness of the attack. The remedy for Catholics can only be found in our parochial schools."

This is a very ultra position. It is certain that modern history cannot be radically changed. In coming out of a condition of mediæval ideas and civilization into a condition of newer thought and advanced civilization, and in tracing the conflicts and wrecks of the old fabrics, consequent upon putting new wine into old bottles, some things will be found in the records of that progress not complimentary to some classes of people. But we ought all of us, however related to the past, to be able to look upon the history of those events with calmness, and treat each other magnanimously. The kind of education which teaches people to do this is the very kind most important to enable diverse peoples to live and act together in a republic. The argument is in favor of our public school system, and shows why and how it should be maintained.

The Protestant ultraism to which I referred declared that "No Roman Catholics should be elected to the School Board; that no Roman Catholic teachers should be employed in the public schools"—an absurdity which cannot be allowed in a country where all religions are equally tolerated and education is equally provided for all. We Protestants will have our prefences, and will show them in our votes, but we cannot afford to advocate such dogmas as those just quoted. In so doing we would ourselves introduce sectarianism into the public schools—the very thing we complain of the Roman Catholics for doing.

How to Do It.

If all classes are to use the public schools several conditions must be faithfully observed.

1. There must be no religious instruction in them. If attempted it will be likely to savor of some particular sect. To attempt it would be inconsistent with the American system of government, and perilous to the successful administration of the school system. A purely secular basis is the only basis on which all citizens can unite. Then no one's doctrines are assailed or slurred. There is abundant opportunity for parents, Sunday-schools, and churches to

look after the religious education, the public school occupying only about one sixth of the hours of the year. The public school can succeed only on a completely non-sectarian, absolutely secular basis. On any other plan it is doomed.

We have no doubt that some great elements of morality may and should be taught—reverence for God, honesty, loyalty to law and government, the duty of worship, chastity, rights of property, etc. Morality relates to right action, right relations between man and man. There are many of these elements of morals common to all religionists.

2. The *administration* must be without sectarian bias or partiality. The people will never knowingly consent to have any sect or denomination interfere with, control or bias the public school. Every denomination must be served alike; otherwise it will justly claim its share of the funds. This must be honestly and squarely done.

3. In the department of historical studies—almost the only one where differences are likely to arise—an unswerving rule must be adhered to. All necessary facts should be taught with perfect indifference to the likes or dislikes of any Church. Historical truth cares for nothing but cold facts. Says Rev. Dr. Quint, in the *Congregationalist:* * "If, in the study of

---
* August 2, 1888.

history, the school comes against some incident which ought to be taught, the plain fact should be stated, whatever it may be—taught naturally, and in the right spirit, with no intent or appearance of slurring any body, and no effort to misrepresent present views. It should make no difference whether it is or is not unpleasant reading for any nation or for any sect. It would not be at all agreeable to Congregationalists to have it stated that their Puritan forefathers imprisoned Baptists and hung Quakers; but, if that is a fact, it cannot be blotted out of history, and if it is presented as a mere fact, and without an attempt to shadow any body but those who did it, we cannot complain. Tetzel did something in regard to indulgences which was the occasion of a tremendous conflict in the world's history. What he did is easily ascertained, and school history cannot ignore it. If his Church sustained or did not sustain him in what he did, that, too, is a matter of history. There is no difficulty in stating the facts in a calm, unimpassioned judicial manner. If, for any reason, the facts should be unpleasant to his Church, that Church must do as the Congregationalists do when the treatment of the Quakers is referred to. The State cannot inquire whether any Church likes or dislikes the record of past ages. This is a fair platform upon which all citizens can stand; and on that platform they will stand, and not pervert nor ignore history, either from policy or fear. Its teachings should not, however, ascribe to any denomination an interpretation of its doctrines, either by inference, omission, or direct statement, which that Church disclaims. Pupils must not be taught that Congregationalists now believe in hanging Quakers because Congregationalists hung Quakers two hundred years ago."

4. In the selection of teachers the School Board should know no denomination. Instances have been known where, for a number of years, every teacher in the public schools belonged to one particular denomination, and every member of the school committee also. Not long ago there was a teacher in the high school of one of our New England State capitals who had a Catholic wife who was an assistant, teaching French and botany, and a very superior teacher. This gentleman, himself a Protestant, and attending a Protestant church, was dismissed solely because he had a Catholic wife. These things should not be allowed to occur.

5. Great wisdom should be exercised, in the administration of the public school affairs, to guard against the appearance of unfairness. When sectarian questions arise they should be met openly, carefully, with cautious examination, and full statements should be frankly made to the people. If there is an unseemly

haste, or an appearance of privacy, or a disposition to shun a frank statement of the case, a sensitive people will suspect some sectarian or political manœuver. Perfect fairness, inflexible firmness, and an unquestioned frankness will succeed.

6. The public schools must not only be managed in a non-sectarian, but also in a non-partisan, way— kept free from the control of any political party, however dominant. In New York city, the public school system is thoroughly honeycombed at every point by the vermin of party politics, and such politics — saloon-dominated, priest-ridden, and money-grabbing politics—as have long characterized that locality. The best thing for the schools is not done, but "soft" places are given to unworthy persons, and school appointments are made for the ends of the dominant party. This evil has reached a pitch where a voluntary committee of citizens is said to be forming for the purpose of watching the educational authorities, and bringing the State machine into accord with the reasonable demands of the community. "The same influence," said the *Boston Herald* of August 1, "is creeping over the schools in Boston, where it seems to be the height of ambition with some to get an election to a place on the School Board, and it is not unknown in other cities. This possibility of corruption exists in the very na-

ture of a free government. It is not the fault of State education as such." The people should wisely discriminate and select, where such sacred and important interests as the education of the young are to be intrusted to men in responsible positions, that they be not committed to such persons as will wrestle with one another over the appointment of their favorites to posts of responsibility in the schools.

Things to be Avoided.

The sectarianism which must be avoided, if Catholic and Protestant children are to be educated together in the same schools, and if the public school system is to be preserved in its integrity, is of a twofold character.

First, there is the Roman Catholic sectarianism which continually echoes the demand for a share of the public school money; which, in some instances, has put members of brotherhoods and sisterhoods into the public schools as instructors, breathing the religious airs and wearing the garb and other insignia of Rome; which on the Sabbath preceding school elections has advocated its candidates from Catholic pulpits and distributed its ballots in the churches; which allies itself with the low saloon and money-grabbing element, as in New York city, for the accomplishment of Catholic ascendency and the control of school matters; which improves every opportunity in the schools to push historical, sectarian, and ethical, questions into disputed and sensitive arenas; and which so administers the work of school boards and school instruction as to provoke suspicion that they are seeking to Romanize the common school system.

Secondly, there is a Protestant sectarianism, no less baneful in its influences, which denies to Roman Catholics a place upon the School Board or as teachers in the public schools, notwithstanding, in some instances, one half of the pupils are from Roman Catholic families; which insist upon retaining as a part of the public school system forms of worship to which Roman Catholics object; which would retain in the text-books passages touching upon disputed grounds between Protestants and Roman Catholics; which is continually on the *qui vive* for the slightest suspicions of any purpose of the Romanists to capture the public schools; which foams at the mouth whenever reasonable concessions are made in favor of conscientious scruples; which is intolerant toward estimable, experienced, broad-minded men who advocate fair-play when heated controversialists rave; which sometimes denies to Roman Catholics the rights of citizenship, and which, at this late day, insists upon putting the Protestant Bible back into the public schools.

Examples of Intolerance.

I will now cite two instances of intolerance—one Protestant and the other Roman Catholic—both of them examples of what is to be deprecated and avoided.

The first, a case of Protestant intolerance, we quote from the *Christian Register*.* It occurred some years ago, in Charlestown, Mass. "A graduate of Harvard College was appointed to the position of sub-master. He was a thorough scholar, a natural gentleman, an excellent teacher. After a while, however, it was discovered that he was a Catholic, although he did not introduce his special religious beliefs into the school-room. At the close of the year the question of his re-appointment came up. The School Board was made up entirely of Protestants, and they declined to re-elect him. One member of the Board asked a postponement of the matter for two weeks. In that time he secured the signatures of the parents or guardians of every child in the school, favoring his re-election. Nevertheless, in spite of this overwhelming appeal from the constituency of the school, the committee, under the lead of a narrow-minded Baptist clergyman, dismissed him because he was a Catholic. Of the sixty teachers, if

---
* July 19, 1888.

we remember the number correctly, under the jurisdiction of that Board, every one was a Protestant. It would be hard to find any thing in the annals of Catholicism more humiliating or disgraceful than such a course of action in an American school. This is an example of the extreme of injustice to which Protestantism may go when it yields to the sectarian spirit in the management of the public schools."

Some years ago a correspondent of the *New York Evangelist* gave an instance of Roman Catholic intolerance in the public schools of Pennsylvania, in a locality where the Romanists held the sway.

Loretto, in Blair County, on the summit of the Alleghanies, was originally a Romish settlement, and named in honor of "Our Lady" of that name. To this day the Romish catechism is taught in the regular course in the public schools, supported by the people, under the school law of the State. When Protestant parents, of whom there is a sprinkling in the town, protest, they are summarily told, "if they do not like it they may keep their children at home."

Such intolerance as these two cases show must be discarded, if we are to keep all our children in the public schools.

An Example of Good Sense.

I will now cite another instance in which a Protestant teacher and a Roman Catholic priest both showed great forbearance, commendable discrimination and wisdom—an example of the spirit to be cherished in order to make our public school system acceptable to both Catholics and Protestants. I quote from an editorial in the *Christian Register :* *

"One of the most successful teachers in Boston taught forty-seven years in the public schools. He had a school in which eight out of every ten were foreigners, and from fifty to sixty per cent. of the whole number were Catholics. In this term of nearly half a century, this master of a Boston school never had any trouble with his pupils on the question of religion. He managed with tact and discretion. Instead of compelling his scholars to recite the Lord's Prayer with him, he simply required that they should maintain a respectful deportment while he said the prayer aloud himself, those being permitted to join in who wished to. The only time when there seemed any danger of a religious collision was when he punished a Catholic boy, not for refusing to say the prayer, but for not maintaining a respectful deportment when prayer was said. The priest to whom the boy appealed wrote a note to the teacher, thanking him for the action he had taken. Yet this same priest was at that very time suing the city of Boston because another school-master, under direction of an in-

---

* July 19, 1888.

judicious member of the School Committee, had whipped a boy for refusing to say the Protestant version of the Lord's Prayer. The priest saw the difference between the two cases. In one case, the boy was punished for refusing to say a form of prayer which was contrary to the usages of his own church. In the other case, he was simply punished for bad behavior. The incident showed that the Protestant school-master and the Catholic priest could see distinctions with a difference, and yet have no difference over their distinctions."

Such a spirit will help to conserve the public school system. For the continuance of the public school system we plead, and ask that Protestants and Catholics may so combine and harmonize in its management and use that it may be preserved. We believe that the existence of this system, supported and controlled, absolutely and entirely, by the State, is a fundamental need of this Republic, and that the logical trend of the Roman Catholic demand is the destruction of this school system.

QUESTION VIII.

What may we Expect Romanists to do in the Future, and How shall we Preserve our School System?

THE hierarchy will doubtless take out of the public schools all the children they can influence by all the arts they can bring to bear upon the parents. Bishop McQuaid said, "The Catholics will go on supporting their parochial schools, as they have a right to do, trusting to the sober second thought of the American people to do them justice." A large number of Catholic children, however, will remain in the public schools.

The Romish population is too open to the influence of American ideas not to have a tendency to revolt from this heavy burden, and from the manifest disadvantage on the part of their children in those schools, however severe the priestly infliction. This tendency to revolt from priestly dominance will be skillfully manipulated. The power of the confessional, of the pulpit, of pastoral visitation, and the awful power which belongs to men who can deny the sacraments, will all be used to draw the Catholic

What to Expect of the Romanists. 239

population into absolute acquiescence with the parochial school demands. This tendency to revolt should be adroitly as well as vehemently supported by Protestant discussion, clear, broad, kindly and cogent.

But whether they continue to patronize the public schools or not, one of their papers * says that Romanists will continue to elect their candidates to public school boards, will put in all the Roman Catholic teachers they can, and in every possible way exert a controlling influence in public school matters, so long as they are taxed for the support of the system. The hierarchy will still maintain an attitude of persistent, determined opposition. The Church of Rome will propose no compromise, but will persist in her course, as she has done in the past, only more determinedly. It is a long contest upon which we have entered. We must adjust ourselves to it. We must not deceive ourselves with vain hopes of speedy peace, nor be deceived by Rome's specious maneuverings.

The editor of the *Christian Union* has put the points very effectively:

The universal diffusion of Catholic education means something more than the opening of schools in every parish; it means a steady and unrelenting attack on our common schools; not on that *abstract* thing called the

---
* The *Pilot*.

Common School System, but on every school in every locality where the Catholic voting population has any strength. This result was inevitable. Catholics have the same indisposition to pay taxes which characterizes the great majority of men of all faiths. They are compelled to support their own Church schools; they are not disposed to support the common schools in addition. Wherever the way is open they will, as a matter of course, use their power to control or cripple the common schools. The great struggle between our schools and this vigilant, uncompromising foe, will not be fought out in Congress or in legislatures, in newspapers or pulpits. It will be fought in every school district in the country. There will be no great or decisive battle, but a long series of skirmishes. Every school-meeting will be contested, and on the result of these minor contests the struggle itself will turn. Henceforth eternal vigilance will be the price we shall pay for our common schools; henceforth no man who cares for his community or his country can afford to shirk a duty which has been more honored in the breach than in the observance.

In many communities these foes of the common schools will not lack for allies who will, consciously or unconsciously, work with and for them; men who will fail to see that they are being used as tools by a power which has never failed of the highest sagacity in using those who are too short-sighted or too selfish to comprehend the real issues involved. The only reply which must be made to the establishment of the parochial school must be the increased efficiency of the common school. Sooner or later the best school will win. Our Catholic fellow-citizens know the value of education; they love their children, and after the *first stages* of this movement are past they will care more for the interest of their children than for the commands of the Church. In matters not distinctively religious, the great body of American Catholics will never submit to dictation from Rome; they are too intelligent and too independent. In the long run, therefore, the best school will win; and the only way to meet the parochial school is to meet it with a common school so superior to it in its educational opportunities and facilities, that no citizen can be in doubt where his children will gain most. In many communities there are those who fail to see this obvious truth, and who see in the reduced attendance upon the common schools, in consequence of the establishment of the parish schools, an opportunity to cut down school expenses. This is a time to spend, not a time to save; and all intelligent men know that there are times when liberal expenditure is not only the *highest* economy, but the *only* economy. These persons are ignorantly falling into the net spread for their feet, from which they will extricate themselves with great difficulty hereafter. If they alone were to fall in the loss would be small; but there is danger that communities may be dragged in with them, and that interests of the very highest importance may be permanently sacrificed.

The foes of our schools will strive in every district where they can command sufficient strength either to elect their own committees, and so control the schools, or to cut down the annual expenses, and so reduce their efficiency. There are two important and obvious duties which no man will neglect who cares for his country or his community; namely, he will attend every school-meeting, and will oppose, in season and out of season, every effort to reduce the efficiency of the schools by reducing the taxes. Let us clearly understand what this struggle means, and let every man choose between the common school and the parochial school. The men who neglect their duties, or who strive to cut down necessary school expenditures, are the enemies of our school system. If economy must be enforced let it be enforced at some other point. *THE COMMUNITY WHOSE ECONOMICS ARE IMPOSED ON ITS CHILDREN IS A COMMUNITY WHICH HAS YET TO LEARN THE RUDIMENTS OF PUBLIC WELL-BEING.*

QUESTION IX.

As to the Pretensions of Rome as an Educator.

WHO is this Church of Rome, that comes to us with this demand? Who is this that claims that our school system is godless and impious, unfit for the education of her children? Who is this that would rend asunder our public school system, the palladium of the American republic? Who is it that claims that God has given to her the *exclusive function* of educating the rising youth? What has been her record in the work of education? What superior enlightenment has *she* imparted to the nations that have long been under her dominion? What morals and piety has she taught them? What type of civilization has she imparted? What progress in the sciences, and in philosophy, and in social amenities? How has she treated the profound original investigators, like Galileo, who have pushed their inquiries beyond the old dusty beaten paths into new realms of thought and discovery? Has Rome been the patroness of learning? And have the countries over which she has held sway been the best developed nations in education, morality and religion?

We only need to ask these questions in any intelligent presence. The answer is ready in every mind, a negative answer—the consensus of the average thought, outside of Romanism, every-where—and indorsed by many Roman Catholics themselves. That such a body, with such a record, should come before this great Protestant nation with such demands as she makes is not only an absurdity, but an affront. It is hardly necessary to turn on the light of history to make the absurdity of her claims appear more clearly than they already appear.

And yet it is well to refresh our minds, that our convictions may be clear and strong.

Let us look at—

I.—The Historic Record of Rome in Respect to Education.

Rome has one thing in her favor. She is old, and has lived long enough to place herself unmistakably on record. Her record runs mostly through the period since the decay and destruction of ancient literature. The facts of her history are largely in the hands of the world.

We ask how it has been under an exclusive Roman Catholic regimen, continued for many centuries, as in some nations? Has the Church of Rome been a conspicuous promoter either of secular education or of morals? If her theory, that *all* education is the exclusive function of the Church, is true in principle; if it is productive of the best results, and develops the best communities; then she presents strong claims to be permitted to work out her plan at almost any reasonable sacrifice.

It must not be denied that the Church of Rome has always done educational work, but chiefly among limited classes of people. The education of the Middle Ages was either that of the cloister or the castle, standing in sharp contrast to each other; the object of the one, to form the young monk; and of the other, the young knight. The illustrious monasteries—Monte Cassino, Fulda, and Tours—kept alive the torch of learning through the Dark Ages; but while their services should be acknowledged they should not be overrated. Their instruction was limited to a small class, was not of a very high or general character, and was confined chiefly to ecclesiastical matters. Beyond those a few rudiments were taught in a narrow circle.

Under the *renaissance* and the Reformation there was some advance and improvement. The fourteenth and fifteenth centuries witnessed the rise of universities and academies in almost all of Europe. Still this culture was only for a few, and, under the leadership of Rome, was never extended to the masses.

Luther brought the school-master into the cottage and laid the foundation of the German system, by which the child of the humblest peasant may receive the best education the country affords. Other Protestant reformers followed this plan. The Protestant schools became the best in Europe, and the monkish institutions of Rome decayed. The Catholics would have remained behind in the race if it had not been for the Jesuits.

THE JESUITS.

The sons of Loyola for a time made great improvement upon the old monkish methods. "They gave the best education," says the *Britannica*, "of their time, in order to acquire confidence; but they became the chief obstacle to the improvement of education; they did not care for enlightenment, but only for the influence they could derive from a supposed regard for enlightenment." After a while governments found it necessary to check and suppress their colleges.

Their methods "degenerated into surveillance," "tracking the soul to its recesses, that they might slay it there and generate another in its place," a "tool subservient to their purposes." "They taught the accomplishments which the world loves, but their chief object was to amuse the mind and stifle inquiry." "Whatever may have been the service of Jesuits in past times," says the *Britannica*, "we have little to hope for from them, in the improvement of education, at present. Governments have, on the whole, acted wisely by checking and suppressing their colleges. The *ratio studiorum* is antiquated, and difficult to reform. In 1831 it was brought more into accordance with modern ideas by Roothaan, the general of the order. Beckx, his successor, has, if any thing, pursued a policy of retrogression. The Italian Government, in taking possession of Rome, found the pupils of the Collegio Romano were far below the level of modern requirements."

THE MASSES IGNORANT.

In short, the story of Roman Catholic education in past centuries has been that very few outside of the nobility, the priesthood, and the religious orders have been educated; that even their education has not been of the highest order; that the bright, scholarly men of Romanism have been rare exceptions, even among her best-educated sons, and that the masses of the people have been left in ignorance.

Dexter A. Hawkins, in *The Christian Advocate:* *

---
* New York city, January 1, 1880.

Some years ago, while spending a winter in Rome, at the house of a cousin of the late Cardinal Antonelli, papal Secretary of State, I investigated, under a commission from one of our States, the condition of public education in Rome and the papal States, where the Romish Church had absolute control of all affairs, both spiritual and temporal.

The public schools had accommodations for only a small portion of the children of school age. The instruction was of the most meager character, consisting chiefly of the catechism, with very little reading or writing, a smattering of the four simple rules of arithmetic, and little geography beyond that of the papal States—a territory containing 3,000,000 of inhabitants, and about three times the size of the State of Connecticut. The mass of the people could neither read nor write.

A primary school in a log school-house in the back settlements of our country, in its instruction, course of study, and proficiency of its pupils, was far superior to the parochial schools even in the city of Rome.

I described to Cardinal Antonelli the free public schools and the state of public education in Massachusetts, giving that as a model of the American system. His reply was that he "thought it better that the children should grow up in ignorance, than to be educated in such a system of schools as the State of Massachusetts supported; that the essential part of the education of the people was the catechism; and while arithmetic and geography, reading, and writing, and other similar studies might be useful, they were not essential."

His cousin, in speaking of the state of society in the Holy City, remarked that "its leading and most important institutions were a church, a monastery, a nunnery, and a foundling asylum."

The same eye-witness, after long official residence in Rome, said : *

While visiting Ireland a few years ago I was gratified to see the island dotted over with national schoolhouses, neatly built of brick or stone by the British Government, in order to try to elevate the Irish race from the slough of ignorance, idleness, and bigotry into which centuries of priestly instruction had brought them: But while driving across the country one day I found standing by the roadside, near one of these school-houses, a Catholic priest with a switch in his hand, with which he scourged home the Catholic children as they approached the national schoolhouse. On conversing with this priest, I found he appeared to sincerely believe he was doing God's work in preventing the children from attending the free public school. I did not suppose such a spectacle would ever be seen in our country. But I learn that a child in Massachusetts has within a few weeks been scourged upon his naked back by a Catholic priest for attending a free public school.

The state of public education in the Catholic part of Ireland, when taken hold of by the English Government a few years ago, was nearly as low as in the papal States when Victor Emmanuel took possession, turned the priests out of the schools, and, advised by the American Minister, began the establishment of a national system modeled after that of New England.

Under the parochial schools of the Romish Church both the Irish and the Italians had fallen in intelligence so far behind other races that they were becoming mere "hewers of wood" and "drawers of water," and occupiers of the most menial positions

---

* *The Christian Advocate*, January 1, 1880.

for the nations that sustain a system of free public education abreast of the age.

THE STORY OF ITALY, SPAIN, ETC.

What is the story* of Italy's ignorance? Under the new Italian Government, in 1860, there were opened 33 great model schools, since which time the condition has begun to improve; but in 1864, out of a total population of 21,703,710 people, there were 16,999,701, or about 80 per cent., who could neither read nor write. And yet Italy has 22 institutions called universities, 12 founded between 1119 and 1443, having, in all of them, 12,580 students in 1878. These are chiefly fitting for priests and monks, the masses not being educated. Why, we will soon see. What is the educational condition of Spain? In 1860, out of a total population of 16,301,851, 11,800,000, or 70 per cent., could neither read nor write. Spain has 58 institutions which are called colleges, with 13,881 pupils, and a few institutions of a higher grade; but the masses are left uneducated. Brazil, dominated by the papacy for centuries, presents a pitiable spectacle in respect to education. *The Statesman's Year-Book* says: "Notwithstanding the efforts of the Legislature, in recent years, for the spread of education, it is still in a very backward state, and the public schools were frequented, in

---

* *The Statesman's Year-Book,* 1881.

1874, by only 140,000 pupils." But the population in 1872 was 9,448,233. The institutions in Italy and Spain called colleges are all of them, in quality and scope of education, very inferior to the colleges we are acquainted with in Protestant countries.

In our day the Church of Rome reiterates her claim that the exclusive function of both secular and religious education is the divine right and duty of the Church. If it is, indeed, the divine right of the Church, as she has always claimed, is she willing to be tested by the results? Confessedly, the actual outcome from the working of any divinely-constituted system should be beneficent. What are the exhibits from the countries which for long centuries have been wholly Roman Catholic? Do they present the highest morals and intelligence? Surely, either the Church of Rome has not worked the system she has always claimed as her exclusive right, or, working it, the system has failed. Which horn of the dilemma will Rome accept? In either case her claim to this exclusive function has nothing to commend it.

Victor Hugo's Testimony.

Victor Hugo knew the record of Rome well, and when the Roman Catholic ecclesiastics, not long ago, tried to get control of education in France he broke out in his characteristic apostrophes:

Ah, we know you! We know the clerical party; it is an old party. This it is which has found for the truth those two marvelous supporters, ignorance and error. This it is which forbids to science and genius the going beyond the Missal, and which wishes to cloister thought in dogmas. Every step which the intelligence of Europe has taken has been in spite of it. Its history is written in the history of human progress, but it is written on the back of the leaf. It is opposed to it all.

. . . . .

For a long time the human conscience has revolted against you, and now demands of you, "What is it that you wish of me?" For a long time you have tried to put a gag upon the human intellect. You wish to be the masters of education, and there is not a poet, not an author, not a thinker, not a philosopher, that you accept. All that has been written, found, dreamed, deduced, inspired, imagined, invented by genius, the treasures of civilization, the venerable inheritance of generations, the common patrimony of knowledge, you reject.

. . . . .

You claim the liberty of teaching. Stop; be sincere; let us understand the liberty you claim. It is the liberty of *not* teaching. You wish us to give you the people to instruct. Very well. Let us see your pupils. Let us see those you have produced. What have you done for Italy? What have you done for Spain? For centuries you have kept in your hands, at your discretion, in your school, these two great nations, illustrious among the illustrious. What have you done for them? I shall tell you.

. . . . . .

Italy, which taught mankind to read, now knows not how to read. Yes! Italy is, of all the States of

Europe, that where the smallest number know how to read.

Spain, magnificently endowed Spain, which received from the Romans her first civilization; from the Arabs her second civilization; from Providence, in spite of you, a world—America—Spain, thanks to you, rests under a yoke of stupor, which is a yoke of degradation and decay. Spain has lost the secret power it obtained from the Romans, the genius of art it had from the Arabs, the world (of America) it had from God; and in exchange for all that you have made it lose, it has received from you the INQUISITION; the Inquisition, which certain of your party try to-day to re-establish; which has burned on the funeral pile millions of men; the Inquisition, which disinterred the dead to burn them as heretics; which declared the children of heretics infamous and incapable of any public honors, excepting only those who shall have denounced their fathers. . . .

This is what you have done for two great nations. What do you wish to do for France? Stop! you have just come from Rome! I congratulate you; you have had fine success there; you have come from gagging the Roman people, and now you wish to gag the French people. . . . Take care! France is a lion, and is alive.

After this master-piece of sarcasm by this great writer (if more is needed) look all over Mexico, Central America, and South America, after nearly four centuries of almost unlimited dominion, by the Roman Catholic Church. See the deepest, densest ignorance, the grossest morals, and the most unpardonable loitering in the march of human progress which can be found in any part of Christendom.

Rome does not come with the right kind of a record to justify American citizens in periling their educational system at her behest. If the entire work of education is the exclusive right and function of the papal Church, under divine appointment, where was there ever such recreancy to a high trust as has been exhibited in the history of that Church? Such is the Church which, under the pretentious claim of a divine right, now asks the most enlightened nation on earth to dismember and ruin her school system—the bulwark of her intelligence, liberty, and progress—and resign the rising youth into her ignorant and sacrilegious hands.

SCIENTIFIC INNOVATION PUNISHED.

Some one, perhaps, asks: "Has not Rome produced great men in every department of science?" I answer in the language of an ex-Romanist: "Rome can show us a long list of names which shine among the brightest lights in the firmament of science and philosophy. She can show us her Copernicus, her Galileo, her Pascal, her Bossuet, her Lamennais, etc., etc. But it was at their risk and peril that these giants of intelligence raised themselves into the highest regions of philosophy and science. It is in spite of Rome that those eagles soared up above the dark and obscure horizon where the pope offers his big toe to be kissed and worshiped as the *ne plus ultra* of human intelligence; and they have been punished for their boldness."

We are familiar with the story of Galileo, how he was treated. That mighty intellect was bruised, fettered, degraded, and silenced. Do I need to cite Pascal, Lamenais, and others, excommunicated for advanced ideas? What kind of a chance would Sir Isaac Newton and Benjamin Franklin, Stephenson, Fulton, Morse, and Ericsson, have had in the Roman Catholic Church, which stifles private judgment, conscience, and intelligence in the search of truth? Besides, while Protestant nations are marching with such giant strides to the conquest of the world, why is it that papal nations remain stationary or settle into decadence? Is it not because their religion stifles the noblest impulses of the human mind?

Such is the past record of Rome outside of the United States in respect to education. We see, however, some indications of a somewhat different policy pursued by this Church in this country. Let us examine and understand it.

II.—Rome's Record in Respect to Education in the United States.

The first Roman Catholic College in the United States was the Jesuit College founded at Georgetown,

D. C., in 1789. In 1830 the Romanists had four colleges. In 1886 her record shows eighty-six colleges,* so-called—that is, they bear that designation. Many of them are in their infancy—foundations for colleges. As with other colleges, theirs must have a beginning, and it is often, with such institutions, small and feeble. Some never come to maturity. Probably not over sixty of them can be said to have approximated to the rank of colleges. Most of them include preparatory departments and even schools of lower grade, the students of all classes being reckoned in the total.

Considering that the Romanists have been building so many churches all over the land this is a strong record. They had also in 1886 nineteen theological seminaries and nineteen female colleges, the latter in no case, however, deserving to be considered, even approximately, with Wellesley and Smith Colleges, either in number of students or quality of education. Besides these the Roman Church has academies, select schools, and conventual schools. In the three higher classes of institutions the students reported are:

In colleges...	14,007 †
In theological seminaries......................	1,214
In female colleges.................................	3,645
Total..	18,866

* See pp. 128, 129.
† Comprising those in the preparatory course.

EDUCATIONAL PRETENSIONS OF ROME. 257

It is due that we say these statistics show that Romanism has not been idle or sparing of efforts in educational lines in this country.

When we look at these facts as they stand alone they seem extraordinary. But compare them with other denominations. Take the three highest classes of institutions:

	Institutes.	Students.
Roman Catholics	124	18,866
Methodist Episcopal Church (North)	144	26,491
Methodist Episcopal Church, North and South	217	31,337
Baptist, North and South	125	16,420
Lutherans	81	5,549

COMPARISON.

The Baptists have but one college older than the first Roman Catholic college at Georgetown, D. C., dating only twenty-two years further back than that institution; namely, Brown University. The Lutherans founded a theological seminary about the same time the Roman Catholics established their first college, and the first Methodist college dated forty one years after the first of the Roman Catholic, at a time when they had four colleges. Romanism had been in America two hundred and seventy years before Methodism came; had the first chance to the whole of North and South America, to the fertile fields and the rich mines of gold and silver. But now the Northern Methodist Church has twenty more higher institutions of learning and eight thousand more students; and the two

17

leading Methodist Churches, North and South, have ninety-three more institutions and forty thousand more students than the papal Church. And, moreover, Methodism has not transferred eight or ten millions of people from the Old World to help build her up here; nor has she obtained, as Romanists have done, large sums of money from Europe and Mexico to aid her in her work. Methodism has been re-enforced by few accessions from abroad, but has gone forth into the highways, the hedges, the frontiers, and gathered her people by moral and spiritual transformations.

Relatively, then, considering her large educational pretensions, her opportunities, and her foreign help, the Roman Catholic Church has nothing to boast of in the line of education.

So much for the numerical exhibit of the educational institutions of Romanism in the United States.

It is important next to consider:

III.—The Quality of the Education Afforded by the Roman Catholic Church.

While we talk of the more advanced educational institutions of the Roman Catholic Church, we must not overlook the fact that the instruction imparted in them is inferior to that of other American colleges and seminaries of the same reputed rank. Only in one study do Roman Catholic colleges exceed non-Catholic colleges—the Latin. As to logic, they *seem* to devote more attention to that than non-Catholic colleges; but it is the old logic of the school-men, its tricks, etc., and not the broader views of later and better treatises. As to Greek, many non-Catholic colleges we are acquainted with require more Greek, in order to admission to their lowest classes, than most Catholic colleges give their students in their whole college course. In only a few of them does the Greek course equal that in Protestant colleges. Catholic colleges do little in the department of the natural sciences. An atmosphere of mediæval sentiment pervades their institutions, and the catechism receives more prominence in their curriculum than any thing else except Latin.

It must be confessed that it is impossible to speak on this question with all the definiteness that may be desired in regard to some of the practical details; but the main features are clear and convincing.

Taking, first of all, the colleges and universities, the question which arises is, How does the curriculum of studies in the best Catholic colleges compare with that of the best non-Catholic colleges? We are aware that this, of itself alone, cannot fully decide the quality of the education given; but it is an important part of the question, showing the scope and breadth of the field traversed. It is generally understood that the Jesuit colleges maintain the highest rank for scholarship of any of the Roman Catholic colleges. I have lying before me the latest catalogues of eighteen Roman Catholic colleges, among which are those of five Jesuit colleges; namely, the Georgetown College, D. C., founded in 1789, and chartered as a university in 1815; the St. John's College, Fordham, N. Y.; the St. Francis Xavier's College, Cincinnati, O., founded in 1831; the College of the Holy Cross, Worcester, Mass., founded in 1843; and the Boston College, 761 Harrison Avenue, Boston, founded in 1863. In these institutions, following the method of other Roman Catholic colleges, a seven years' course of study is prescribed, the last four years corresponding to the usual classical collegiate course, in non-Catholic colleges, for the degree of A. B. These five Jesuit colleges do not vary much in their courses of study. The following is an abbreviated statement of the collegiate course of study in the St. John's College at Fordham, New York:

LATIN.

1st year: Syntax reviewed. Idioms. Prosody. Exercises in Prose and Verse. Sallust. Virgil. Cicero in Catilinam.
2d year: Principles of Latin Style; Prose and Verse Composition. Livy. Horace. Virgil. Cicero.
3d year: Cicero's Orations—De Oratore, Ad Brutum. Horace. Juvenal. Persius. Tacitus. Prose and Verse Composition.
4th year: No Latin.

GREEK.

1st year: Grammar (completed). Prosody. Xenophon's Cyropedia. Herodotus. Homer's Odyssey.
2d year: Principles of Greek Style; Prose and Verse Composition. Plato's Apologia. Demosthenes's Olynthiacs. Homer's Iliad. Sophocles's Œdipus Rex.
3d year: Demosthenes. Thucydides. Sophocles. Pindar. Longinus. Æschylus. Prose and Verse Composition.
4th year: No Greek.

MATHEMATICS.

1st year: Algebra and Geometry.
2d year: Trigonometry. Surveying. Analytical Geometry.
3d year: Calculus.
4th year: Dana's Mechanics. Astronomy.

HISTORY.

1st year: Ancient.
2d year: Modern.
3d year: Modern.

ENGLISH.

1st year: Prosody. Composition.
2d year: Du Cygne's Precepts of Literature. Lectures on Style and Poetry. Analysis of selections from the best authors. Critical Study of Shakespeare's Macbeth. Epistolary, Descriptive, and Narrative Composition. Essays, Poems, etc. Jenkins's History of English Literature.
3d year: Du Cygne's Principles of Rhetoric. Lectures on the Principles of Rhetoric, the Construction of a Discourse, etc. Critical Study of the best speeches in Goodrich's "British Eloquence" and of Shakespeare's "Julius Cæsar." The utmost attention is given to English composition. Debates are held every week.
4th year: No English exercises.

ELOCUTION.

1st year: One hour a week.
2d year: "   "   "
3d year: "   "   "
4th year: "   "   "

NATURAL SCIENCES.

1st year: Nothing.
2d year: Avery's Chemistry.
3d year: Avery's Chemistry.
4th year: Olmstead's Natural Philosophy.

In addition to the foregoing, in the fourth year the following *philosophical* studies are pursued : " Jouin's logic, metaphysics, and ethics. First term : Logic and ontology. Second Term : Cosmology, psychology, and theodicy ; the general principles of ethics and of civil society. The lectures are given in Latin. The students are required to speak Latin and defend their theses every week in that language. Such defense is often public before the faculty."

RELIGIOUS INSTRUCTION.

1st year: De Harbe's Catechism.
2d year: "   "
3d year: Lectures on the Evidences of Religion.
4th year: "   "   "   "

An examination of the foregoing curriculum will show the character and extent of the culture contemplated in the Jesuit institutions, except their universities, which have law, medical, and other departments. Its inferiority to the courses of study in other American colleges will be readily seen.

1. The standard of admission is inferior. Harvard, Boston, and Wesleyan Universities, Amherst and Dartmouth Colleges, and others of like rank, do not differ much in their requirements for admission. Six

books in Virgil's Æneid, with the Eclogues, four books of Cæsar, five orations in Cicero, and in some a portion of Sallust and Ovid, besides Arnold's Latin Prose Composition, are required, in Latin ; four books of Xenophon's Anabasis, three books of Homer's Iliad, the Greek Reader, and, in some of them, one book in Herodotus, are required, in Greek ; in algebra, through quadratic equations in all, and in some of them the whole of Greenleaf's, Loomis's, or Olney's larger books, and plane geometry. But in the foregoing Catholic curriculum we find Sallust, Virgil, and Cicero in the studies of the freshman and sophomore years. The list of preparatory studies, in some Jesuit colleges, makes no mention of algebra or geometry. Four Jesuit Colleges—Georgetown, D. C , St. Francis Xavier's, Cincinnati, Boston College, and the College of the Holy Cross—include algebra, but not geometry ; while St. John's, at Fordham, N. Y., omits geometry until after the collegiate course is commenced. In some colleges the Greek Reader is the only preparatory Greek read.

2. The courses of study are not as broad as in the non-Catholic colleges. Less attention is devoted to natural sciences, mental and moral philosophy, political economy, etc., and the elective system of studies has been only sparingly adopted. Nor do they furnish as ample or as valuable facilities for pursuing

such inquiries. With the larger departments of modern investigation the Church of Rome has had little sympathy, preferring to confine herself to an old routine.

3. Most Roman Catholic institutions devote little attention to the Greek, and more to the Latin language than the non-Catholic colleges. The study of Latin in Catholic colleges generally continues through four years, while Greek seldom occupies more than two years. In some of them the students are required to converse and to conduct extemporaneous discussions in the Latin language. No such exclusive prominence is given to any single language by the non-Catholic colleges; but it is believed that the drill in translation and construction is not less thorough, while the knowledge of the Greek gained by the graduates is far superior to that imparted by the Catholic institutions.

Thus far the Jesuit colleges. Other Roman Catholic colleges are considerably inferior to these. In the Augustinian College at Villanova, Pa., the studies of the freshman year are English grammar, parsing in Pope's "Essay on Man," arithmetic, and algebra commenced. In Latin, Sallust and Virgil's Bucolics; and, in Greek, the grammar and the Gospel of St. John. Cæsar is the only Latin author read before admission to college; and in Greek only the first and second parts of Arnold's exercises. Latin, Greek, and mathematics extend through the four years of the college course. Natural philosophy is studied only in the sophomore year, and the only other natural science specified is chemistry, in the junior and senior years. Logic is a study in the fourth year. Besides these, rhetorical, historical, and religious studies are continued through the entire course.

In St. Vincent's (Benedictine) College, in Westmoreland County, Pa., only the Latin Grammar is required in Latin, and no Greek or algebra, prior to admission to the college course.

Arithmetic and English grammar are studies of the first and second year in some of these lower grade colleges. In many of them, biology, zoology, geology, mineralogy, astronomy, and political economy are wholly omitted. Aside from the Latin language the quality of the drill in these institutions is not very well known. The instruction in the natural sciences in almost all Catholic colleges is meager and imperfect, though they are advancing somewhat. The moral and mental philosophy is that of the papal scholastics of the olden times, based upon peculiar dogmas of Rome. The subtleties and sophistries of logic receive particular attention.

Among the Catholic colleges of highest rank may

be mentioned the University of Notre Dame, at Notre Dame, Indiana, magnificently provided with buildings and grounds, and Saint Francis College, Baltic Street, Brooklyn, N. Y., the latter under the Franciscans (O. S. F.), and the former under the Congregation of the Holy Cross (C. S. C.). Others of these so-called "colleges" are inferior to the best Protestant academies and high schools. The discipline in the Catholic colleges is severe, rigid, and peculiarly exclusive, having supreme reference to the promotion of the Catholic faith. In all of these institutions which have boarding departments no student is permitted to leave the grounds without permission. No books, other than text-books and works of reference recommended by the professors, may be held by the students, unless by permission of the president. Students are not allowed to receive newspapers except from the reading-room, which is under the direction of the president. Letters received and sent away are subject to the supervision of the college authorities. No private pocket-money is allowed, but must be deposited with the treasurer.

An Interior Inspection.

A recent writer in the *Christian Union* * gives an interesting interior view of a Catholic College.

---

*June 14, 1888.

It does not need to be said that the Catholics do not believe in co-education. Even in the lower schools the sexes are kept carefully apart, though putting them together would generally enable the parish to have graded schools, giving to each recitation just double the time without making the classes any too large. But this educational gain would be at the sacrifice of a principle of most vital importance. The Sacred Congregation de Propaganda Fide, in its letter to the bishops of the United States in 1875, assigned two fundamental reasons for its condemnation of our Public School System :

"1. The system .... excludes all teaching of religion.

"2. Certain corruption likewise ensues from the fact that in the same schools, or in many of them, youths of both sexes are congregated in the same room for the recitation of lessons, and males and females are ordered to sit on the same bench (*in eodem scamno*); all which have the effect of lamentably exposing the young to loss in faith and endangering of morals."

Such being the dangers involved in teaching the little tots of both sexes together, the Church of course avoids the greater scandal of educating young men and women in the same building (*in eodem domo*).

In order to get some impression as to what the Catholic colleges for men were like, I visited one morning that of St. Francis Xavier, on Sixteenth Street. This college, by the way, is but one of four which the Catholics maintain in this city. The building is a costly and imposing one. On being presented to the president, a large man with an imperious bearing—a typical prelate—I stated the name of the paper which I represented, and my desire to visit some of the recitations, in case such visits were permitted. "What are your qualifications for the task?" was the somewhat overwhelming question immediately put to me. When I recovered my mental equilibrium I spoke of my university degree—the first time I had ever had occasion to make use of it. This seemed satisfactory, and the prelate himself conducted me through the college.

The first recitation we entered I found that my degree was not so all-sufficient as I had supposed. Though the subject was rhetoric the recitation was entirely in Latin. As I had only spent seven years upon this branch, and in that time, like most college boys, had only managed to stammer through seven or eight hundred pages of Latin literature, I had to confess that I knew practically nothing about it. The president was not at all displeased at this, and took a great deal of pride in the Latinity of the class. Meanwhile I borrowed a text-book and followed the recitation as best I could. I found that the young men were quite familiar with the book, but did not discover any particular readiness in the expression of ideas of their own. In case there is mental discipline in cramming the memory with words which the student does not care to remember after the period of recitations, then this drill in rhetoric was valuable. This question, however, the reader has probably settled for himself, and upon its stettlement must depend his estimate of the educational value of a Catholic college.

After leaving the recitation in rhetoric the president asked me if I would not like to attend one in philosophy, and I gladly assented. We found the class discussing Hume's famous argument against miracles. Again I borrowed a text-book and managed to catch the drift of the discussion. Meanwhile the president talked with me of the advantages of using Latin instead of English in the study of these branches. It cultivated, he said, clearness in thinking and conciseness of expression, since the English language was no such medium for philosophical thought as the Latin. To all this I listened politely, thinking of the days when Latin was considered a better medium for the expression of every kind of thought. The president himself was remarkably familiar with Latin, and there was no doubt as to his sincerity in regarding it as a superior medium of instruction. Very soon, however, his opinions received a curious comment. The professor suddenly changed the recitation from Latin into English. The president expressed his surprise at this, and the professor explained that when he had gone over the lesson once in Latin, he found it well to review it in English, "in order to make sure that the class thoroughly understood what they had been reciting."

I did not ask to be conducted into any more recitations. I had formed a much more definite impression of the teaching than I had expected in so short a time. Unfortunately, it was not an impression which I can expect others to accept, since my own experience in college and out of college had rendered me a prejudiced witness. To those who have admitted that students should either learn twice as much Latin in our American colleges or none at all, and have preferred the former alternative, the course at St. Xavier's will commend itself. The students were twice as familiar with Latin as I had ever been, and the innumerable difficulties of that language did not retard them one half as much in their study of rhetoric and philosophy, as they had retarded me in the study of classic literature and history. Nevertheless, there was a gross sacrifice of the knowledge of rhetoric and the knowledge of philosophy, to the knowledge of facts about a dead language which could throw no light upon any subject in which men of to-day are interested. The Catholic Church, in its religious instruction of the common people, held on to the Latin language long after it had ceased to be the language of the common people; and in its intellectual instruction of students it has held on to the same language long after it has ceased to be the language of students. The teaching was adapted to a time when all literature worth reading was in Latin. That time passed away several centuries ago.

After visiting the recitations I had a talk with the president respecting various points of interest relating to the scope of the instruction. There was one point which impressed me favorably, not because it was a new idea, but because it was a good idea which seemed to have been well carried out. Attention was given to the gentlemanliness—I might almost say courtliness—of the manners of the students. This, too, may be survival from the time when the clergy of the State Church were cultured courtiers, allied to the aristocracy and out of sympathy with the people. But, whatever its origin, there is no doubt as to its value.

Only one other point is worthy of mention, and this is merely of a piece with the other mediævalism of the curriculum. In St. Xavier's College there is no regular professor of science. In one of the Catholic colleges of this city (St. John's, Fordham), there are four, but usually the curriculum is marked by the comparative absence of such instruction. There was also no professorship of history and political economy. In short, the spirit of the old cloisters still prevailed. It was intellectual life apart from the world, not intellectual life in the world and for the world. The students were separated as far as possible from the currents of thought of to-day.

EDUCATIONAL PRETENSIONS OF ROME. 271

THE HIGHER EDUCATION OF CATHOLIC WOMEN.

The Roman Catholic academies, select schools, and colleges for females, have been supposed by many American parents, particularly in wealthy and aristocratic circles, to afford advantages for education superior to our non-Catholic schools of like grade; and many daughters have been sent thither for instruction. Academic departments connected with convents have also been patronized for such supposed advantages, and daughters of Protestant parents have thus been lured into the Roman Catholic Church. Close inquiry in regard to the education imparted in these institutions leads to the conclusion that instruction in the fine arts, in the languages, and in the sciences is far inferior in all elements of true culture to that imparted by the non-Catholic schools. They pander to the vanity of wealthy and aristocratic patrons, and aim to make their daughters showy rather than truly cultivated. The whole system is superficial in its plan and execution. Those who come forth well educated become such not by any superior advantages furnished by Roman Catholic schools, but by reason of natural ability or personal application.

The same writer just quoted in the *Christian Union*, and in the same article, gives an interior view of this department of education:

For the higher education of Catholic women I visited the Academy of the Sacred Heart on Seventeenth Street. This is one of the two Catholic schools for women which are given in the *City Directory* under the head of colleges. I was graciously received by the Lady Superior, who assured me that she would take pleasure in conducting me through her school. This she did, talking all the while with a pleasing enthusiasm about different features of the Academy, telling me the history of the educational sisterhood to which she belonged, explaining the character of the instruction which it aimed to give, and, above all, telling of the devotion of the scholars, narrating little incidents showing how deep it was, and how it lasted until after the children had grown into womanhood. I cannot tell all this as it was told me, but must content myself with summing it up in as few words as possible.

In the first place, this Academy of the Sacred Heart is not a college at all, nor even a high school. In its curriculum some of the higher branches, such as geometry and philosophy, do indeed appear, but the classes in them are extremely small, there being only one in the class in geometry. The aim of the school is not so much education as "finish." The Order of the Sacred Heart is French in its origin and its control. The system of education is not very different from that in France under the *ancien régime*. Then, as we know, the series studies were avowedly given less importance than the accomplishments. Two hours would be devoted to writing, geography, history, and arithmetic, and four to catechism, drawing, dancing, and music. A thorough grasp of the principles of one of the higher branches would have jarred with this notion of what was becoming to a fine lady. In the place of these she was trained in the art of entering a room, of courtesying, of managing her train, and all the little niceties of speech, manner, and address which went to make up a grand lady. It was of this ancient schooling that the course of instruction at the Academy of the Sacred Heart reminded me, though these characteristics were not so strongly accentuated. The superioress assured me that only a few minutes each day were devoted to religious exercises, and that Protestant and Jewish (!) pupils were not obliged to study the catechism and church history.

I was taken every-where—into the beautiful little chapel, into the play-rooms, the music-room, the recitation-rooms. But I heard no recitations. The superioress told me that visitors were never invited to these, and that if they should be the girls would be so embarrassed that they could not do themselves justice. I was, however, taken into a play-room where nearly thirty of the little girls were singing in concert French songs as they went through different figures. The exercise corresponded to the marching in college gymnastics, but was infinitely prettier and more pleasing. The superioress told me that there were no classes in dancing; but these games employed many of the steps and cultivated quite as much grace of movement. The sister in charge was a bright, sweet-faced young French woman, and it was perhaps her spirit which made the young girls enjoy the games so thoroughly.

The girls of the school ranged apparently from five to seventeen. This fact emphasized the comparative absence of any higher education. The course for the older pupils did not compare with that in a New England or western high school, and not a great many of the pupils were of the high school age. This fact, however, is not so significant in New York city as it would be in the educationally more progressive sections of the country, for in New York, excepting one large normal school and one city college, there are no public high schools, though there are, of course, numerous private schools which give a corresponding education to the daughters of the rich.

There was one thing which pleased me in the appearance of the girls. Though they were all the children of wealthy parents (the tuition being one hundred dollars a year, with instrumental music sixty dollars extra, vocal music eighty dollars, drawing sixty dollars, etc.) nevertheless they were all dressed in a simple though pretty blue uniform. The superioress said that they had just introduced it this year, and had found, somewhat to their surprise, that the girls and their parents gladly adopted it. It put an end to vulgar competition in dress. Some of the girls wore blue ribbons and some red. The superioress explained that (like the old French convent schools again) they were divided into two parties, and that the contest between them was respecting mistakes in French. Even at recess-time the girls were expected to speak French, and if a "blue" heard a "red" make a mistake she immediately demanded her ribbon. Those who did not lose their ribbons at all in a given time —I forget how long—were awarded prizes.

But the supreme aim, the avowed aim, of the entire course of instruction was neither education nor finish, but the winning of the girls to the love of the Church. The sisters in charge were fine types of womanhood, and the spirit of the school was charming. The lady superior told me, and I believed it, that the girls often came to them with their troubles, and sometimes came in tears merely because a sister had seemed severe, when the sister herself had no recollection of it. Every little while the superioress would herself have a talk with each of the girls alone, and at these times she, too, gained their friendship. Defective, therefore, as I found the intellectual education—the training to think and to know—there was nevertheless something about the instruction which might well be imitated in our public schools. It cannot, however, be imitated while people tolerate that teacherships shall be in any respect the patronage of school boards. It cannot even be insured when competitive examinations are made the test of fitness. It can only be secured when school boards and superintendents have the same loyalty to the municipal corporations that the Catholic clergy have to their ecclesiastical corporations, and through their loyalty select teachers according to merit, taking into account something else besides intellectual qualifications. The real education of girls includes sweeter manners and purer tastes, and these come only from personal contact with fine women. If the public schools are to have all the good qualities of the finest of Catholic schools, then Protestant young women of cultivation and refinement must give up the immoral idea that their position exempts them from the obligation to earn their own living by service, and must remember that the greater their advantages the greater their obligations toward those who are without them.

Parochial Schools.

The parochial schools of Romanism are the lowest class of their educational institutions, and, as might be expected, the condition, previous advantages, and social surroundings of the mass of the pupils are, for the most part, of a very low grade. The character of the educational drill, as observed by visitors, has been pronounced to be of an inferior quality, the course of study meager and very imperfect, and the discipline harsh. Exceptions there doubtless are, in schools and in pupils, some of which have been highly commended. The educational institutions of Romanism are feeling the stimulating influence of the higher attainments of Protestant institutions, and are doubtless in course of improvement. But their histories, geographies, reading-books, and other text-books, afford evidence of Roman Catholic manipulation. Papal ideas, dogmas, and versions of history are infiltrated through them. Catholic saints, holy days, institutions, and the mediæval ages are glorified. The minds of pupils are thus turned backward rather than forward, belittled rather than enlarged, and facts of history long and well-established are presented in a distorted light and often wholly omitted. Pupils in these institutions are thus educated out of joint with their times and in conflict with the facts of universal history.

Religious Instruction.

Roman Catholic tenets form a part of the daily instruction in all their educational institutions of every class. No distinction is made on the ground of religious belief, but all are required to be present at the public exercises of religion. The Catholic catechism and lectures on the Catholic religion are specified each year in the collegiate courses of study, and are also found in all their schools of every grade. Out of eighteen catalogues of Roman Catholic colleges in my hands only one or two contain any thing like the following. "Students who are not Catholics will not be required to participate in any distinctively Catholic exercise, nor will any undue influence be exerted to induce a change of belief." Some other catalogues say: "The exercises of religious worship are Catholic, and every student, no matter of what denomination he may be, will be required, for the sake of order and uniformity, to attend them." This is the usual practice in all Catholic institutions. The religious education—by catechism, lectures, prayers, and other processes distinctively Catholic—is connected with secular training. The catalogue of the Georgetown College says: "No distinction is made in the reception of students on the ground of religious belief, but all the boarders are required to be present at the public exercises of religion." "Catholics are instructed in their religion by means of the catechism, which forms one of the regular recitations, and weekly catechetical lectures, which are attended by all." The catalogue of Seton Hall College says: "All students are required to assist at *mass* twice a week, and Catholics to go to confession and communion monthly, unless their spiritual director should otherwise direct them." Mass is observed regularly in all these colleges.

Roman Catholic Text-books,

as seen by an eminent critic,* are at least very peculiar and defective. He says:

Here is a Catholic school-book used in high schools and sometimes in colleges, a modern history by Peter Fredet, Professor of History in St. Mary's College, Baltimore. I turn to the appendix of it and come upon a most amazing series of notes. Here are dissertations pouring copious, loathsome, mucilaginous, but not adhesive, whitewash on the massacre of St. Bartholomew and on the Inquisition. Here are apologies for the greatest atrocities Rome has committed. We are told here deliberately that Romish priests had nothing to do with the death of most of those who suffered in the Inquisition; that at the moment of execution the priests appeared at the side of the man only to inspire him, if possible, with sentiments of repentance; that all the priestly council did was to pronounce the individual guilty and deliver him over to the secular authorities. We are told here in a foot-note that John Huss was placed under the custody of the magistrates of Constance, who, following the jurisprudence of the age with regard to such transgressors, consigned him to the flames. You think that I exaggerate, but here I read, when the Spaniards are reproached for the rig-

---

* Rev. Joseph Cook.

ors of the Inquisition, their answer is that by punishing a few obstinate individuals they saved their monarchy from the civil wars which desolated Germany, Switzerland, and Holland, and did not, after all, cause so much blood to flow as the Calvinistic reformation did. That is what is stuffed down the throats of the brightest Catholic youth in this country.

He says Bismarck was justified in his horror, when he said that the saddest sight in France was the manipulation of the historical text-books by Romish ecclesiastics.

Here is a Fifth Reader, which I bought lately at the Romish bookstore in this city, and it is full of portraits of Romish archbishops, and the contents have been carefully selected to give sectarian impressions. I open this Sixth Reader and I find it also full of foot-notes and of selections such as indicate the sectarian bias of the whole work. There is Michael Angelo making a picture before one pope, and here I turn to some of the foot-notes and I read a little biography of the Most Rev. John Hughes. It is in unguarded places that the purpose of the Roman priesthood comes out, and the last sentence in this short notice of the archbishop reads: "Both by speech and pen he labored untiringly to secure that Catholic training for Catholic children on which the future of the Church must, humanly speaking, depend, and his labors are still bearing most abundant fruit." I turn on here to a little notice of Mrs. Jameson, and the statement I find of most importance is the following: "Though not a Catholic, Mrs. Jameson pays graceful homage to that faith which has been the basis of all that is true and noble in art since the beginning of the Christian era." Just so, indeed. And I ask your attention to the following important statement: "Orestes Augustus Bronson, the most original and philosophical thinker that America has yet produced." Now what if I were to call up the scholars out of the two or three thousand parochial schools in the United States and ask them to recite? Why, what they would give us in answer to our questions would be these text-books—these precious statements about the Catholic authorities, and these whitewashed pages concerning the Inquisition, the edict of Nantes, and the massacre of St. Bartholomew; these subtle insinuations of Catholic doctrine concerning mariolatry and the infallibility of the pope, and these presentations of American history in such a manner as to make the impression that the Jesuits were the fathers of the best part of our civilization here. This is what we should hear from these young lips.

Another eminent critical authority [*] says concerning *An Abridged History of the United States*, by John R. G. Hassard, LL.D., with an introduction by Rt. Rev. J. L. Spalding, D.D., Bishop of Peoria:

This volume belongs in "The Young Catholic's School Series." It is written with the definite purpose, avowed by Bishop Spalding in the Introduction, of giving a Roman Catholic interpretation of the United States history. Without charging on the manual any violent perversion of facts it is enough to say that this end is very adroitly carried out in the book. Catholic agencies are magnified, frank criticism is employed where it counts for little, matters of greater importance are passed over in silence, the edge and nobleness of the Protestant history are blunted, and the point is pretty effectively made to stand out everywhere that what the country needs for the perfection

---

[*] The *Independent*.

EDUCATIONAL PRETENSIONS OF ROME.   281

of citizenship is Roman Catholicism, and that the best that is in it has come from this source.

Strange are the omissions and misleadings of the Catholic text-books. One of them, in its preface, complains that "The manuals of geography hitherto used in our schools are not only objectionable on account of their misstatements, but are still more objectionable and defective on account of what they suppress or fail to state."

It is interesting (says Mr. Edwin D. Mead) * to go through these books and observe what they "fail to state," and then observe some of the things to which they are able to give so much space. There is room to state that Ireland "is noted," among many other things, "for the unwavering fidelity of its people to the Catholic faith;" but there is not room to state that the Netherlands are noted for any thing besides their "low situation, numerous canals and windmills." There is room to speak of "many Catholics" exiled to Siberia, but of nobody else; to note that the States of the Church are "at present usurped" by the King of Italy, but to say almost nothing else about the whole history of Italy. A primary object every-where is to make these books for school children serve the purposes of theological and sectarian controversy.

How about America? Here is Sadlier's smaller geography †—a very popular book in the parochial

---

* Address on *The Roman Catholic Church and the School Question.* Boston: George H. Ellis. 1888, pp. 37, etc.

† *Sadlier's Excelsior Introduction to Geography.* Designed for Junior Classes. By a Catholic Teacher. New York: William H. Sadlier. See also *O'Shea's Comprehensive Geographies.* New York: P. O'Shea.

schools, and, like the other books in the series, a beautiful book. It contains probably all the history of the United States that some of the younger and poorer children, who leave school early, ever get. If they do get more I could quickly show you that they are quite likely to get what is worse. Let me read to you the section devoted to the history of the United States (Lesson XXXIII, p. 22):

What can you say of the United States?—It is the most populous and powerful country in America.
By whom was this country originally inhabited?—By the Indians.
By whom were the Indians dispossessed of their lands?—By the Spanish, English, and French colonists.
Who were the first explorers of great portions of our country?—Catholic missionaries.
Who discovered and explored the upper Mississippi?—Father Marquette, a Jesuit missionary.
Where, in many of the States, were the first settlements formed?—Around the humble cross that marked the site of a Catholic mission.
What political division is the United States?—A republic.
How long has it been a republic?—One hundred years.
To what nation did the thirteen original States belong?—To England.
When did they declare themselves independent?—July 4, 1776.
Why did they declare their independence?—Because they were unjustly oppressed by England.
What is the war called which occurred at this time between the United States and England?—The War of the Revolution.
What Catholic nation very materially assisted the Americans during this war?—France.
How long did the War of the Revolution last?—About eight years.
At its close who became the first President of the United States?—George Washington.

This is the whole lesson. This is the general account of the colonization and early history of the

United States. And this is a good sample of the proportion of the rôle assigned to Jesuit missionaries all through these books. ... The descendant of the New England Puritans, or of other worthies whom some of us have been in the habit of thinking as standing for something in this American enterprise, is moved to ask the Jesuit, when he reads of all his accomplishments in these books, "Did any body help you found the American republic?"

Under the special head of New England, in this particular geography, comes this further historical information, so admirably calculated to clear up any thing left doubtful as to the genesis and significance of New England in particular:

> What was the first settlement in the New England States?—A Jesuit mission on Mount Desert Island (in 1612).
>
> By whom was this settlement destroyed?—By the English.
>
> What people made a permanent settlement in Massachusetts in 1620?—The Pilgrim Fathers.
>
> Who were they?—English Protestants who, being persecuted by their Protestant fellow countrymen, took refuge in America.
>
> How did they act in their new home?—They proved very intolerant, and persecuted all who dared to worship God in a manner different from that which they had established.

That is all. The important significant thing about the founding of New England is supposed to be told—there is no room for any thing more than the leading facts. Now, ladies and gentlemen, you do not need to be told, and the makers of this book do not need to be told, that this is not history. History is not history at all save as its proportions are preserved. The Jesuit missionaries were heroic men, and they are most interesting figures—we are glad our own Mr. Parkman has written so much and so well about them. But their settlements and efforts were sporadic, and have had almost no influence upon the main currents of our

American life and the development of our institutions, whose sources are here left almost unnoticed. The "Jesuit mission on Mount Desert Island" should not be mentioned in a primary text-book. It is questionable whether even Father Marquette should be mentioned in a book which has no space to tell how the present North-west became what it is. The boy or girl who learns history from such books learns no history.

These geographies are stamped on the title-page as by a "Catholic teacher." Many of the books are marked as belonging to a "Catholic Educational Series." Here is the *Young Catholic's Fifth Reader;* almost every portrait in it is that of a bishop. "This *Third Reader*, in common with other books of the Catholic National Series, has one chief characteristic," says the preface, "namely, a thoroughly Catholic tone, which will be found to pervade the whole book." * About that there is no doubt. From the first story, on "Bessie's First Mass," to the pieces on "How to be a Nun," "Saint Bridget," and "The Saint Patrick Penny," the "thoroughly Catholic tone" never fails. The Catholic name and atmosphere and effort are every-where. Ladies and gentlemen, that is bad. My good Catholic friends, that is bad for you, bad for your children. It is not good for any of us to let our denominationalism be the "chief characteristic" of any of our books, much less our children's books. We do not want, any of us, Catholic reading-books, nor Quaker spelling-books, nor Jewish geographies, nor Baptist histories, nor Presbyterian grammars, nor High Church cook-books, nor Unitarian geologies, nor Trinitarian arithmetics.

My Catholic brother, are you doing your duty as a

---

* *The Third Reader.* Catholic National Series. By Right Rev. Richard Gilmour, D.D., Bishop of Cleveland. New York: Benziger Bros.

citizen of this free republic? Are you doing your duty to your children if you let them get their history from books in which every "stronghold of bigotry and intolerance" is always an anti-Catholic place? Is it right to let them be taught that "the holy see has been God's instrument in conferring upon Europe all the real good she enjoys?" Is it right to teach them that "to Catholics are due nearly all the valuable inventions we have?" Is it right to teach them that "the only bond of unity among Protestants is a common hostility to Catholicity?" Is it right to teach them that the English free-thinkers, from whom Rousseau and Voltaire drew some of the ideas which wrought the French Revolution, were men who "denied the difference between good and evil?" Is it right to represent the Thirty-Years' War as a Lutheran rebellion assisted by "the Protestants of France," saying no word of Cardinal Richelieu's hand in the matter? Is it well to harp so much on Salem witchcraft, and to say nothing of the six hundred condemned in one district in France by Boguet, of the fifty who suffered at Donay, of the fact that the "witches' hammer"—one of the inventions not catalogued by Bishop Gilmour—was the work of two German Dominicans? Is it right to record the reported answer of the Duke of Guise to his Huguenot would-be assassin, "If your religion teaches you to assassinate me, mine obliges me to pardon you," and to fail even to mention the assassination of William the Silent by the paltry wretch Gérard, an assassin fortified for his task by "holy communion," and applauded as the doer of a laudable and generous deed by his most Catholic majesty of Spain, who, upon the assassin's execution, elevated his family to a place among the landed aristocracy? Is that the honest way of teaching history?

. . . .

But it may be urged that this is all nobody's business. The Catholic priest may say that he has nothing to say about any books used in any Protestant private school, and that people have a right to do what they please in their own affairs. My good friend, that argument is quite out of date. You are a hundred years behind the times when you say that. You shall go to school to my friend's five-year-old boy if you have not got beyond that. "Let Jack alone," Will said to Dick, who was quarreling with Jack about his sled; "the sled is his, he has a right to do whatever he will with his own." "No, sir," retorted Dick, firmly; "he has not a right to do whatever he will with his own; he only has a right to do what is right with his own." It is not our policy in this republic to foolishly or hastily or oppressively meddle with any society or with any man. There will never be any interference with any man who, for religious reasons or any other, chooses to educate his children otherwhere than in the public schools, so long as that education is done in any just, proper, and respectable way. But our people do not recognize the right of any body to do whatever he pleases with his own. The interests of the State are paramount to the caprice of any man or any body of men; the whole community is under sacred obligations to each child born into it, and every one of us is on his good behavior. There is no society among us whose affairs are or can be simply its own affairs; and if rank abuses or the teaching of palpable and baneful untruths become common and regular in any private school in Boston, whether on Moon Street or Chestnut Street or Marlborough Street, then it is inevitable that sooner or later there shall be such State supervision as shall stop it.

Inferiority Acknowledged by Eminent Roman Catholics.

A very candid and eminent Roman Catholic, Mr. Orestes A. Bronson, LL.D., confirms this view. Speaking of Roman Catholic colleges, he said:

They practically fail to recognize human progress. . . . As far as we are able to trace the effect of the most approved Catholic education of our day, whether at home or abroad, it tends to repress rather than quicken the life of the pupil, to unfit rather than prepare him for the active and zealous discharge either of his religious or his social duties. They who are educated in our schools seem misplaced and mistimed in the world, as if born and educated for a world that has ceased to exist. Comparatively few of them (Catholic graduates) take their stand, as scholars or as men, on a level with the graduates of non-Catholic colleges; and those who do take their stand do it by throwing aside nearly all they learned from their Alma Mater, and adopting the ideas and principles, the modes of thought and action they find in the general civilization of the country in which they live. . . . The cause of the failure of what we call Catholic education is, in our judgment, the fact that we educate not for the future, but for the past.

We do not mean that the dogmas are not scrupulously taught in all our schools and colleges, nor that the words of the catechism are not duly insisted upon. We concede this, and that gives to our so-called Catholic schools a merit which no others have or can have. There can be no question that what passes for Catholic education in this or any other country has its ideal of perfection in the past, and that it resists, as un-Catholic, irreligious, and opposed to God, the tendencies of modern civilization. . . . The work it gives its subjects, or prepares them to perform, is not the work of carrying it forward, but that of resisting it, driving it back, anathematizing it as at war with the Gospel, and either of neglecting it altogether or taking refuge in the cloister, in an exclusive or exaggerated asceticism, always bordering on immorality, or of restoring a former order of civilization, no longer a living order, and which humanity has evidently left behind and is resolved shall never be restored.

The *Christian World** bears the following testimony:

Some statistics have lately been in circulation through the press which are calculated to convey very erroneous impressions respecting the part of Roman Catholicism in American education. Of 303 colleges and universities in this country it is said that the Roman Catholics have 54, the Baptists 48, the Methodists 32, the Presbyterians 25, the Congregationalists, Lutherans, and Episcopalians 16 each, while the remainder are distributed among the less influential and numerous denominations. Now any one who has even a superficial knowledge of our educational institutions knows that these figures mean little or nothing; that many, if not most, of the colleges here enumerated are little more than high schools, and that it is pre-eminently true of the Roman Catholic "colleges" that of the fifty-four there is not one that is a first-class institution worthy to be named by the

---
* October, 1872.

side of Harvard, or Yale, or Princeton, or the universities of Virginia and Michigan, or a score of other institutions under Protestant influence in and around our own city. In fact, any one who will take the pains to examine their curriculum will find that, save in the single branch of the Latin language, they are scarcely above Phillips Academy, at Andover, or the Boston High School. Now, it is in the very nature of things that such institutions can exert only an insignificant influence upon the community in the way of promoting the higher education.

The *Catholic World* was only a little in advance of the *Christian World* * in confessing the same facts:

It is high time for us to apply to our own publications a little of that free examination which we have bestowed upon others, and to let argument among Catholic writers be something more than the foolish wrangling of ambitious rivals. In the article to which we have alluded we said that few of the Catholics papers had a circulation of more than 10,000; and some people found fault with us for that. We wish we could give them 25,000 or 50,000 apiece; but it will not mend matters to say that all Catholic papers are powerful organs of public opinion when we know that they are nothing of the sort. Most of them are doing excellent service within their own sphere; but why affect to deny that their sphere is a narrow one and their means are small? We have tried to impress upon the Catholic public the duty of supporting the Catholic press to the utmost of their ability. We have shown that where

---

* June, 1872.

Protestants attack us in a million printed sheets we give a feeble * answer in perhaps ten thousand. We number 8,000,000 souls, yet our newspapers, with very few exceptions, languish for want of readers, and *our colleges are not creating a literary class among the laity.*

The *Catholic Review* † published a statement by Bishop Cosgrove, of Davenport, Iowa, in which, complaining of the small support given by Catholics to Roman Catholic papers, he says: "We find that about one Catholic in forty is a subscriber to one of them. We find the combined circulation of all the Catholic papers of the country to be less than that of a single issue of the *Police Gazette.* We find it less by thousands than the journal (*The Christian Advocate*) published by another single establishment, the Methodist Book Concern. Protestant exchanges charge that our people are ignorant; that they lack intelligence, . . . and usually they have the best of the argument, for the facts are very stern and hard to face." The editor of the *Review* declared these complaints well founded.

In 1881 the *Freeman's Journal* called the parochial schools "apologies, compromises, systemless pretenses," in which "a smattering of the catechism is supplied to fit the children for the duties of life."

---

* Scarcely over 5,000,000 at that time. † March 7, 1885.

A point has cropped out, more than once, in our discussions which should receive more distinct notice, though it will be briefly treated.

IV.—The Roman Catholic Church does not believe in the education of the masses.

There are good reasons for making special mention of this point. When did she ever exhibit a concern for the education of the people? We have noticed that wherever she has done her educational work in other countries it has been in certain classes and for specific ends. Her ideal of civil government does not require the education of the whole community. Why, then, is the Roman Catholic Church pursuing such a different policy in this country from that she has followed in the countries where she has long been in the ascendency? In those countries, we have noticed, the masses have been left in ignorance; but here she professes a great concern for the education of her people. Why? Rev. Dr. McGlynn, who claims that he is still a good Roman Catholic in all the essentials of that religion, shall answer this question. He said (in part before quoted):

The extraordinary zeal manifested for getting up these sectarian schools and institutions is, first of all, prompted by jealousy and rivalry of our public schools and institutions, and by the desire to keep children and other beneficiaries from the latter; and, secondly, by the desire to make employment for and give comfortable homes to the rapidly-increasing hosts of monks and nuns who make so-called education and so-called charity their regular business, for which a very common experience shows that they have but little qualification beyond their professional stamp and garb. It is not risking much to say that if there were no public schools there would be very few parochial schools, and the Catholic children, for all the churchmen would do for them, would grow up in brutish ignorance of letters; and a commonplace of churchmen here would be the doctrine taught by the Jesuits in Italy, in their periodical magazine, the *Civita Cattolica*, that the people do not need to learn to read; that all they need is bread and the catechism, the latter of which they could manage to know something of even without knowing how to read. A confirmation of this is to be found in the very general illiteracy in countries where churches and churchmen have been exceedingly abundant and have exercised temporal control. It is a remarkable fact that in Italy, France, and other so-called Catholic countries, in spite of the hostility to the government schools, the clergy do not establish parochial schools. The ecclesiastical authorities of Italy, while willing enough to impose on our Catholic people of America so heavy a burden, do not dare to try to impose a similar burden upon their people nearer home.*

Thus spoke Father McGlynn only one year ago.

It is not often that Roman Catholics are as frank in declaring their real sentiments as the *Catholic World* was, when, a few years ago,† it said:

---

* *North American Review*, August, 1887. † April, 1871.

We do not indeed prize so highly as some of our countrymen appear to do the simple ability to read, write, and cipher. . . . Some men are born to be leaders, and the rest are born to be led. . . . The best ordered and administered State is that in which the few are well educated, and lead, and the many are trained to obedience, are willing to be directed, content to follow, and do not aspire to be leaders. . . . In extending education and endeavoring to train all to be leaders, we have only extended presumption, pretension, conceit, indocility, and brought incapacity to the surface. . . . We believe the peasantry in old Catholic countries two centuries ago were better educated, although for the most part unable to read or write, than are the great part of the American people to-day. . . . For the great mass of the people the education needed is not secular education, which simply sharpens the intellect and generates pride and presumption, but moral and religious education, . . . which teaches them to be modest and unpretending, docile, and respectful to their superiors.

Such is the language of the *Catholic World*, edited and conducted by the Paulist Fathers, of which Fathers Hecker and Hewitt are conspicuous, probably the most progressive and literary of all the orders of the Roman Catholic priesthood.

One time, in a large town in Indiana, a company of gentlemen were interested to introduce a new railway into the place. One of the number called upon the Roman Catholic priest to secure him not to oppose the coming of the road into the town. The gentleman was unfortunate in one of his suggestions to the priest, for he said, among other things: "This new road will add to the general intelligence of the place." "I don't want it," said the priest, instantly; "my people know too much already. If they know any more I can't do any thing with them."

Pope Gregory XVI., in his celebrated encyclical of August 15, 1832, said:

If the holy Church so requires, let us sacrifice our own opinions, our knowledge, *our intelligence*, the splendid dreams of our imagination, and the most sublime attainments of the human understanding.

QUESTION X.

Has Romanism adopted a More Enlightened and Liberal Policy in our Times and in our Country?

IN discussing this question we are first of all brought face to face with the utterances of the famous papal encyclical, issued only twenty-four years ago, in which the Pope formally set at naught some of the most vital principles of modern society.

This letter, issued December 8, 1864, condemned as errors *eighty* of the leading and ruling principles of modern civilization. He stated them negatively, but we take the liberty to put them into the corresponding affirmative form,* retaining the original numbers of the encyclical.

The fundamental principle of democratic government is *that all civil power emanates from the people*—they are the sovereigns; but the Romish Church denies this, and holds that:

(39.) *The people are not the source of all civil power.*
(19.) *The Romish Church has a right to exercise its authority, without having any limits set to it by the civil power.*

---

* We give it in the form and with the comments of Dexter A. Hawkins, Esq., a late member of the New York Bar.

(24.) *The Romish Church has the right to avail itself of force, and to use the temporal power for that purpose.*

(26.) *The Romish Church has an innate and legitimate right to acquire, hold, and to use property without limit.*

In our country, churches and religious corporations, as well as all other corporations, can hold property only when authorized so to do by statute, and for the uses specified by statute, and then only to the amount fixed by statute. The Romish Church opposes all this, as it prevents it from swallowing up the property of the country. In England, before the statutes of mortmain, it had got possession of one third of the property of the kingdom; and so astute were the priests in evading these statutes that it took four hundred years to perfect them sufficiently to protect the public against the rapacity of this Church.

Blackstone says that but for those statutes ecclesiastical corporations would soon have engulfed the whole real estate of England. With all these precautions the civil power had finally to resort to confiscation to restore enough of the lands to the people to insure the prosperity of the realm.

In Italy, Spain, and Mexico the civil government, for like reasons, though it was Roman Catholic, has been compelled to resort to confiscation.

In this country, if we should admit that this Church has the innate power of acquiring, holding, and using property without limit, we should soon have to resort to confiscation to save something for the people. History repeats itself.

(27.) *The pope and the priests ought to have dominion over the temporal affairs.*

Hence, in all countries, when not prevented by law,

they always have and always will interfere in politics and elections, and threaten with spiritual penalties voters of their faith in order to get control of the State.

(30.) *The Romish Church and her ecclesiastics have a right to immunity from civil law.*

An essential principle of our Government is, on the contrary, that every person and every corporation, whether lay or ecclesiastic, is equally answerable to the civil law.

(31.) *The Romish clergy should be tried for civil and criminal offenses only in ecclesiastical courts.*

In 1853, just after the free governments in Italy had been crushed out, and the influence of this Church restored, I attended trials in the courts in Florence for a month, and almost daily questions and cases arose involving in some way the Church or ecclesiastics; and in every instance the judges promptly held that the civil power could not entertain any case or question affecting the Church or ecclesiastics, but that all such must be referred to the tribunals of the Church.

(42.) *In case of conflict between the ecclesiastical and civil powers the ecclesiastical powers ought to prevail.*

Under this principle the Romish Church, in countries where it is in full power, has set aside and annulled laws and judgments on the ground that they were in conflict with the policy and rules of the Church.

(45.) *The Romish Church has the right to interfere in the discipline of the public schools, and in the arrangement of the studies of the public schools, and in the choice of the teachers for these schools.*

It has exercised this right in every country where it had the power to do it. If it had the power here it would re-write or throw out from our public schools a large part of the text-books, and substitute the catechism; and no teacher would be permitted to instruct in either public or private schools unless first approved by this Church, as was the case formerly, but not now, in Italy, Spain, and Austria.

(47.) *Public schools open to all children for the education of the young should be under the control of the Romish Church, and should not be subject to the civil power nor made to conform to the opinions of the age.*

In countries where it has the power no school is allowed to exist, nor is any one allowed to teach, unless first approved and permitted by this Church. Many schools have been closed and teachers punished in Italy, Spain, and Mexico for attempting to go on without this approval and permission. In our free country any one has a right to establish a school and to teach in it without the permission of any Church or even the civil authorities. To acquire and impart knowledge is one of the sacred and inborn rights of our people.

(48.) *While teaching primarily the knowledge of natural things the public schools must not be separated from the faith and power of the Romish Church.*

(53.) *The civil power has no right to assist persons to regain their freedom who have once adopted a religious life—that is, become priests, monks, or nuns.*

(54.) *The civil power is inferior and subordinate to the ecclesiastical power, and in litigated questions of jurisdiction should yield to it.*

(55.) *Church and State should be united.*

(78.) *The Roman Catholic religion should be the only religion of the State, and all other modes of worship should be excluded.*

In every country, whether monarchy or republic, where the Romish Church has obtained sufficient power it has excluded all other forms of worship and made public worship in any other form than their own a crime severely punishable. Under the present constitution of the Romish Church it cannot change these guiding and ruling principles, even if it would; for that would destroy the doctrine of infallibility. It cannot refuse obedience to these doctrines without ceasing to be itself.

Under such a regimen what opportunity is there for the progress of society?

Some who have followed this discussion may be inclined to think that I have not been sufficiently liberal toward the Roman Catholic Church as it stands before the public at the present time. They recognize the fact that her former history has been bad, and substantially as I have described it, but are disposed to more charitably construe her present attitude, especially in the United States.

The Catholic University at Washington, D. C.

It may seem strange to some, just in the wake of the laying of the corner-stone of a great Roman Catholic university in our national capital, to which so much attention has been given of late by the public press, that either the amount or the quality of Roman Catholic education should be called in question. On the 24th of May last a most imposing ceremony of laying the corner-stone of this American Catholic university was conducted in the presence of a great array of prelates and statesmen, and of President Cleveland. The Right Rev. John Lancaster Spalding, D.D., Bishop of Peoria, Ill., delivered an eloquent address, in which he discoursed upon the debt of modern science to Christianity, the advantages of a "True University," the qualities of a "Cultivated Christian," etc.

The *Catholic World*,* in setting forth the reasons for this university, and for locating it in Washington, D. C., says: "The Church is an intellectual body," etc. "That this is not known to non-Catholics is the greatest misfortune that the Church suffers from." Indeed? Is it not the greatest misfortune to the Church that, after having been so long in the world and so prominent before the public and in all history, it has never yet impressed the world that it "is an intellectual body?" The Church has at last reached the period, says the *Catholic World*, when "the intellectual side of Catholicity can only be adequately revealed by a university," and that, too, at a point "when the supreme activity of American life—the political—reaches its culmination." It is, indeed, high time that "the intellectual side of Catholicity" was "*adequately revealed.*" But what a confession

---

*August, 1888.

the statement implies for a Church claiming such great antiquity! If Romanism was one of the younger religious bodies, as the Disciples, or the Free Will Baptists, or some other denomination which has come into being within fifty or one hundred years, the language would not imply such a humiliating acknowledgment. This writer is not through with confessing; but, in his case, privacy is removed from the confessional, and it is the ear of the world into which the confession is poured. He expresses the hope that henceforth there will be "a gradual cessation of that distrust and suspicion that Catholicity is inimical to free institutions—a sentiment which is the greatest obstacle, in many minds, to Catholic truth." A great task is this which he assigns to Romanism, to live down so bad a record of hostility to freedom, extending through so many centuries, written in blood and torture, authenticated in all history, perpetuated in monuments, again and again renewed, every decade, by fresh utterances against the right of private judgment, and the re-assertion of the very same old dogmas, whose logical sequence is intolerance toward all non-papal ideas and institutions.

It was, indeed, the more necessary for the Romanists to make this act conspicuous, because the Church of Rome has suffered in its reputation as an educator from the palpable facts of her own history. The practical results of her long exclusive sway in Southern Europe, South America, etc., etc., have not been favorable to her reputation. Unlike Protestantism, the history of the Roman Catholic Church may be searched in vain, through some centuries, for another example of the founding of a university on a scale at all proportionate to what is *claimed* for the one to be established in Washington, D. C. Romanists needed to make an educational demonstration. It was eminently spectacular in tinsel and titles, but conspicuously wanting in the scientific spirit and method. But the most glowing prospectus of this new Roman Catholic university falls far below many of the American universities, both State and denominational. If the curriculum of studies in this new papal university is based upon fundamental principles of the "infallible Church," its students will be faced toward mediæval times; and, blindfolded by absolute authority, and with ears closed to the ringing notes of modern progress, they will be driven backward over the dusty pathways of tradition and decay. No university foundation, with however generous endowment, or imposing structures, or high-sounding titles, can deliver Rome from her rigid, iron bondage. Her education is cloistered in offensive, unalterable dogmas, limited by the Missal and cramped by scholasticism.

Are New Ideals Possible?

Her ideals are all in the past, ill-timed, and coldly rigid. Corner-stones, and high battlements, and turrets, and domes, and magnificent endowments, and titled professors, will not compensate for cloistered thought, iron-clamped dogmas, and a mediæval atmosphere—the invariable products of a policy dictated from the Vatican; for no Roman Catholic, all over this habitable globe, can get away from the leading-strings of the propaganda at Rome.

Does some one say that the founding of that university may be an attempt to inaugurate a new era in Romanism? Roman Catholics will not thus speak. Intelligent papists know that Rome has no new eras; that new eras do not enter into her conceptions. She discounts the new, and bestows all her premiums upon the old. There may be new phases in her external history, but no new doctrines, no new policy, no breaking away from any thing which is her essential self. She may dispense with fire and fagot, with the sword and gibbet, and allow her Inquisitions to slumber, when she is *obliged* to, having no power to use them. But she enforces upon her people the same old dogmas, and absolute submission to her authority. She does this now, as ever, by the arts of the confessional, by withholding the sacraments, by the terrors of excommunication.

But some will ask, Did not Bishop Spaulding, in that corner-stone address, eloquently portray a new policy, more in harmony with American ideas of progress, which was to characterize that university? In that corner-stone address Bishop Spaulding presented a singular spectacle, though not altogether novel, of a papal ecclesiastic posing before the American public in the attitude of one struggling to throw off bondage to the past, and present the Roman Church in harmony with the spirit of modern progress. He said, "Like the old, the Church can look to the past." Yes, indeed, its visual focus has been long fixed upon the past, and she has continually pointed her people to past ages for their ideals, their standards, their authority. He then says, "Like the young, she can look to the future." Whether she can do so is yet to be seen. Born in the Dark Ages, and all her ecclesiastical and doctrinal theories shaped, hammered, and fixed by the schoolmen, the logicians of that murky period, her mental vision, like the eye of the owl, is adapted to see only in the dark. How can minds long accustomed to seek for truth amid the shadows and mists of the Dark Ages bear the brighter light of modern ideas?

But do some inquire, "Will not a new country, a republic, like the United States, call for some modifications of Romanism here?" Her possibilities will doubtless be, and indeed are already, limited by her environment, so that she cannot act the part she used to act in the old papal countries in Europe. But that is a different matter from changing her fundamental dogmas, and the inevitable logical sequence of those dogmas. Still living on that old basis, if the old opportunities return, who can affirm that Rome will not reproduce the terrible scenes of the olden times?

But we will let Bishop Spalding speak again. He proceeds, "If there are Catholics who linger regretfully amid glories that have vanished, there are also Catholics who, in the midst of their work, feel a confidence which leaves no place for regret, who understand that the earthly environment in which the Church lives is subject to change and decay, and that new surroundings imply new tasks and impose new duties." Well said, Bishop Spalding! But how do Roman Catholics succeed who turn their faces to their new environments, and attempt the "new tasks" which "new surroundings" "imply?" How far do they break away from Rome's old paths? What opportunities has Romanism had afforded her amid the favoring circumstances of the new civilization of the United States, and how often have many American Protestants looked to see the sons of Rome improve these splendid opportunities for rehabilitation! Many Protestants have sincerely looked and hoped for it, and have construed, as favorably as possible, every indication which has afforded a chance for a favorable construction of her policy. But each break of light through the clouds has been followed by a darker overcast of the ecclesiastical firmament.

Papal Infallibility Indorsed by American Prelates.

When, within the clear recollection of many of us, the dogmas of the immaculate conception and the infallibility of the pope came up for decision and formal proclamation at Rome—the former in 1854 and the latter in 1870—it was felt, now the American prelates have an opportunity to resist the retrograding policy of Rome, and insist upon turning the face of the papacy toward the advancing sun. These dogmas were as purely mediæval as any that could have been cited, as pernicious in their influence, and by logical sequence, too, the most relentless and odious in practical results. Though held in some form for centuries, they were brought up for formal definition and proclamation in two sessions of the Ecumenical Council at Rome. How did the American bishops perform their part? One by one, some very reluctantly, but, finally and fully, all assented to the monstrous dogmas. They lost their opportunity.

When the dogma of the infallibility of the pope was proclaimed eighty-eight members of the council voted against it. Who were they? Were they prelates from the United States, the nation of advanced ideas of liberty and progress? Let us see. Twenty-five were from Austria, 25 from France, 11 from Germany, 8 from the British dominions, 6 from Italy, 6 from Turkey and Persia, and only 4 from the United States, out of over 50 present from this country. Roman Catholic prelates from this country of liberal ideas fell behind those of even Austria, France, and other portions of papal Europe, in the spirit of modern progress.

What was the object in view in proclaiming the infallibility of the pope? It was, says the *Catholic World*, "to give the papacy more complete spiritual supremacy over the conscience." When the council was called every bishop, archbishop, and cardinal all over the world was required to be present. To be absent without due cause, the reason to be decided by an authority, was to expose the absentee to a heavy penalty. A circular was sent out intimating that although the *right and duty of proposing matters to be acted upon by the Council belonged only to the pope* and his associates in Italy, yet others might be submitted to the committee intrusted with the programme of business at Rome, who should exercise the right of deciding what they considered most important to the general Church; but it was distinctly stipulated that such matters "must not run counter to the constant belief of the Church and her inviolable traditions." There was, then, no chance for any reform measures.

The council came together in December, 1869, and the discussion of the question of the infallibility of the pope was reached May 13, 1870. The proposition was to proclaim that the pope is infallible when he teaches *ex-cathedra*.* This was not wholly a new doctrine, but the Church was to define and proclaim, in formal words, a doctrine which had always been held and acted on in some form, but not with the *exclusive* † power with which he was now to be invested. It did not refer to the pope's life and conduct, but to his official teaching of doctrine, and means that in such teaching he cannot fall into error.

When the vote on this proposition was taken, July 11, 451 voted in favor of it, 62 conditionally in favor of it (*placet juxta modum*), and 88 unconditionally against it. Of these 88 four out of over 50 were from the United States (the Archbishop of St. Louis and the Bishops of Pittsburg, Little Rock and Rochester). Of 62 who voted conditionally against it 4 were from the United States (the Archbishops of Oregon City, and New York, and the

---

* See *Deharbe's Catechism*, pp. 142, 143.
† See paragraphs near the close of this chapter, where it is more fully explained.

Bishops of Monterey and Savannah). Three American bishops were absent and one had died.

How came the absurd dogma to be approved? Many bishops went to the council opposed to its proclamation—conspicuously some American bishops. Said a correspondent of the *New York Tribune*, describing the work:

On the arrival of the fathers in Rome they found themselves in the position of boys in a public school. Their business was cut out for them—what they were to do, how they were to do it, and to what limits they might go, was accurately laid down. The head master kept them well in hand. They fretted and remonstrated, but were compelled to submit. New regulations, still more binding, were issued. Remonstrances were sent in; some very energetic action was contemplated. "Should they leave Rome?" "Should they absent themselves from the council?" were questions deeply pondered. "Gross and unmannerly interruptions, hisses and howls, and harsh epithets greeted speakers who exercised a little freedom in uttering adverse views, while the cardinal president rung the bell to call the speaker to order, and if he failed to succeed, the speaker was pulled down from the pulpit." "In short, the man who ventured to differ from the Roman court was regarded almost as a criminal by a portion of the council and by the pope." "The council," it was said, "was summoned not to discuss, but to obey."

Those who differed from the managers of the council were called "heretics," "Jews," "Gallicans," "falsifers," "Protestants." Thus was the approval of the dogma wrung out of the council, every American bishop at last giving his assent. So that it was currently said in Rome, "The bishops who came as 'pastori' (shepherds), leave Rome as 'pecore' (sheep), and may go and gambol; for, having shorn themselves, they are light as lambs."

This is but a single instance in which the bishops of the United States, the land of the advancing sun, have ignored the sentiment of Bishop Spalding, that " new surroundings imply new tasks and new duties," and indorsed one of the darkest and most retrograding dogmas of the Middle Ages.

Mediæval Ideas of American Romanism.

Bishop Spalding goes on to say: "The splendor of the mediæval Church, its worldly power, the pomp of its ceremonial, the glittering pageantry in which the pontiffs and prelates vied with kings and emperors in gorgeous display, are gone or going; and were it given to man to recall the past the spirit whereby it lived would be wanting." But the dogmas of the mediæval Church remain, all reiterated, taught, and enforced. The triumph of the dogma of the infallibility of the pope shows the power of the mediæval spirit and the mediæval logic. Its formal proclamation was the inevitable logical sequence of premises laid down in mediæval times and continually cited even to our day.

The trouble is a logical one. The theory of the papacy was wrought out and its premises laid in the Dark Ages, and not until the premises are discarded can Romanism radically change. These old premises they have long drilled into the priesthood and young students of theology; and they propose to drill all their children and youth, from the parochial schools to seminaries, colleges, and universities, in the same dogmas, and thus hold them in the iron clamps of mediæval logic. What is the reason? The American school system, they fear, will loosen them from the old moorings.

Dr. Orestes A. Bronson wrote:

The opposition to us represented by "Native American" and "Know Nothing" sorties or movements is not in opposition to us as orthodox Christians, nor, in itself considered, to us as foreigners, but simply as the representatives of a civilization different from the American, and in many respects inferior and opposed to it."

Mr. Bronson also said:

What passes for Catholic education prepares its subjects for neglecting civilization, taking refuge in an exaggerated asceticism always bordering on immorality or restoring a former order of civilization.

The polar star of Rome is still fixed in the old mediæval firmament. Even the most advanced Roman Catholic writers in our times continue to glorify the Dark Ages for their superior virtues.

The editor of the *American Catholic Quarterly Review*, the leading periodical of Romanism in the United States, in July, 1888, said, "the most prominent characteristic of them (the Middle Ages) was their faith. They were emphatically 'Ages of Faith.' In this respect they present a marked contrast with the skepticism, the infidelity, and disbelief of modern times." The writer admits that there was "barbarism, darkness," etc., even among Roman Catholics, but among those who "disobeyed the faith which they believed;" nevertheless, he says, "in their Christian *Catholic* aspects" they were well nigh perfect, and "the most prominent characteristic," "under those aspects, was their faith."

How much evidence of a new liberalizing spirit does this leading Catholic periodical exhibit? Was it "faith" or an unquestioning credulity which is here glorified?

What else can the proposed great University at Washington do than follow in the same old methods? Nothing could please Protestants more than to see it break away from the old ideals; but how can it? It will be held in the leading-strings of Rome.

What a Catholic Layman Says.

A Roman Catholic layman said, in the *Independent* of August 9,* that it is impossible for a member of that Church to express an opinion which does not coincide with the governing powers of the Church. It is prohibited. What chance is there for any mental progress in such a body? How can a man look to a future essentially different from the past? How can Bishop Spalding's ideal for the new University at Washington ever be realized? He says "the face of hope turns to the future," "leaving their dead with their dead;" and yet papists are continually busy with "schemes for bringing back the things that have passed away."

This writer in the *Independent* says: "The Protestant, who can speak his mind socially, politically, and morally, cannot realize how utterly impossible it is for a Roman Catholic, be he priest or layman, to say what he really thinks. A curious and very interesting evidence of this was given quite recently by Archbishop Walsh, in connection with recent pronouncements on Irish affairs. He said that while Protestants were obliged to decide on such matters † according to their conscience, Roman Catholics were bound to obey the voice of God as made known by the pope,

---

* 1888.   † Referring to the last papal pronouncement.

and were not allowed the exercise of a private conscience. 'Happy Protestants!' a Roman Catholic friend of the writer's exclaimed, with some emphasis; 'they are allowed to have a conscience, and are informed that it is their duty to use it; whereas we Catholics are denied a conscience, practically, since we are not to use that which we possess.' In fact, it is the plain teaching of the Roman Catholic Church that *the conscience, once submitted to Rome, must remain forever submitted.*"

On such a basis as that, and affirmed, too, by a Roman Catholic, and verified by the Roman Catholic catechism, how can the great University projected at Washington ever become any thing but a mausoleum of the ideas of the dead past? How can there be any great change or reform in the papal Church, even in the favorable circumstances afforded in America, except by some great moral convulsion like the Lutheran Reformation? How, then, can Bishop Spalding's ideal of a new order of things amid the "new surroundings" be realized, so long as it is true that the change and decay of earthly environment makes no change in the essential character and elements of that Church?

This layman proceeds, "It is unhappily the case in America that there is a very strong feeling against any change of religious opinion; and this feeling naturally finds an outcome on individuals who change.

It is also an unhappy fact, undeniably and infinitely harmful, that a considerable number of priests who have abandoned the Roman Catholic Church are of immoral character and degraded habits. Men of honor and self-respect do not wish to be classed with such men, and would endure any sufferings sooner than have the name of being one with them, even in sympathy. Hence an immense and crushing difficulty lies in the way of those who see the many evils in the Roman Catholic Church. They are powerless to reform it from within, and equally powerless to reform it from without." . . .

"Any other body of men may effect a reform in the discipline of their Church, or may leave it without reproach, if they believe that their conscience prompts them to do so. But it is not so with the Roman Catholic, be he priest or layman, be he ever so honorable, be his career ever so blameless, be his convictions ever so strong. He is maligned, sneered at, and persecuted by the Church he was striving to reform, and for the prosperity of which he would give his life blood; and he is suspected and discouraged by the very men who denounce this Church for refusing liberty of conscience to her children, and yet, such is human nature, discourage those who act on this principle." . . .

"One of the best and most amiable bishops

of the Roman Catholic Church was a friend of the writer. He went to the Vatican Council,* and intended to vote against transferring the collective † infallibility of the Church to the personal infallibility of the pope. His determination was strong and resolute, and there were, as it was known later, a large number of bishops who had formed a similar determination. They were marked men. Every influence was brought to bear on them to change their determination—personal persuasion, entreaties, threats. The eyes of the world were on the council, and it was necessary to make it appear absolutely free and absolutely unanimous. I saw that bishop after his return, heart-broken, infinitely sad. He died soon after. 'But why,' I said, 'did you vote against your conscience?' 'What was my conscience,' he replied, 'in comparison with the conscience of the pope? How could I believe myself right when so many wiser and holier men believed me to be wrong?'

"It is well known that Dr. Newman offered some serious private objections to this definition, and it is said that Archbishop Kenrick simply left the council, rather than vote against his conscience or against the holy father's desire.

---

* The Council that sat in Rome 1869-70, and proclaimed the dogma of the infallibility of the pope.

† The old doctrine was that the Church in its councils, etc., was infallible.

"A letter by Bishop Strossmayer, published in the *Kölnische Zeitung* soon after the council, puts this fact very clearly:

"'The Vatican Council was wanting in that freedom which was necessary to make it a real council, and to justify it in making decrees calculated to bind the consciences of the whole Catholic world. . . . Every thing which could resemble a guarantee for the liberty of discussion was carefully excluded. . . . And, as though all this did not suffice, there was added a public violation of the ancient Catholic principle—*quod semper, quod ubique, quod ab omnibus*. The most hideous and naked exercise of papal infallibility was necessary before that infallibility could be elevated into a dogma. If to all this be added that the council was not regularly constituted; that the Italian bishops, prelates, and officials were in a monstrously predominating majority; that the apostolic vicars were dominated by the propaganda* in the most scandalous manner; that the whole apparatus of that political power which the pope then exercised in Rome contributed to intimidate and repress all free utterances, you can easily conceive what sort of *liberty*, that essential attribute of all councils, was displayed in Rome.'"

Thus was the personal infallibility of the pope de-

---
* The cardinals in Rome and vicinity.

clared and defined as a dogma. "It is only now that *the personal power* and the personal claim of the pope to exercise that power *in politics* is being enforced, that the multitude has begun to realize what was done in the Vatican Council."

Under such a regimen as that, what grounds are there for confidence that any amelioration can take place in the essential character of Romanism? There is no chance for reform. The Roman Catholic Church is ruled by a knot of determined, dark-minded, desperate men in Rome, who hold the Church close to her mediæval moorings, and will let nothing slip from their relentless grasp. The parochial school system is a part of their plan. It means, more than anything else, the instilling of the most ultra mediæval dogmas of Rome, through the catechism, into the minds of the children—not mere instruction in regard to morals and practical religion, but the dogmas pertaining to the hierarchy, the absolute authority of the Church, bishops, and priests, subjection to the pope and to whatever orders may come from Rome.

We have been accustomed to read the extreme declarations of absolutism by European Romanists, and to make some allowance for them, on the ground that they were proclaimed by men who had all their lives been so familiar with absolutism in civil government that their ecclesiastical ideas had been unconsciously tinged and shaped by their surroundings. Many of our good American citizens have thought such sentiments could not be proclaimed and tolerated even by the Catholic Church, in the United States, amid the modifying influences of American ideas and American society. They will probably be surprised at the list of utterances which have been made, not by European Romanists, but by representative Romanists in the United States. We therefore ask careful attention to declarations made by

AMERICAN ROMANISTS ON THE RIGHT OF PRIVATE JUDGMENT AND CIVIL AND RELIGIOUS LIBERTY.

In 1852 the *Rambler*, a Roman Catholic periodical in England, contained the following remarkable utterances:

Religious liberty, in the sense of a liberty possessed by every man to choose his own religion, is one of the most wicked delusions ever foisted upon this age by the father of all deceit. The *very name of liberty* —except in the sense of a permission to do certain definite acts—*ought to be banished from the domain of religion.* It is neither more nor less than falsehood. *No man has a right to choose his religion.* . . . None but an atheist can uphold the principles of religious liberty. . . . Shall I therefore fall in with this abominable delusion? Shall I foster that damnable doctrine that Socinianism, and Calvinism, and Anglicanism, and Judaism, are not, every one of them, *mortal sins, like murder and adultery?* Shall I hold out hopes to my erring Protestant brother that I will not meddle with his creed if he will not meddle with mine? Shall I tempt him to forget that he has *no more right to his religious views than he has to my purse, to my house, or to my life-blood?* No; *Catholicism is the most intolerant of creeds.* It is intolerance itself, for it is truth itself. We might as rationally maintain that a sane man has the right to maintain that two and two do not make four as this theory of religious liberty. Its impiety is only equaled by its absurdity.

The above extract was indorsed by the leading organ of the Roman Catholic Church in the United States. The *Freeman's Journal,* of New York, Archbishop Hughes's own paper, in its issue of June 26, 1852, referred to the above extract, and said, " *We willingly indorse every word of it.*"

The *Shepherd of the Valley,* published in the interests of the papacy in St. Louis, also indorsed it.

That excellent magazine, the *American and Foreign Christian Union,* is an authority for the following utterance, in its issue for March, 1852, in which the whole paper can be found, as quoted from the *Shepherd of the Valley,* a Roman Catholic organ at St. Louis, Mo.:

The radical tendency which has taken such universal and firm hold upon the American people is without doubt *hurrying us to the pit.* Radicalism is simply Protestantism pushed to its last consequence—Protestantism as it really is—not a religion, not a positive system or collection of systems, but the incarnate demon of rebellion against all authority and law. . . . . *"The doctrine of the right of private judgment is the most absurd of all doctrines.* . . . "The Catholic has no mission to propagate democracy. It is not the Gospel, and he who thinks that the temporal or eternal welfare of man depends upon its spread had better give to his catechism some of that time which he has hitherto devoted to his daily paper."

November 23, 1851, the *Shepherd of the Valley* had uttered even more startling sentiments:

The Church is of necessity intolerant. Heresy she endures when and where she must; but she hates it and directs all her energies to its destruction. If Catholics ever gain an immense numerical majority religious freedom in this country is at an end. So our enemies say; so we believe.

Who will say that such declarations are not the logical sequences of Catholic dogmas?

The New York *Tablet*, another Roman Catholic periodical, has been quoted as uttering these views:

No self-appointed missionaries of self-created societies have any rights against the national religion of any country, and no claim even to toleration. The Catholic missionary has the right to freedom, because he goes clothed with the authority of God, and because he is sent by authority that has from God the right to send him. To refuse to hear him is to refuse to hear God, and to close a Catholic church is to shut up the house of God. The Catholic missionary is sent by the Church that has authority from God to send him; the Protestant missionary is sent by nobody, and can oblige nobody in the name of God or religion to hear him. Our Protestant friends should bear this in mind. *They have as Protestants no authority in religion, and count for nothing in the Church of God.* . . . They have from God no right of propagandism, and *religious liberty is in no sense violated when the national authority,* whether Catholic or pagan, *closes their mouths or their places of holding forth.*

About thirty-five years ago, when Rev. Mr. Hastings was the chaplain of the American Embassy at Rome, the *Freeman's Journal* declared that, if he should "make a single convert, he would be kicked out of Rome, though Mr. Cass should bundle up his traps and follow him."

Mr. Bronson, in his *Quarterly Review* for October, 1852, expressed similar views. He said:

All the rights the sects have or can have are derived from the State, and rest on expediency. As they have, in their character of sects, hostile to the true religion, no rights under the law of nature or the law of God, they are neither wronged nor deprived of liberty, if the State refuses to grant them any rights at all. . . . The sorriest sight to us is to see a Catholic throwing up his cap and shouting, "All hail, Democracy!"

Again Mr. Bronson[*] said:

---

[*] *Quarterly Review,* April, 1854.

The power exercised over sovereigns in the Middle Ages was not an usurpation, was not derived from the concessions of princes or the consent of the people; but it was hers (the Church) by divine right; and who so resists it rebels against the King of kings and Lord of lords. This is the ground on which we defend the power exercised over sovereigns by popes and councils in the Middle Ages. . . . All history fails to show an instance in which the pope, in deposing a temporal sovereign, professes to do it by the authority vested in him by the pious belief of the faithful, generally received maxims, the opinion of the age, the concessions of sovereigns, or the civil constitution and public laws of Catholic States. On the contrary, he always claims to do it by the authority committed to him as the successor of the prince of the apostles, by the authority of his apostolic ministry, by the authority committed to him of binding and loosing, by the authority of Almighty God, of Jesus Christ, King of kings and Lord of lords, whose minister, though unworthy, he asserts that he is; or in some such formula which asserts that his power is held by divine right, etc. . . . The principal Catholic authorities are certainly in favor of the divine right. . . . The Gallican doctrine was from the beginning the doctrine of the courts, in opposition to that of the vicars of Jesus Christ, and should therefore be regarded by every Catholic with suspicion.

Soon after, a writer, over the signature "Apostolicus," in the *Baltimore Clipper*, said:

I say, with Bronson, that if the Church should declare that the Constitution and every existence of this and any other country should be extinguished, it is a solemn audience of God himself, and every good

Catholic would be bound, under the penalty of the terrible punishment pronounced against the disobedient, to disobey.

The *Freeman's Journal*, January 14, 1854, said:

Trembling mayors and embarrassed governors shall yet appeal to Catholic bishops to lend them their most active exertions toward poising on its basis the fabric of our republic and the hopes of the Constitution.

Scarcely ten years later, the Mayor of New York called upon Archbishop Hughes · to assist him in quelling the Irish riot. The American people will not soon forget that during the late civil war his holiness, Pius IX., was the only European ruler that officially recognized the Southern Confederacy * as an independent government, that he made haste to interfere in the civil affairs of this country, most presumptuously proceeding to appoint Archbishops Hughes, of New York, and Odin, of New Orleans, as arbitrators to settle our national difficulties, and also volunteered a solemn admonition to the chief rulers and people of the United States.

Passing to a later period, we find similar utterances in the *Catholic World:* †

---

* He addressed Jefferson Davis as the "Illustrious Honorable President." This action, following soon after Archbishop Hughes's visit to Rome, in the second year of the war, coupled with the facts that after that the enlistments among the Catholics nearly ceased and the papal population became hostile to the war, are very significant.

† January, 1870.

My right of conscience is the law for the State, and prohibits it from enacting any thing that violates it. MY CONSCIENCE IS MY CHURCH, THE CATHOLIC CHURCH; and any restriction of her freedom, or any act in violation of her rights, violates or abridges my right or freedom of conscience.

The *Catholic World* * said:

The Catholic Church is the medium and channel through which the will of God is expressed.... While the State has rights, she has them only in virtue and by permission of the superior authority, and that authority can only be expressed by the Church.

The same periodical declared, at another time: †

She (the Church) does not and cannot accept, or in any degree favor, liberty, in the Protestant sense of liberty.

In 1870 a Roman Catholic priest in St. Louis absolutely refused to give testimony in a court of justice, on the ground that by the authority of the pope the priesthood were under no obligation to obey the civil law. Roman Catholic authorities declare: "A priest cannot be forced to give testimony before a secular judge." ‡ "The rebellion of priests is not treason; for they are not subject to civil government." §

The *Catholic World* ‖ said:

---

* July, 1870. † April, 1870. ‡ *Taberna*, Vol. II, p. 228.
§ *Emmanuel Sa.* ‖ December, 1870.

It has always been the Catholic interpretation of this passage (Matt. 17, 23-26) that the successors of St. Peter are by divine right sovereigns, owing no subjection, even in temporals, to any civil authority; and that whatever obedience they have voluntarily rendered at certain times to emperors has been merely a condescension, like that of our Lord himself on the earth, practiced for the sake of the common good.

AMERICAN ROMANISM OFFENSIVE IN ACTS.

When we have been compelled to read of collisions between the clerical and secular authorities in some European countries over the question of education— as in France or Belgium—we have been accustomed to assure ourselves with the thought that under the conditions of American society, with its freedom, tolerance and enlightenment, there is no opportunity for such friction and antagonism—that there is no likelihood that Roman Catholic priests in America will attempt to exercise very arbitrary powers or that their laity will submit to them. But, as before noticed, we have had numerous cases with shadings as dark as in many papal countries.

A correspondent of the *Lutheran Observer* gave* the following succinct account of the Roman Catholic church case, at Williamsport, Pa.:

"Father Stack, who is the priest of the "non-German Catholics" of this city, has somehow been administering

---
* January, 1872.

the affairs of his parish so as to displease his bishop, O'Hara, of Scranton. Without specifying any reasons for his action, the bishop ordered Father Stack not to "exercise any priestly functions in Williamsport. This prohibition binds *sub gravi*." This phrase, *sub gravi*, was explained to mean, under penalty of the divine displeasure. The bishop ordered the German priest here, Father Koepper, to take possession of the keys of the Church of the Annunciation and hold them until further orders. But Father Stack, without having the fear of the bishop before his eyes, and not even dreading the *sub gravi*, procured a set of duplicate keys and went into his church and held service, and with a boldness which gives the conduct of the priest an air of the heroic, he applied to the court for a preliminary injunction to restrain Bishop O'Hara from exercising extra-judicial authority in displacing him without due process of trial, as required by the canons of the Church. It seems the bishops of the Romish Church of this country have been in the habit of exercising the most absolute power in displacing and removing their priests, and often to the disgust and injury of these subordinates. Though others have dared to complain of the arbitrary power of the bishops, yet no one has had the courage thus far to resist them, by appealing to the courts for protection, but Father Stack. At first he was joined in his application for an injunction by a number of the members of his church, but after reflection they became alarmed at the boldness and impiety of resisting their bishop, and withdrew their names from the application, and left the priest to go to law by himself. Nothing daunted by being thus forsaken of his friends, he proceeded alone to the encounter.

Father Stack was aware that there is a law of the Church, enacted by the Council of Trent, requiring, though practically disregarded, that "the superior must inquire against his subject respecting those things only founded upon evil report, and then cite him and give him the chief points of the accusation, and make known the evidence and names of the witnesses, and shall receive the legitimate defenses of the same subject, and only on the proof of a grave offense shall he remove him from his administration. The father knew that he had enjoyed no such right of trial, and was not going to permit himself to be put under discipline without a hearing. He says he is testing the legitimacy of a prevalent jurisdiction, not only for his own sake, but for the sake of the entire Catholic priesthood in the country; and it is gratifying to the popular sense of justice to know that Judge Gamble sustained the injunction, and permitted Father Stack the use of the Church of the Annunciation and the liberty of "exercising priestly functions in Williamsport," himself not fearing the *sub gravi*.

The Right Rev. Bishop justified himself in his affidavit before the court for not heeding the exact provisions of the canon law enacted by the Council of Trent, on the significant ground, "That because of the want of *temporal power* to establish the same by the holy see, and for want of sovereign legislative enactments of the States in this Union, in which they are restricted, as well by the Constitution of the United States as those of the several States, the Catholic Church is and only can be a missionary church in the United States." That is to say: 1. That *if the holy see had "the temporal power" and " sovereign legislative enactments" in this country, it would use civil force, when necessary, in the administration of ecclesiastical discipline;* and 2. *Because the Constitution of the United States and those of the several States do not lend themselves to the Church of*

Rome, as instruments of religious tyranny, that the Church must itself assume unusual and despotic power.

In April, 1873, the Cincinnati *Gazette* gave an account of the sad and strange death of a Roman Catholic citizen of Kalamazoo, Michigan. It seems the man lent a priest a sum of money to help build a parish church, which the Catholic bishop refused to recognize subsequently as a loan. "The poor man, fearing a foreclosure of the mortgage on his farm, brought suit in chancery against the bishop. For doing this he was forbidden to partake of communion by the bishop during the episcopal visit, and the edict of excommunication was read to him. Fearfully frightened, he asked what his offense had been, and was told that he was excommunicated for having sued a bishop of the Church. Being a devout believer in the powers of the clergy he was frightened nearly out of his wits, and implored the bishop to revoke the excommunication. This was done on condition that he would withdraw his suit. He complied with the demand, and the interdict was removed. It was too late, however, and the wretched man sank beneath the weight of his fancied guilt and died. The matter has created much excitement in Michigan, as might be expected. Senator Emerson has introduced in the Legislature a bill punishing by a fine of one to five thousand dollars, or imprisonment from one to five years, any bishop or priest who shall excommunicate, or threaten to excommunicate, any member to prevent him from commencing any suit or collecting any claim."

The case of Mr. Parker, of Holyoke, Mass., against Father Dufresne of that city, was well stated in the Boston *Daily Advertiser*, November 12, 1879:

> It appears that Parker went to hear Father Chiniquy, a French Catholic convert to Protestantism, preach, as did others of Father Dufresne's parish. When Father Dufresne heard of it he called on all who had gone to hear Chiniquy to acknowledge it. Parker did not confess, and was excommunicated. Afterward the priest, as the complaint phrases it, " fraudulently, willfully, violently and maliciously intending to injure the plaintiff in his business," publicly in the church forbade any person belonging to his church " having or using any hacks belonging to that hackman that has been to Chiniquy's church," threatening to turn them out of the church, and to refuse to baptize their children, marry them, or attend their funerals. It was alleged that a funeral party which came to the church in Parker's carriages was turned away, the priest saying that he would perform the service " when they knew better than to come in those hacks, and not before."
>
> The answer of the priest was that, if it should appear that he uttered the words alleged, the acts were done " in the proper exercise of his priestly duties and authority as the duly settled and installed pastor of the French Roman Catholic Church, of which the

plaintiff was a member;" that the language was not uttered unlawfully or maliciously to injure his business, but "in the lawful exercise of his authority, and for the proper regulation and discipline of his said church and the congregation worshiping therein, and by the authority and consent of his ecclesiastical superiors, and in the proper discharge of his duties and functions." The real question, it will thus be seen, was whether church discipline could legally be exercised in a manner to interfere with a man's right to conduct a lawful business and break it up by forbidding patronage of him.

The case was tried before Judge Bacon, who, in his charge to the jury, presented the law of the matter substantially as follows: The law provides a remedy for a man whose lawful business is interfered with by fraud or threats which injure it. It is not lawful for any one to interfere with another's business by threatening and intimidating those who trade with him. The case must be considered, not with regard to any religious communion, but solely with regard to the law and the evidence as affecting the common rights of all American citizens. He instructed the jury that, before they could return a verdict for the plaintiff, they must be satisfied that the defendant used the language charged, at least the material part of it constituting a threat, and that the threats were made to deter the defendant's customers from employing him, and maliciously either in fact or in law. If he had no ill-feeling or spite toward the plaintiff, yet if the declarations were without justifiable cause, and were of a nature tending to injure the plaintiff, they were malicious in a legal sense. It would be no excuse that he believed it to be his duty, nor that ecclesiastical authority upheld him. "There is no ecclesiastical authority to be recognized under our Government which allows a wanton and unreasonable interference with a man's private business, not connected with the Church from which he has been excommunicated. The Church may excommunicate him, but must not pursue him further and interfere with his private business. . . . In other words, our laws do not allow any ecclesiastical authority to interdict a man from pursuing his ordinary business, or to prevent even the members of the same denomination from which he has been excommunicated to deal with him."

Father Scully, in the enlightened city of Cambridge, within three miles of the State-house of Massachusetts, is a priest who asserts the exclusive power of forgiving the sins and saving the souls of his parishioners, and of inflicting eternal damnation upon those who disobey and refuse to send their children to his parochial schools. What would not such an ecclesiastical tyranny do if it had the civil power on its side? What physical pains and penalties would it not resort to to enforce its behests? One boy was currently reported, in the best journals, as having been flogged by this priest so badly as to be disabled from sitting up for some weeks. Put with this the terrible anathemas and excommunications prompted by a freak of personal pride and passion, and nothing can be conceived more alien to our institutions or more repugnant to American ideas of liberty. More than this, when complaint was attempted before the archbishop, it was credibly reported that parties calling were refused a hearing. Yes, an archbishop who is a graduate from Boston public schools, who has been credited with unusual breadth, good humor, intelligence and candor, gave his indorsement not only to Father Scully's purposes, but also to the means he used for carrying them out. These items were currently mentioned in the newspapers and elsewhere, and we have seen no denial of them. These things are significant of the spirit and tendency of the papal priesthood in the United States.

What guarantee have we that these methods will be limited to educational matters? They will be formidable enough if aimed only against the public school system so fundamental to American life and institutions. But they are applied to other matters. How many priests have attempted a spiritual coercion over their flocks in regard to voting in elections?

Pope Leo XIII. on Liberty.

The latest, and one of the most important encyclical letters of Pope Leo XIII. was issued from Rome on the 20th of June, 1888. It is an exposition of the doctrine of "Liberty" as held by the Church of Rome. But such a doctrine of liberty! It is only liberty to submit to Rome and do what Rome dictates. I am not slurring the document.

There can be no other rational interpretation of it. Look at the premises laid down in the first paragraph. When reasoning with Roman Catholics we must remember that they are skillful logicians—that is, in the old tricks of logic laid down by the schoolmen of the Middle Ages. Now let us notice the argument* introduced as the basis for the whole letter. The Pope says:

Man, indeed, is free to obey his reason, to seek moral good, and to strive after his last end. Yet he is free also to turn aside to all other things, to follow after false dreams of happiness, to disturb established order, and to fall headlong into the destruction which he has voluntarily chosen.

He says man's will is naturally free, but has an infirmity or weakness under which it is liable to act wrongly and fatally wrong. He then proceeds:

The Redeemer of mankind, Jesus Christ, having restored and exalted the original dignity of nature, vouchsafed special assistance to the will of man, and by the gifts of his grace and the promise of heavenly bliss he raised it to a nobler state.

Christ having made this provision for enabling and strengthening man's will, Pope Leo says, he has committed it to his Church to dispense. I will give his words:

---

* We quote from the letter as published in the *Boston Pilot* August 11, 1888.

This great gift of nature has ever been, and always will be, constantly cherished by the Catholic Church; for *to her* ALONE *has been committed the charge of handing down to all ages the benefits purchased for us by Jesus Christ.*

Here we have the pivotal point of this great Encyclical. The Catholic Church is the repository, the dispenser, of this grace which enables men to exercise true liberty. It "has been *committed*" "*to her alone*," and can be obtained only in her fold, in implicit, unquestioning obedience to her dictation.

This is the latest utterance of Rome. The pope discourses upon the necessity of law and conformity to it—a doctrine which Protestants recognize; but we teach a voluntary obedience to law, the act of individual choice—very different from a blind unquestioning submission to the dictation of an imperious hierarchy.

He contends that "the profession of one religion is necessary in the State; *that one* must be professed which alone is *true*," the religion of the "*Catholic States*." "This religion," therefore, "the rulers of the State must preserve and protect." He speaks of the theory of "the separation of Church and State" as a "fatal theory." He says that "liberty of conscience should be restricted to *the true religion*" (the Roman Catholic) "and within these limits boldly defended."

That is the whole story about liberty—there is no liberty to be recognized, or which has any claim to be respected, outside of the Roman Catholic Church. Pope Leo XIII. did not need to proclaim this doctrine at this late day. It has for centuries been the declared policy of Rome, and has been illustrated in flames and blood, and the agonizing tortures of the Inquisition. These utterances, in the year of grace 1888, are specially commended to the candid attention of such Americans as think Romanism is essentially modified in our times and in our country.

We hear much about the attachment of the Roman Catholics to the political institutions of the United States. The *American Catholic Quarterly Review* * says it is "because under those institutions they enjoy greater religious freedom than they do in Europe, and also because the Catholic Church in this country is less trammeled and less interfered with, and is much more prosperous than it is under most of the governments of European countries." European countries have had bitter experiences with Romanism, and have found that it cannot be trusted. Hence the close restrictions there environing the papacy. The larger liberty enjoyed by the Church in the United States should certainly be appreciated, but the *ad captandum* utterances complimentary to American institutions

---

* July, 1888.

are too illogical, from a Roman Catholic standpoint, and consequently too specious and insinuating, to be trusted. This *Review* further says that Archbishop Ryan, of Philadelphia, "has expressed these ideas, not only in this country, but also in Europe, and notably in Rome, only a few months ago, in his address to the sovereign pontiff of the Church, at the formal presentation of a copy of the Constitution of the United States by President Cleveland, in honor of the fiftieth ordination to the priesthood of Leo XIII. . . . In confirmation of this we make the following brief quotations from that address:

In your holiness's admirable Encyclical, "*Immortale Dei*," you truly state that the Church is wedded to no particular form of civil government. Your favorite theologian, St. Thomas Aquinas, has written true and beautiful things concerning republicanism. In our American republic the Catholic Church is left perfectly free to act out her sacred and beneficent mission to the human race. . . . We beg your holiness, therefore, to bless this great country, which has achieved so much in a single century; to bless the land discovered by your holy compatriot, Christopher Columbus; to bless the prudent and energetic President of the United States of America; and, finally, we ask, kneeling at your feet, that you bless ourselves and the people committed to our care.

In reply to Archbishop Ryan his holiness said:

As the Archbishop of Philadelphia has said, they (the Americans) enjoy full liberty in the true sense of the term, guaranteed by the Constitution—a copy of which is presented to me. Religion is there free to extend continually, more and more, the empire of Christianity, and the Church to develop her beneficent activities. As the head of the Church I owe my care and solicitude to all parts of the world, but I bear for America a very special affection. . . . Your country is great with a future full of hope. Your nation is free. Your Government is strong, etc.

This is the way American citizens are flattered, and the dust fully blinds many eyes. We are familiar with this kind of glorification of the liberty of our republic. We do not fully credit them when papal prelates utter their compliments and their patronizing platitudes about the institutions of the United States. We cannot forget Rome's dogmas, Rome's logic, Rome's record, Rome's diplomacy, and Rome's subtlety in all the past; nor can we ignore the inevitable trend of her administration. May heaven forgive us if we inflict any injustice. We have sincerely tried to appreciate all they have said; but we cannot see how an intelligent logical person can harmonize their politico-ecclesiastical dogmas with the platitudes with which they seek to disabuse American minds. If the fault is ours we must rest under the aspersion, until the prelates of Rome shall have so lived down their long and oft confirmed record as to furnish a rational basis for confidence.

We ask if there are not clearly-defined utterances from high Roman Catholic authorities which justify us in withholding confidence? Yes. Pope Leo XIII. himself states the attitude of the Church on this question in a way that excites the deepest distrust. He says, in his late Encyclical on Liberty, June 20, 1888:

Although in the extraordinary condition of these times the Church usually acquiesces in certain modern liberties, *not because she prefers them in themselves*, but because she judges it *expedient* to *permit* them, IN BETTER TIMES SHE WOULD USE HER OWN LIBERTY.

Yes, doubtless. This apparently quiet utterance has a deep meaning. "In better times"—that is, when the Church possesses the power, "she will use her own liberty." Will American citizens give her this supreme power? Answer, ye loyal sons of America!

He speaks in one place of "the excesses of an unbridled intellect." Every son of Rome is *bridled* in intellect; and what excesses of bridled intellect we have in the example of Alexander VI., in the St. Bartholomew massacre, in the slaughter of the Waldensians and the Huguenots; in the burning of Latimer, Cranmer, John Rogers, etc.; in the tragic, heart-rending scenes of the Inquisition! If such the excesses of bridled intellects, directed by Rome, let the intellect of the world be *un*bridled. Do Bishop Spalding and the founders of the new Catholic University propose to throw off the bridle of the papacy? No. They are still to be Pope Leo's nags, bridled and driven by him. And they propose to gather the children of papists into parochial schools, that the Roman hierarch may bridle *them* and drive them along the dusty, deeply rutted paths of the papacy in abject submission to the dictation of foreign ecclesiastics. Thus curbed and reined, they propose in due time to thrust these children and youth upon us as American citizens, with their eyes turned askant to Rome, obeying every look and nod of the pontiff whose lust for dominion covets the submission of these United States to his dictation.

Such is the Encyclical. We join with the *Independent* in saying, "It is really not an essay about liberty, but an essay against liberty of thought and speech and worship."

The reason why we have introduced this latest papal Encyclical is that the American people may have the latest Roman Catholic utterance of the highest authority in regard to liberty, that they may also see that Rome has not essentially changed, and that they may know how utterly disqualified is the Roman Catholic Church to train the children, or any part of the children of this free republic. The more of them she trains in her dogmas the more difficult will be the work of molding, establishing, and conducting the affairs of this republic.

Revolt.

Said a Catholic layman in a recent article in the *Independent*,* "There is at present a deep stirring of thought among Roman Catholic laymen, which is none the less earnest because, for obvious reasons, it cannot voice itself exteriorly. And this opinion is the result of careful consideration, on the part of one who has had special and exceptional opportunities of knowing the opinions of both priests and laymen of the Roman Catholic Church." But he says no public expression of opinion at all at variance with the governing powers of the Church is tolerated. He thinks, however, it must yet break out into utterance. He further adds, "How deeply the papal questions of the hour are trying men's souls will never be known until the day of account. . . . There is as deep an agitation in the Roman Catholic Church to-day as there has ever been. The fire smoulders; when and where the flames will break forth God only knoweth. But for those who desire truth to prevail there is a terrible responsibility, if they 'break the bruised reed or quench the smoking flax.'"

The *New York Herald*, edited by a gentleman of

---

* August 9, 1888.

the Roman Catholic faith, and of princely generosity to the poor of Ireland, said (October 14, 1880), "The people have an opportunity to see just what sort of an institution the (Roman) Catholic Church is in politics, and to understand what a farce it would be to pretend that free government can continue where it is permitted to touch its hand to politics. . . . This is a Protestant country, and the American people are a Protestant people. They tolerate all religions, even Mohammedanism; but there are some points in these tolerated religions to which they object and will not permit, and the vice of the (Roman) Catholic Church, by which it has rotted out the political institutions of all countries where it exists, which has made it like a flight of locusts every-where, will be properly rebuked here when it fairly shows its purpose." The article added an assurance that the *Herald* was "in the fullest possible sympathy with American opinion on this important topic," and a few days later (October 30, 1880), the editor, recurring to this subject, wrote, "In all it then said the *Herald* has the sympathy of many loyal and devoted (Roman) Catholics." Will not such sentiments soon find fuller and freer utterances among Romanists?

On Christmas day, 1884, Pope Leo XIII., addressing his cardinals, sent to the Christian world a greeting which contained the following utterances:

It is with deep regret and profound anguish that we behold the impiety with which Protestants propagate freely, and with impunity, their heretical doctrines, attacking the most august and the most sacred dogmas of our very holy religion, even here at Rome, the center of the faith and the seat of the universal and infallible teacher of the Church; here, where the integrity of the faith should be protected and the honor of the only true religion should be secured by the most *efficient means.*

It is with sorrow of heart that I see the temples of heterodoxy multiplying under the protection of the laws, and liberty given in Rome to destroy the most beautiful and most precious unity of the Italians, their religious unity, by the mad efforts of those who arrogate to themselves the *impious* mission of establishing a new Church in Italy, not based on the stone placed by Jesus Christ as the indestructible foundation of his heavenly edifice.

Theory of the Papacy.

It is an old dogma of Rome, never changed or modified, that both the ecclesiastical and temporal authority, exercised and still claimed by the popes, is invested in them by divine appointment. In support of this doctrine they appeal first to the New Testament, and next to the tradition of the Church, handed down, as they claim, in unbroken continuity from the apostles to the present time. According to their theory, the apostle Peter was indicated by Christ as superior to the rest of the apostles in faith and spiritual discernment, and as the one invested with special pre-eminence. The Church, too, which Peter was to found and preside over (at Rome, as they claim), was predestined to a superiority among other churches, and St. Peter's personal superiority was to be vested in perpetuity in his successors at Rome.

Such is the theory at the basis of the exclusive authority exercised by the Roman Catholic Church. The evidence on which these claims rests is very ambiguous and conflicting, most of it of more than doubtful genuineness, and scattered through a period of so much obscurity that the conclusions reached, after the greatest research, are feebly conjectural, too indefinite to constitute the basis for the monstrous assumptions on which the papacy is predicated and acts. But Roman Catholics have accepted the basis as sufficiently genuine, and on these premises, logically, unblushingly, and always, they plead supreme authority and power. How, then, can Rome change in her essential character?

Popery is wholly

OUT OF SYMPATHY WITH MODERN IDEAS AND PROGRESS.

The evidence abounds. That enlightened statesman, Count Cavour, prime minister of Victor Emmanuel, showed a thorough comprehension of the genius of Romanism for the repression of free thought, and declared that he would seek the overthrow of the papal dominion, not by fire and fagot, the favorite weapons of Rome for long ages, but by the introduction of modern improvements. He said:

I will attack Rome by railways, by the electric telegraph, by agricultural improvements, by establishing national banks, by gratuitous education on a large scale, by civil marriages, by the secularization of conventual property, by the enactment of a model code embodying the most lenient laws in Europe, and by the suppression of corporeal punishment. I will place the spirit of modern expansion face to face with the old spirit of obscuration; I am quite certain the former will triumph. I will establish a blockade of new civilization around Rome. If she undergoes a modification she will come to us; if she remains unchanged she will, by constant comparison, become so disgusted with her state of inferiority that she will throw herself into our arms to escape destruction.

This policy has extended in Italy, and internal improvements are visible; but the noble administrator passed away in the midst of his labors, and the new policy has felt the loss of his vigorous hand.

Reform and Progress Handicapped by Recent Action.

The world has never seen organic Romanism so far removed from the influence of modern progress as since the Vatican Council of 1869–1870. Prior to that time a collective infallibility was indeed ascribed to the pope, but his personal official infallibility had never been formally proclaimed as a dogma of the Church. Heretofore all matters of dispute in regard to doctrine and ecclesiastical affairs were settled by an Ecumenical Council, which was the supreme tribunal. As a typical illustration may be cited the action of the Council of Constance (1414-1418), deposing three popes from their positions. That council held every thing in its own hands, claiming and exercising supreme jurisdiction in matters of faith and administration, to which all parties, popes included, must submit in obedience. Pope Martin V. himself formally assented to and indorsed the attitude of that body.

The Council of Trent (1545-1563), if it did not create, confirmed and established the essential features of the modern Romish Church, giving a stamp of permanency to some things before more or less problematical. Since then the Romish Church has rested her dogmas, laws, and regulations upon the decisions of that council. The Church, dating from Trent, has at least one point of difference from the Church ante-Trent. The strong reformation current within the Church, in the prior period, was expelled by the action of the Council of Trent, and the Church has since borne the stamp of an anti-reformation character. "Ever since," says Uhlhorn (Das römische Council), "her course has been onward to a more perfect suppression and elimination of all reformatory and evangelical elements. Out of the mediæval Catholic Church has issued the specifically Romish Church, and the direction of her development is set forth by the statement that the Catholic character retreats more and more behind the specifically Romish."

Uhlhorn allows that there has been a species of improvement in the Catholic Church since the Council of Trent, such as in the general character of her clergy and a correction of the more scandalous abuses, and there has been a small measure of progress. But there has been a retrograde in dogmas, as seen in the authoritative sanction of two such dogmas as the immaculate conception of the Virgin Mary and the infallibility of the pope (both during the pontificate of Pius IX.).

By the recent Vatican Council the most extreme ultramontane theory was established, the pope being raised to the character of an absolute infallible monarch, without peer, rival, or associate in authority, to whom even an Ecumenical Council stands only in an advisory relation, with no power to amend his decrees nor even to convene for advisory purposes except as summoned by his mandate. What more explicit assertion of unqualified sovereignty than the text of the dogma:

If any shall say that the Roman pontiff has the office merely of inspection or direction, and not *full and supreme power of jurisdiction over the universal Church*, not only in things which belong to *faith and morals*, but also to those which relate to *the discipline and government* of the Church spread throughout the world, or assert that he possesses merely the principal part and not *all the fullness of this supreme power* . . . *let him be anathema.*

The Vatican decree of papal infallibility declares:

. . . We teach and define that it is a dogma divinely revealed that the Roman pontiff, when he speaks *ex cathedra*—that is, when in discharge of the office of pastor and doctor of all Christians, by virtue of his supreme apostolic authority, he defines a doctrine regarding faith or morals to be held by the universal Church, by the divine assistance promised to him in blessed Peter—is possessed of that infallibility with which the divine Redeemer willed that his Church should be endowed for defining doctrine regarding faith or morals; and, therefore, such definitions of the Roman pontiff are *irreformable of themselves,* and *not from the consent of the Church.*

Since the aforesaid declaration was made, the most eminent Roman Catholic prelates have interpreted it as having a well-nigh universal breadth, bringing within the scope of papal infallibility, for decision by his short *ex cathedra* process, matters of science and history, if the pope is pleased to regard them as related to faith and morals. Thus it is proposed to supersede the old processes of reasoning, examination, and investigation, and receive the oracular decision of the Roman pontiff. Receptiveness and docility are to supplant individual thought and pains-taking inquiry. How does such a theory comport with modern progress?

Cardinal Manning defines the Vatican dogma as maintaining that infallibility extends to all that is opposed to revelation, to all that is scandalous or offensive to pious ears, and to all matters pertaining to the proper custody of Catholic belief. He says: *

It extends to certain truths of natural science, as, for example, the existence of substance, and to truths of natural reason, such as that the soul is immaterial, that it is "the form of the body," and the like. It extends, also, to certain truths of the supernatural order which are not revealed, as the authenticity of certain texts or versions of the holy Scripture. There are truths of mere human history which are not revealed, without which the deposit of the faith cannot be taught or guarded in its integrity. For instance, that St. Peter was Bishop of Rome, that the Council of Trent and the Council of the Vatican are ecumenical —that is, legitimately celebrated and confirmed; that Pius IX. is the successor of St. Peter by legitimate election. . . . That there is an ultimate judge in such matters of history as affect the truths of revelation is a dogma of faith.

In pleading for papal autocracy and infallibility the argument, from need, is very prominent with Catholic

---

* *The Vatican Council and its Definitions.* 1871.

writers. They have this ridiculously short cut: "An infallible tribunal is needed; therefore there is an infallible tribunal;" or as Mr. J. H. Newman* puts it: "The absolute need of spiritual supremacy is at present the strongest of arguments in favor of the fact of its supply."

HEREAFTER, IF ANY PRIESTS OR PRELATES OF ROME DESIRE TO HAVE THE CHURCH MAKE ANY MODIFICATION OR ANY INNOVATION IN DOCTRINE, OR CHANGE IN HER ESSENTIALLY ROMISH POLICY, THEY ARE UTTERLY POWERLESS.

This is evident, because by the absurd action of the notorious Vatican Council they have surrendered that power to the pope, giving to him full and absolute authority in such matters. But the pope cannot proclaim any doctrine contrary to the teachings of the Council of Trent, because that was an Ecumenical Council, and the dogmas of Ecumenical Councils are held to be infallible. There is, therefore, no chance for any progress or essential reform. The way is blocked. The ratchet is set. Nothing but a convulsive upheaval can break up and destroy the iron clamps which now bind the papacy.

---

*Essay on Development.

Professor George E. Fisher, D.D.,* says:

The proclamation of the pope's infallibility in religious doctrine and in ethical teaching has raised, as far as we can now see, a new barrier in the way of Christian union. It sharpens the antagonism between the Protestant and the Roman Catholic position. The boundary between the two religions is no longer in a degree vague and fluctuating. An absolutely tangible issue is presented. As long as this dogma of papal infallibility is upheld we can see no room either for a gradual reformation of doctrine in the Roman communion or for a reunion of the two sundered branches of the Western Church.

In this retrograde movement in the Romish Church, handicapping all progress, modification, and reform, the Catholic prelates of the United States, as we have seen, acted a prominent part—a relatively larger and less enlightened part than the prelates of the old countries of papal Europe—in the Vatican Council. So hopeless is it to look for any material modification and improvement of the essential character of Romanism in the United States at the close of the nineteenth century.

In the light of these facts, let American citizens seriously ponder the hostile attitude of the Roman Catholic Church toward our public school system, and her pernicious influence upon the future prospects and citizenship of the multitude of children trained in her parochial schools.

---

* In the *Congregationalist*.

THE LIQUOR PROBLEM IN ALL AGES,

By Rev. DANIEL DORCHESTER, D.D.

A New Edition, Revised, and Including the Newest Phases of the Temperance Movement, from 1883 to 1888. 728 Pages Octavo, Beautifully Bound, and Printed with Large Type. Price, $2 50. Sent by Mail on Receipt of Price. Subscription Agents Desired.

COMMENDATIONS OF THE NEW EDITION, 1888.

The *Boston Journal* said: "Dr. Daniel Dorchester's work upon *The Liquor Problem in All Ages*, revised, and in a supplementary chapter brought down to the year 1888, presents a valuable account of liquor legislation and other efforts made toward temperance in this country and abroad. The tables of statistics, reports, and other evidence are of great use in estimating the growth of the temperance movement. Doctor Dorchester's historical accuracy is well known, and his enthusiasm upon this subject enables him to comment with much force upon encouraging facts."

Mrs. J. Ellen Foster, President of the W. C. T. U. of Iowa, said: "I thankfully welcome the new edition of your great work, *The Liquor Problem in All Ages*. The volume of temperance sentiment in our age and country is so great; its crystallizations in society, in law, and in politics are so many and varied; its related issues in our changing civilization are so multiform, that we do well to study foundation principles and historic data. In this I have been greatly helped by your book. I feel the bed-rock of truth under my feet as I read its pages. Surely, one needs to find the 'sure foundations' in these troublous times. The author has, with great care in detail, brought the work down to the last acts of this Drama of Progress, and with characteristic judicial poise set forth this many-sided contest of the powers of darkness with the ever-rising sun of truth. I'd like, if it were possible, to turn book-agent, and go from house to house with this wonderful volume."

Rev. Albert H. Plumb, D.D., said: "The new edition of *The Liquor Problem* is greatly increased in value. The mass of recent information packed into the long supplement makes the volume complete as a compendium of the freshest and weightiest facts up to the present year. I have turned to it again and again for needed implements in temperance work. The entire book, with its histories, its diagrams, its tables, its voluminous testimonies and powerful reasoning, is a characteristic monument to the patient research and judicial wisdom of its industrious and able author."

The *Watchman* said: "Dr. Dorchester's eminence as a statistician assures his readers that where facts are concerned he speaks with care, and is unassailable. An important feature of the book is eleven colored diagrams strikingly illustrating the economic aspects of intemperance and its relative progress to the population in the British Isles and in the United States. It is a storehouse of facts and principles worthy to be meditated on by thoughtful readers and serviceable to temperance workers. It is a handsome as well as useful volume, copiously illustrated."

PHILLIPS & HUNT, Publishers,   805 Broadway. N. Y.

CHRISTIANITY IN THE UNITED STATES

FROM THE

First Settlement down to the Present Time.

By DANIEL DORCHESTER, D.D.

800 pages. 8vo., with Maps, etc.

In Cloth, - - $4.50.   Half Morocco, - - $6.00.

PHILLIPS & HUNT, 805 Broadway, New York City, and
CRANSTON & STOWE, Cincinnati, O.

COMMENTS.

The *Watchman* says: "The author has placed all interested in the study of religion in this country under great obligations. The plan of the work contemplates a succinct account of every considerable religious movement in our land since the discovery of America. . . . The reader will be especially impressed with the impartiality of the chapters recounting the origin and growth of the Roman Catholic Church in this country. . . . He seems to have risen to the philosophical conception which was foreign to the mind of D'Aubigne, and which is imperfectly perceived by the average controversialist."

The *Western Christian Advocate* says: "It is the work of an investigator, and may be made to do invaluable service in the hands of students of the religious history of our country. In all respects the work is worty of the highest commendation."

The Rev. Philip Schaff, D.D., LL.D., says: "*Christianity in the United States* is a most valuable contribution to our American church history. It more than fills the place for our generation which Dr. Baird's book did for his."

The Rev. Joseph Cook says: "You have made what ought to be a great and growing circle of readers profoundly your debtors by this contribution to the study of the ways of Providence in the education of the foremost Christian republic of all time."

The *Independent* says: "*Christianity in the United States*, by Dr. Dorchester, is a really great book. I have looked over it (in proof sheets) and am amazed at the thoroughness and accuracy which characterize this stupendous undertaking. It is a perfect mine of information, and I am glad that so competent and careful a man as Dr. Dorchester has had the courage and patience to work out such a splendid result."

The *Christian Union* says: "Thoroughly fair-minded, it is full of facts, which, judged from the stand-point of the secular reader, are of the greatest importance and interest. . . . The volume fills its niche, and will be of service in popularizing a knowledge of the past and present of our churches."

The *Examiner* (Baptist) says: "The history of various Christian bodies in the United States is more candid, comprehensive, and accurate than we should know how to find in any other single book."

THE WHY OF METHODISM.

By DANIEL DORCHESTER, D.D.

16mo.   70 cents.

PHILLIPS & HUNT,   -   805 Broadway, New York City.

WHAT IS SAID OF IT.

The Boston Daily Traveler says: "Dr. Dorchester has made clear to thousands of the great Church of which he is one of the leading clergymen the reasons for their own faith which many have perhaps only dimly seen. Methodist Episcopal polity is a puzzle to outsiders, and is not always clear to insiders. Both these classes will find Dr. Dorchester's volume of great interest."

The California Christian Advocate says: "It is the most powerful and convincing argument on Methodism ever issued, and it is in a form so condensed that any one can read it through in a day. If, after reading this book, any Methodist wants to get out of the Church, all the doors and windows ought to be opened, so that he may go quickly."

The Rev. W. F. Warren, D.D., LL.D., President of Boston University, says: "It ought to be placed in the Reading Course of the 'Oxford League;' also, in the proposed course for the class-leaders of our Church."

The Michigan Christian Advocate says: "The view is by no means narrow and technical, but is a comprehensive and intelligent survey of Methodism. . . . It would be a good book to scatter broadcast in the Church, and will be especially appropriate in our Sunday School libraries."

The Northern Christian Advocate says: "Dr. Dorchester worthily represents his Church. . . . The book is well worthy of a wide circulation."

The Peninsula Methodist says: A most opportune and valuable volume. . . . This is another book that should be in every Methodist home and in every library under Methodist control."

The Central Christian Advocate says: "The chapter on 'Polity' is of especial value. The pastors will do well to place this volume in the hands of persons who have recently joined the Church and those about to join. It is an admirable volume."

The Christian Advocate says: We give this little book, in its statements and figures, the strongest commendation, and wish that it could be circulated among our laymen and preachers as widely as possible."

The Methodist Review says: "Viewed as a brief and popular presentation of the question, it is one of the best books of its class hitherto produced. In strong and pithy style it treats of the origin, the character, the inference, and the polity of Methodism."

THE PROBLEM OF RELIGIOUS PROGRESS.

By DANIEL DORCHESTER, D.D.

603 Pages. Price, $2.

PHILLIPS & HUNT, 805 Broadway, New York City.

COMMENTS.

This is pre-eminently a book for the times.—*Christian Guardian.*

Whoever takes up this book intending only to glance at a few of the statistics will probably be mistaken, for, having begun to read, he will wish to keep on to the end. This at least was our experience, notwithstanding the work is so largely one of statistics, by which we are not easily entranced. The reader is impressed with the great care taken in preparing the computations, the evident candor with which they have been prepared, and the magnitude of the problem to which they have been applied.—*The Watchman.*

A remarkable book. Nothing issued from the press in recent years can surpass it in interest for the Christian Church. . . . The book cannot fail to have an extensive sale among all Christian denominations. No brief notice can do justice to its contents. Its pages must be studied. Its chapter on missions is worth many times the price of the book.—*Methodist Mission Rooms.*

One of the best books that has appeared recently.—*Western Christian Advocate.*

Dr. Dorchester deserves much consideration as a collater of facts and a close reasoner upon them. . . . The general result of his reasoning is instructively re-assuring. . . . As the main value of the tables necessarily resides in their accuracy it is interesting to note the unwearied pains with which Dr. Dorchester has supplied himself with the freshest and most authentic returns, and the skill with which—when such a course was the only one—he has freshened outworn estimates into what may fairly be taken as present probabilities. . . . We hesitate not to say that, in our judgment, this is the most important contribution which has thus far been made to a subject grave and full of interest. Every clergyman needs the pluck which such a volume is calculated to breed.—*Congregationalist.*

If any one doubts the permanency of the Christian religion, or imagines that it is to be swept away by a few blatant infidels, he has only to turn to the pages of this valuable volume to be re-assured.—*New York Evening Express.*

We scarcely remember to have read a book so well sustained throughout, and containing so much clear thinking and so many valuable facts in similar compass. Let every minister read it, and every despairing Christian use it as a tonic, and especially should those who have to contend with skeptics and revilers fortify themselves by the mastery of its contents.—*Rev. J. M. Buckley, D.D.*

The book embodies a solid array of facts, the force of which cannot be evaded.—*The Methodist.*

www.ingramcontent.com/pod-product-compliance
Lightning Source LLC
Chambersburg PA
CBHW021942240426
43668CB00037B/488